W9-CMJ-400

Caribbean Creolization

Caribbean Creolization

Reflections on the Cultural Dynamics
of Language, Literature, and Identity

~ ~ ~

Edited by
Kathleen M. Balutansky
and Marie-Agnès Sourieau

University Press of Florida

Gainesville · Tallahassee · Tampa · Boca Raton · Pensacola · Orlando · Miami · Jacksonville

~

The Press University of the West Indies
Barbados · Jamaica · Trinidad and Tobago

Copyright 1998 by the Board of Regents of the State of Florida
Printed in the United States of America on acid-free paper

Published by the University Press of Florida (ISBN 0-8130-1558-8)
Published simultaneously in the Caribbean by
The Press University of the West Indies (ISBN 976-640-060-1)
All rights reserved. Published 1998

03 02 01 00 99 98   6 5 4 3 2 1

Library of Congress Cataloging-in-Publication Data (UPF)
Caribbean creolization: reflections on the cultural dynamics of
language, literature, and identity / edited by Kathleen M. Balutansky
and Marie-Agnès Sourieau.
p. cm.
Includes bibliographical references and index.
ISBN 0-8130-1558-8 (alk. paper)
1. Creole dialects — Caribbean Area. 2. Languages in contact—
Caribbean Area. 3. Caribbean literature — History and criticism. 4.
Group identity — Caribbean Area. 5. Caribbean Area — Civilization. 6.
Caribbean Area — Languages. I. Balutansky, Kathleen M., 1954– .
II. Sourieau, Marie-Agnès.
PM7834.C37C36   1998
417′ .22′09729–dc21   97-34954

03 02 01 00 99 98   6 5 4 3 2 1

Cataloguing in Publication Data (UWI)
Caribbean creolization : reflections on the cultural dynamics of
language, literature, and identity / edited by Kathleen M. Balutansky
and Marie-Agnès Sourieau.
p. cm.
Includes bibliographic references and index.
ISBN 976-640-060-1 (alk. paper)
1. Creole dialects — Caribbean area. 2. Creole dialects — cross-cultural
studies. 3. Language and culture — Caribbean area. 4. Caribbean
literature — history and criticism. I. Balutansky, Kathleen M.
II. Sourieau, Marie-Agnès.
PM7831.C36 1998   417.22–dc20

Contents

Preface

The idea for this anthology was born while the editors were both at the University of Virginia, collaborating on several projects linking the francophone and anglophone Caribbean. As we discussed the growing interest—in American universities and colleges—in the cross-cultural reality that governs Caribbean literature and culture, we noted that much of the critical and theoretical writing on the subject is produced by scholars from North American and other universities. These scholars, furthermore, tend to focus on a single cultural and linguistic corpus, or to rely on the critical or theoretical work of a few writers from the same linguistic and cultural Caribbean affiliations. This concentration, though understandable and often inevitable, has the unfortunate effect of limiting our students' understanding of the interconnectedness of the process of creolization in the entire Caribbean region. Our increasing interest in providing a truly cross-Caribbean assortment of opinions that could fully disclose the intricate nature of creolization as a cross-cultural and transnational phenomenon led to this anthology.

The essays collected in this anthology are written by prominent writers from the English-, French-, Spanish-, and Dutch-speaking Caribbean, whose literary corpus has represented their insights into the process of creolization. However, this is not a collection of fiction, poetry, or plays but a series of reflections on the cultural dynamics of language and literature and the interrelation (to use Edouard Glissant's term) of these dynamics in the Caribbean. Our main goal in developing this collection was to provide a much-needed forum for reflections on current notions of creolization (that is, creoleness, *Antillanité, Créolité,* etc.), in Caribbean literature and culture.

Although we expect that most readers of the anthology will be scholars and students of Caribbean literature and culture, we hope that the collection will also be of interest to a general public eager to understand the complexity of multiculturalism in the New World.

We thank all our contributors for their generosity and patience with the long process that brought the collection to realization. We also want to thank Saint Michael's College and Fairfield University for their financial and institutional support during the last stages of the project, and we extend our thanks to the members of their respective staffs who cheerfully performed various administrative tasks that facilitated the production of the manuscript.

We are grateful to Walter J. Petry, Jr., and William M. Abbott for their insightful suggestions. We are particularly grateful to John Howland, Jr., for his comments and invaluable advice throughout the various stages of the editing process.

Introduction

> If we assume that métissage is generally the result of an encounter and
> a synthesis between two different components, it seems to us that creol-
> ization is a métissage without limits, the elements of which are mani-
> fold, its outcomes unpredictable. Creolization diffracts whereas some
> forms of métissage may concentrate once more. . . . Creolization's most
> manifest symbol is the Creole language. Its genius rests on its being
> always open; that is, maybe, its becoming fixed only within some sys-
> tems of variables that we will have to imagine as well as define. Thus,
> creolization carries in itself the adventure of multilingualism along with
> the extraordinary explosion of cultures. But this explosion of cultures
> does not mean their scattering nor their mutual dilution. It is the vio-
> lent manifestation of their assented, free sharing.
>
> Edouard Glissant, *Poétique de la relation*, 46–47[1]

> I am only one-eighth the writer I might have been had I contained all
> the fragmented languages of Trinidad.
>
> Derek Walcott, *The Antilles*[2]

To the uninitiated, the process of creolization that Glissant and Walcott
describe above may seem obscure, exotic, or defined by a specific geographical and historical context—the continental and insular Caribbean.
However, far beyond its geographical specificity, Caribbean creolization
offers a glimpse into a phenomenon that is fundamental to the New World
experience.

The term creolization may indeed be new to those not familiar with the
historical and literary study of the Caribbean and Central and South
America, but it is at the heart of historical, social, and literary discussions
that have taken place in the Caribbean for several decades. For those who,
both inside and outside of academia, continue to grapple with the slippery
aspects of what has been called diversity, multiculturalism, transculturalism,
or hybridization of our New World cultures, an understanding of creolization may shed some light on the elusive and ominous social, political,
and even economic meanings of emerging American identities. The following essays on the current cultural dynamics of language and literature

1

in the Caribbean represent the latest writings of prominent Caribbean writers whose reflections may illuminate current discussions of contemporary Caribbean literary production, and definitions of cultural diversity and identity.

If we consider that, from its origins, Western thought was based on the ideology of order prevailing in all domains over chaos, and that in the Judeo-Christian tradition chaos was to be neutralized by universal law, it is not difficult to grasp the fundamental contradiction between the "universalizing" impulse of Western thought and the reality of Western colonialism. In the New World, brute exploitation gave the lie to Western ethics, philosophy, aesthetics, and politics.

In the seventeenth century, sugar cane cultivation and the development of plantation economies created patterns of development that were similar in Brazil, the Guyana coast, the Caribbean islands, and the Caribbean coasts of Central America, Mexico, and Louisiana. The location of the Caribbean archipelago determined that the islands would be at the center of intense economic and cultural exchanges and would serve as a bridge connecting North and South America. As a result of the slave trade and colonial economic exploitation, vast numbers of people from diverse geographic, racial, and cultural origins were forcibly imported to the Caribbean—a region that stands today as a reminder of the disruption and eventual subversion of both the physical origins of these peoples as well as all academic theories of unitary origins. In his study of the black Atlantic world, Paul Gilroy uses ships and sailing as a central symbol for the Atlantic African diaspora because the intense traffic of ships was an essential factor in "the circulation of ideas and activists as well as the movement of key cultural and political artefacts" between Europe, America, Africa, and the Caribbean (4). For Gilroy, from the beginning, economic and cultural exchanges created in the North Atlantic regions a rhizomatic transcultural structure.[3] Gilroy's perspective follows Milan Kundera's earlier reflections on the formation of Caribbean identities which, he remarked, have been determined by similar "median contexts," which he defines as the "middle course between a nation and the world." Kundera stresses the urgency of redefining the concept of "nation" in whose name the call for cultural identity is undertaken (1991, 57). Similarly, Paul Gilroy deplores "the fatal junction of the concept of nationality with the concept of culture," while emphasizing the importance for Blacks of the West in recognizing their connection with their Western intellectual heritage (2).

Gilroy's seminal work on black identity is one of the latest in recent attempts to counter old cultural studies of the Caribbean region that generally emerged from essentialist concepts of ethnicity, nationality, and authenticity. In other words, the cultural, political, and literary discourse about Caribbean identity—not unlike that about African American and Black English identity—had almost exclusively limited itself to binary opposites: White/Black, master/slave, civilized/primitive, autonomous/dependent, etc. This dynamic, of course, was embedded in Europe's academic rhetoric of (unitary) identity. Europe's obsession with linear origins, and especially with "being" as a stable category of integrity and purity, resulted directly from its concepts of ethnic difference and racial classification as well as from its sense of a God-given right to dominate the inferior "other."

From the very beginning these assumptions were constantly challenged, as they continue to be, and Gilroy as well as Kundera join many others who have placed the African diaspora at the heart of the complex unfolding of the drama of modernity. Like others before him (who will be discussed later in this introduction), Paul Gilroy stresses the difficulty of defining the heterogeneous and heteronomous identities of postcolonial cultures: "against this choice (immutable origin, ethnic purity) stands another, more difficult option: the theorization of creolization, *métissage, mestizaje,* and hybridity. From the viewpoint of ethnic absolutism, this would be a litany of pollution and impurity. These terms are rather unsatisfactory ways of naming the process of cultural mutation and restless (dis)continuity that exceed racial discourse and avoid capture by its agent" (2). Here, Gilroy seems to echo Haitian poet, novelist, and critic René Depestre who takes up Kundera's notion of "median contexts" to characterize the restless mutations of creolization (Precolumbian, Latino-American, African, French, English, Spanish, Portuguese, Dutch, Indian, Syro-Lebanese, Japanese, and also North American and Canadian). Says Depestre, "Anthropologically and culturally, they [these median contexts] keep intersecting, inter-penetrating, fertilizing, juxtaposing each other, before venturing with a sensuous and baroque exuberance into the process of creolization that crossbreeds them [or, onto the cross-weaving loom that creolizes them]" (161).

Creolization is thus defined as a syncretic process of transverse dynamics that endlessly reworks and transforms the cultural patterns of varied social and historical experiences and identities. The cultural patterns that result from this "crossbreeding" (or cross-weaving) undermine any academic or political aspiration for unitary origins or authenticity. In *Le discours antillais,* Martinican critic Edouard Glissant remarks that the reality of "the general cultural phenomenon of creolization is all too apparent, although the legitimacy of this concept remains to be grounded, its specificity clarified" (422). In his major theoretical works Glissant explains his vision of the specificity of Caribbean identity, which consists of two main axes, antillanité, or Caribbeanness, and poétique de la relation, or cross-cultural poetics. According to Glissant, these interrelated and interdependent concepts express the racial and cultural pluralism, historical discontinuity, geographical fragmentation and political insularity of the Caribbean experience. Through a cross-cultural poetics, Glissant seeks to express the diversity of his people's collective identity through practice of textual métissage by which he establishes the possibility of a pluralist postcolonial textuality able to forge a new Caribbean identity.

In stating that "creolization carries within itself the adventure of multilinguism along with the extraordinary explosion of cultures" (1990, 46–47), Glissant underscores the unlimited creative dimension of creolization—its infinite openness, its resilient dynamics, its fluidity—all triumphantly conveyed through the multiple facets of the Creole language. The discursive "relation" between this description of Caribbean culture and that offered by Bernabé, Chamoiseau, and Confiant in *Éloge de la créolité* is significant; "At the heart of our Creoleness," the authors of *Éloge* write, "we will maintain the modulation of new rules, of illicit blendings. For we know that no culture is ever a finished product, but rather the constant dynamic search for original questions, new possibilities, more interested in relating than dominating, in exchanging rather than looting" (54).[4]

The weight of history is evident in the terms *criollo* in Spanish, *Creole* and *creoleness* in English, and *créolité* in French. These terms are sometimes synonymous with mestizaje in Spanish or métissage in French, but they involve a variety of semantic fields that have shifted throughout the history of the Caribbean and that even today vary in meanings and connotations in different regions.[5] The very shifting nature of these terms in historical and cultural contexts marks the risk that accompanies any attempt to circumscribe either the concept or reality of "creoleness." In our current context, for instance, the authors of *Éloge's* original interpretation of a francophone *créolité* distinct from that of the anglophone or hispanophone, was promptly revised. In a more inclusive representation of creolization, Antonio Benítez-Rojo sees in the "discontinuous conjunction" of the Caribbean basin "the features of an island that 'repeats' itself, unfolding and bifurcating until it reaches all the seas and lands of the earth, while at the same time it inspires multidisciplinary maps of unexpected designs" (3). Like Glissant's rejection of all boundaries, Benítez-Rojo's definition represents the Caribbean as "a cultural meta-archipelago without center and without limits, a chaos within which there is an island that proliferates endlessly, each copy a different one, founding and refounding ethnological materials like a cloud will do with its vapor" (9).

Significantly, some twenty years before discussions of creolization by Glissant, Bernabé, Confiant, Chamoiseau, and Benítez-Rojo, the poet and historian Edward Brathwaite, in his study of colonial Jamaica, defined creolization as a way of seeing Jamaican society and the Caribbean islands generally, "not in terms of white and black, master and slave, in separate nuclear units, but as contributory parts of a whole" (1971, 307). Rather than stressing the distinctness of cultures, Brathwaite identified "impurity" (or "demographic alliance") as the necessary precondition of the emergence of a purely Caribbean culture in the future. Brathwaite, then, was one of the first to posit that the liberating process of creolization originates from the unrestricted interaction of cultures.

It is from this dynamic that creolization becomes a power for reversing the processes of acculturation (or assimilation), deculturation, discontinuity, and marginalization that have affected the entire Caribbean. As quoted above, Derek Walcott notes in his 1993 Nobel Lecture that he is "only one-eighth the writer [he] might have been had [he] contained all the fragmented languages of Trinidad." He adds, "Break a vase, and the love that reassembles the fragments is stronger than that love which took its symmetry for granted when it was whole" (8).

This is not to say that the region's complex human mixtures, as well as its labyrinthine racial and cultural combinations, are not the result of, or do not result in, a painful pattern of confrontations and ruptures among racial groups and of considerable mutations of personal and cultural identity. Indeed, those who inhabit this region still dwell in a socially, racially, and spiritually fragmented world—one that yearns to imagine itself as a whole. From the early days of slavery to the present, this need has underscored the struggles, conflicts, and upheavals within communities as well as individuals.

Though Gilroy's metaphor of the black Atlantic's "Middle Passage" as a ship is a compelling one, the historical experience of colonialism and slavery in the Caribbean has more often been summed up in a powerful signifier: the plantation. The lives and values of Caribbean peoples have been shaped and controlled by this experience, and its resulting injury is still felt deep in the region's psyche. The pain from these wounds surfaces at the slightest pressure and constitutes the essence of artistic creation. It comes as no surprise then, that even in a 1973 interview, George Lamming could assert that for the Caribbean people "the colonial experience is a live experience in [their] consciousness"; it is "a continuing psychic experience that has to be dealt with long after the actual colonial situation formally 'ends'" (Kent 92).

Indeed, the issue of identity has been raised by every Caribbean writer who confronts the individual or collective question of memory, of belonging, and of being. The fiction of Caribbean writers such as Lamming,[6] contemporary Caribbean poetry (including that of Derek Walcott), the plays of Errol Hill and of the Sistren Collective all make the reader hear, see, and feel the struggles of individuals and communities that spring from a history of slaughter, oppression, and negation.

It is the weight of this history that shaped V. S. Naipaul's early view of the Caribbean as "half made societies that seem doomed to remain half-made"[7] and that leads Walcott to acknowledge, as does Naipaul, that "the basis of the Antillean experience" is "this shipwreck of fragments, these echoes, these shards of a huge tribal vocabulary, these partially remembered customs" (1993, 11). In that regard, Naipaul's symbolic representation of the shipwrecked and hopeless Caribbean—most explicitly illustrated in *The Mimic Men*—is in sharp contrast to that of Gilroy and echoes European thinkers such as Froude, whose words Walcott repeats in his 1993 Nobel Lecture: "the Caribbean is still *looked at,* illegitimate, rootless, mongrelized. 'No people there,' to quote Froude, 'in the true sense of the word.' No people. Fragments and echoes of real people, unoriginal and broken" (6, our emphasis). Pointing to the irony imbedded in the paradox of modernity, Milan Kundera sums up isolation of such multiplicity: "in Martinique, France, Africa, and America meet. Yes, that's beautiful, except that France, Africa, and America couldn't care less. In today's world, reduced to a few megacenters, we can barely hear the voices of the small [centers]. . . . Martinique: the encounter of a marvelous cultural complexity and of an immense solitude" (Kundera 1993, 57–58). It is this solitude that most clearly emerges in the works of Caribbean writers, including Naipaul, who recently has taken a more affirming view of the Caribbean "shipwreck." Indeed, Naipaul no longer seems to see the Caribbean as a shipwreck, as he uses a more positive metaphor—motion—one that also emerges from Gilroy's sense of the significance of ships. Always mindful of universal truths, Naipaul reminds his readers that the "history of the Mediterranean regions, of Turkey, Carthage and Rome, is a history in perpetual motion."[8] In typical Naipaulian fashion, the assertion that "we are made of a multitude of heritages" is immediately followed by the dismissive: "and to me, discussing the questions of culture and identity as if they would be new issues is a matter for superficial chatter" (5). For most people from the Caribbean, however—whether they reside in the Caribbean or in its diaspora—and for those who study their history, cultures, and languages, there is nothing superficial about questions of Creole culture and identity.

Quite to the contrary, it is a constant source of wonder that, despite the fragmentation derived from plantation economies and despite the very painful historical experience of colonialism, the elements of creolization have survived to reveal their spirited adaptability in the formation of new nations. It is no less remarkable that Caribbean writing has managed to move from narratives of existential fragmentation (common in pre-1970s Caribbean literature) to narratives that celebrate new multifaceted and liberated identities (common in "post-colonial"[9] writings of the 1970s and 1980s, especially in women's texts). In his Nobel statement, Derek Walcott speaks for more than a few fellow Caribbean writers when he sees the scene of the "shipwreck" as one of teeming vitality:

> That is the basis of the Antillean experience, this shipwreck of fragments, these echoes, these shards of a huge tribal vocabulary, these partially remembered customs, and they are not decayed but strong. They survived the Middle Passage and the *Fatel Rozak*, the ship that carried the indentured Indians from the port of Madras to the cane fields of Felicity, that carried the chained Cromwellian convict and the Sephardic Jew, the Chinese grocer and the Lebanese merchant selling cloth samples on his bicycle. (1993, 11–12)

For a fuller representation of creolization, add to Walcott's description Depestre's observation that the historical process of creolization (resulting from maroon activity outside of the plantation system) "engendered new modes of thinking, of acting, of feeling, of imagining, of dancing, of praying, of working within the dynamic social body" (164). Add, too, Benítez-Rojo's image of Caribbean culture and its literary expression as a syncretic artifact, made of the interplay of "foreign" signifiers originated in Europe, sub-Saharan Africa, and southern Asia, with "traditional" signifiers, or local codes, an interplay that is "like a ray of light with a prism; that is, they produce phenomena of reflection, refraction, and decomposition. But the light keeps on being light" (21).

These reflecting and refracting images of creolization offer glimpses of a process, not of a product. And this, fundamentally, is why in recent years a few Caribbean writers have critiqued concepts identified in descriptive nouns that imply a static state of being (as in the critiques of the notion of créolité) or of an essentialized synthesis (as in Benítez-Rojo's critique of the notion of mestizaje). In the evolving and revolving process of creolization, the energy of the imaginary's unpredictable and innovative spiraling must keep on whirling.

In order to read and talk about texts that emerge from the process of creolization, Benítez-Rojo suggests an "aesthetics of Chaos" (1–5); Glissant expresses the same notion of chaos in his articulation of the "esthetics of the chaos-monde," the necessarily changing mentalities in mutual exchange (108). What these writers offer is a new poetics for the Caribbean: an affirmation that creolization means "difference"—the right to "opacity," as Glissant puts it (203–9)—and consequently the refusal of universal transparent models. This poetics celebrates the right to borrow or absorb selected components of the "other" without relinquishing one's own dimensions; it is an interplay of mutual mutations. "Capacities for genuine change" are possible, says Wilson Harris, only through "cross-cultural imaginations," by transforming reductive models or "rituals" into new, open aesthetics (1983, xv).

In recent years the increasing number of anthologies in English—offering a sampling of fiction, poetry, or drama by writers from the various areas of the Caribbean—has marked a growing interest in Caribbean writing. Notable general collections include *Contemporary Caribbean Short Stories* (Morris 1990), *If I Could Write This in Fire* (Smorkaloff 1994), and *Rhythm and Revolt: Tales of the Antilles* (Breton 1995). Significant anthologies focusing exclusively on women's writing include *Her True Name* (Mordecai and Wilson 1989), *Creation Fire* (Espinet 1990), *Green Cane and Juicy Flotsam* (Esteves and Paravisini-Gebert 1991). Charles Rowell's recent anthology *The Ancestral House* (1995) includes but is not limited to Caribbean short stories. Other anthologies that have offered a much-needed critical and theoretical examination of Caribbean writing have tended to focus on women writers; most notable are *Out of the Kumbla* (Davies and Fido 1990) and *Caribbean Women Writers* (Cudjoe 1990). Daryl Dance's *New World Adams: Conversations with Contemporary West Indian Writers* (1992) is an excellent presentation of Caribbean writers' critical voices, but Dance's interviews were mostly recorded in the early 1980s, at a time when the discourse on creolization had not yet gathered its current power.

This collection of essays occupies a special space in the discourse of creolization because it draws together prominent writers from the English-, French-, Spanish-, and Dutch-speaking Caribbean and from various Caribbean nations—which are clearly defined political and economical spaces: Cuba, Curaçao, the Dominican Republic, Grenada,

Guadeloupe, Guyana, Haiti, Jamaica, Martinique, Panama, Suriname, and Tobago. Our identification of the writers according to their countries relies on our understanding that each space possesses its own political and ethnic specificity, although we understand that Caribbean cultures flow—as Benítez-Rojo has pointed out both in *The Repeating Island* and in his essay on Cuban creolization included here—into patterns overlapping borders and therefore testify to the subversive, liberating vitality of the process of creolization. Indeed, these essays represent a truly diverse range of reflections on the complexities of the transcultural Caribbean imagination and on its fundamentally paradoxical impact on Caribbean writing. This textual diversity produces a dynamic comparative reading which, in turn, reproduces the manifold dimensions of creolization.

More importantly, however, these essays represent our current moment in the dialectical process of coexistence and interaction among the regions of the Caribbean. Our contributors share an awareness of and support for discrete cultural identity while realizing that creolization is the condition that allows them to reconcile and transcend past alienations. Because creolization involves a cultural process rooted in long-lasting psychological, spiritual, anthropological, and linguistic experiences, the texture of this anthology reproduces the fundamentally eclectic pattern of Caribbean experiences.

The essays are grouped around the two main elements of creolization that affect literary production. Part 1, "Creolization and the Creative Imagination," addresses the search for cultural meaning in all aspects of life. These essays reveal the reality of creolization as the unceasing process of transformation of mythical, existential, religious, social, political, and cultural elements constantly acting upon each other, as Wilson Harris points out in his essay. Antonio Benítez-Rojo examines the unstable states of creolization through the endlessly repeated explosion of the plantation. He shows how the rhythm inscribed in the literary language of recently published Caribbean works refers to the black hole of the plantation, where the paradox of the fragmented Caribbean self lies. On the other hand, Carlos Guillermo Wilson reminds us that the "cradle-hammock" of creolization to which his title refers was also the cradle from which African children were stolen, and that racism survives in the mestizaje cultures of Hispanic nations of the Caribbean and Central America. In the essays by Astrid Roemer, Sherezada (Chiqui) Vicioso, Erna Brodber, and Lourdes Vázquez explorations of creolization take the form of a search for cultural inheritance and for a return to a space that can yield a fuller memory. In these essays creolization is at the crossroads of forgetting and remembering, of an elusive past to be re-imagined and an uncertain future.

The essays in part 2, " Creolization, Literature, and the Politics of Language," focus more specifically on the linguistic terrain that Caribbean literature inhabits and explores. The question of language is at the core of these explorations because in the Caribbean—as in many other parts of the world with a colonial past—most literary texts reflect a struggle with the imposed language of the colonizer in which the texts themselves are often produced. Collins's awareness of her learned academic discourse and Philip's jubilant rejection of that same discourse aptly frame this section, in which all of the essays address master/slave relations in the creole languages of the Caribbean. Both Collins and Philip articulate, in their individual styles, the subversive process of appropriating the inherited "master" language and turning it into their own expressions of identity. Read together, these essays illustrate Benítez-Rojo's observations and show how—through a transformed language and the creation of new techniques, styles, syntaxes, images, rhythms, and meanings—Caribbean writers have overcome cultural displacement and exerted control over their own creation.

In their essays, Frank Martinus Arion and Jean Métellus develop opposing theories of masters' and slaves' roles in the creation and development of Caribbean languages. While Arion rejects the "Great House" theory of the formation of Papiamento, Métellus embraces this theory as he affirms the French origins of Haitian Creole. Taken together, the essays explore the impact of these conflicting theories on literary production as well as on contemporary political struggles for authority.

The essays by Ernest Pépin and Raphaël Confiant, and Maryse Condé explore more directly the role of Creole languages in the production of consciousness and literature. While Pépin and Confiant take on some of the critiques recently leveled on their use of créolité, Condé rebuts the manifesto of the Martinican "school of créolité"—with its rigid linguistic rules and restricting canon—and refuses to be creatively confined to her native land. Like Pépin and Confiant, Condé reaffirms Creole languages as linguistic subversion as well as resistance to colonial oppression, but she claims her need for and right to unrestricted individualism.

Daniel Maximin's poetic opening essay, "Antillean Journey," embodies aspects of both parts of the collection through its claim of a poetic subject and a language of mixed sounds, tonalities, rhythms, and flavors. The collection begins with Maximin's piece because it retraces the ambiguous journey of the French-speaking islands' languages (through his literary elders Aimé Césaire, Léon Damas, Gilbert Gratiant, and through local modes of expression): "Music, Creole, French" are the Antilles' "maternal tongues" linked freely together to express a collective imaginary. The collection ends with Philip's essay as a superb illustration of what Maximin sees as Désirade's task in writing as a Caribbean Creole woman. Through the metaphor of Caribbean people carnivalling and "moving" through the streets of Toronto, Philip shows how cultural, social, and linguistic realities are shaped by the politics and ideologies of a community at a given time, and how these in turn shape her own literary creativity.

Finally, Yanick Lahens's afterword goes beyond the explanatory overview of this introduction and offers a critical perspective on some of the specific issues that the essays raise. Focusing on the issues of unity and diversity that emerge in both the theoretical and practical aspects of creolization, Lahens offers a sober look at the Caribbean. Often taking the uniqueness of Haiti as her point of departure, Lahens reminds the reader that discussions of creolization are very incomplete if they fail to include an understanding of maronnage, the literal as well as figurative flight of Africans from any contact with their enslavers.

As reflections on the many facets of the concept and connotations of creolization, creoleness, créolité, antillanité, métissage, mestizaje, and related concepts, all the essays gathered in this anthology are engaged in repossessing the past, defining present identities, and shaping new liberated poetics—contributing, therefore, to the representation of changing Caribbean aesthetics. Indeed, the contributors to this anthology are articulating new modes of thought which, though nurtured in their specific geographical context, depart from it to reach a global understanding of the world. From the myth of an original—lost—identity to the mosaïc of identities created through cross-cultural associations, the process of creolization actually encompasses the story of all peoples displaced in the movement of colonial empires, nationalistic upheavals, and economic disasters. And, although the word creolization itself is etymologically linked to specific geographical areas (the Caribbean, Louisiana, Guyana, Brazil, Mauritius, Reunion), its cultural and ethnic ramifications encompass broader cultural phenomena that are emblematic of the condition of many cultures in the twentieth century.[10] From this perspective, whether Caribbean creolization is signified as a ship, a shipwreck, a plantation, a crossroads, a cradle-hammock, or a liberating Creole language, what emerges from the essays collected here is a world-view of liberation, redemption, and transcendence.

Kathleen M. Balutansky
Saint Michael's College

Marie-Agnès Sourieau
Fairfield University

Antillean Journey

Daniel Maximin
Translated by Kathleen M. Balutansky

Prelude

Your name is Désirade and you dream of writing. Of a writing free and sweeping enough to spin sentences without boundaries, words without end—a trail of islands suspended on a watery page, at the edge of over-crowded continents. Free enough to celebrate your awakening to the beauty of a world of stowage and drifting, to elevate your verses against forbid-ding obstacles, and to rescue from their silence your desires adrift between shielded mouths and closed ears—without surrendering to the masters of language the keys to the freedom of your words.

Yes, you wish to narrate the fire of your apocalypse. And the course of your reading timidly follows the message of adopted fathers and mothers who managed to stand up to codes of oppression, and had no fear of nam-ing for the future the unnamable and the marvelous in the first languages within reach of their unfettered hearts.

For everywhere—with the power of bamboo lithely tearing exotic lace—poetry uproots consciences from the swamps, from marshes and mangroves, thus discovering nations well concealed in the landscape, the sap of free-dom in upright bodies, the volcano under the mountain, the mahogany wood for the *poteaux-mitans* (center post, used in Vodun ceremony).

A literary heritage comes with neither right of succession nor of initiation.

A single word, offered to strip the borrowed styles of your loneliness.

Travel back to your roots.

And, risking its luster, your obscured leaf will rise in flight.

Thus goes exile.

Antillean Désirade.

You come from a people without mother tongue, with neither private voice nor private domain; with no particular gods. The Antilles: fires without hearth, rested in their pride on three Caribbean rocks, to forge new hearts with seven scattered bloodlines. Africa, Europe, Asia, and America: four continents to create an island.

You are born from a defiant people, accustomed to grasping left-handed nocturnal freedoms.

The master and the slave have created the Creole language, and Creole has served orders and whip, submission and revolt, marooning and drums. And the same French language has served to codify the laws of inequity as well as to convey ideas of enlightenment that validated the revolt against the *Code Noir* (1685 slave legislation issued by France for its colonies). Diderot against Bougainville. Romantic graffiti against imperial walls. Then, the former slaves decreed the law of Creole freedoms. And Blacks, now humanized, undertook the systematic conquest of formal equality through the mastery of European academic, political, and legal discourses:

> I am a man of good thirst, crazed, circling the poisoned ponds.
> Aimé Césaire, *Et les chiens se taisaient* (1989, 67)[1]

(No wonder the colonists always distrusted French written by Blacks, just as the colonial state distrusted the Creole spoken by the colonized.)

From the start, bilingualism—though still insufficiently shared—represented the Antillean's contradictory desires to empower the Antilles to master their own history in the sociojudicial framework of Europe, while at the same time demanding their individuality in celebrating the conniving sociocultural forms of the oppressed:

> Every text written by a Black or a Mulatto diminishes every
> day the number of detractors . . . and adds to the numbers of
> those who are convinced of the moral and intellectual capaci-
> ties of Blacks. (Vaval [1933] 1971, 476)

Then blossomed an initial literature more interested in ridding Blacks of the status of savage inhumanity and in making Europe recognize that the descendants of slaves were worthy of rising to the status of foreign black brothers. And oblivion seemed the shortest path to this metamorphosis: hardly ever did this poetry portray the human condition. No longer denouncing the Antillean hell, poets portrayed instead a paradise without humans, where the celebration of solitude allowed the poet to elude a confrontation with his subjects. Countering the Romantic project of celebrating nocturnal schemes between man and nature, this poetry devoutly burned its memories in the midday sun so as to plant for tomorrow the laurels of better days. Against the Romantic poetry of autumn and memory, nineteenth-century poetry of the Antilles was essentially Parnassian, more concerned with celebrating its mastery of language and lavish scenery than with countering its lack of language and humanity:

> Midday! the air that blazes, and burns, and consumes itself
> Pours into our weak eyes an unyielding clarity
> Everything quivers in space and in the vastness
> The blue sky is cloudless and the horizon without mist
>   Gilbert de Chamberland, "Midi"[2]

> cassias and flame trees are in bloom, this is the month
> Of the blazing island light
> Unknown winds descend from the woods
> The Caribbean spring bursts in the towns.
>   Daniel Thaly, "L'Inutile Paradis"[3]

As every society constitutes itself from its lost paradise, it might have been necessary for these poets to build a dream landscape in order to better overcome the historical nightmare of seasons in hell. Offering a welcoming geography to a new history, the enslaved land transformed into land of love promising the birth of the Antilles. Later, the light of day was wed to the shadows of history with the advent of the journal *Lucioles*,[4] in Martinique in 1927:

> In our countries, countries where the sun sets, shade has come early. Shade is made of light reflecting the path of departed thought.
>   What do we want? To slightly move back the sunset while attracting to our beginning of night the most fertile rays that a sun has left behind in the old Europe.
>   What else do we want? In spite of the red effort of light, the West remains its grave. Thus, in our Islands have not you seen, once the sun is buried, these particles of wandering light rising, zigzagging at the mercy of their lively fantasies, from fires, it is some life flying. "Fireflies" of letters, pregnant with the

thought of a Near-West, pregnant also with the Martinican effort, our writings will carry poems and songs, critiques, studies
and tales in the ashen twilight of our Antilles.

Those who will know us are those who want to extract themselves from their lives and escape, for a time, from the prison
of days. (Graciant)

To escape the prison of words one had to imagine a new language, an
entirely new "credo for mixed-bloods." This fertile play on the absence of
language and the inadequacy of the discourse of European cultures too
old and self-assured to feed the fragile rebirth would be the work of
Gratiant's students from the *Lycée* of Fort-de-France, Césaire and Damas,
also heirs of Mallarmé and of Rimbaud's *"Livre Nègre"*:

> This exceptional sentence of Mallarmé: "My senses lament the
> failure of discourse . . . only it philosophically restores the lan-
> guage's flaws." . . . I strongly believe in these matters and effort
> has been to *bend* the French language, to *transform* it to ex-
> press, let us say: the I, the black-I, the Creole-I, the Martinican-
> I, the Antillean-I. That is why I have been more interested in
> poetry than in prose, to the extent that it is the poet who cre-
> ates his own language. (Césaire 1978)[5]

The poetic act always accompanies the initiation of peoples born blind
to their own renaissance for lack of the reassuring myths that elsewhere
sustain the birth of every society. History and geography, revolt and
métissage, music and insult, the volcano and the mangrove merge in passionate love, transforming islands into an archipelago, without a single
blank page in the saga of the trees:

> [A]nd the sea is leafy, and from the height of its crest I am
> reading a magnificent land, full of sun . . . of parrots . . . of fruit
> . . . of fresh water . . . of breadfruit trees. . . . A land of coves, of
> palm leaves, of screw pines . . . a land of open hands. . . . And
> the world does not spare me. . . . There is not in the world one
> single poor lynched bastard, one poor tortured man, in whom
> I am not also murdered and humiliated. (Césaire 1989, 67, 70)[6]

It is the heart that begets the defiant poet, not the poet who creates a
nation, in spite of the temptation to speak for the sorrows that cannot
speak. Thus was born Damas, the poet, the child born without mother

tongue because of his mother's death; until age seven unable to speak
either Creole or French; reborn as a major poet to recapture, in Paris—the
Paris of exile and of the meeting of Blacks—his words caught between his
suffering and his color:

> Who is to speak
> if not still-born
> my other self. . . .
> Who is to speak if not you
> of all the grief of choosing words
> guiding red roses
> to kill a solitude
> weary of witnessing dawn's
> refusal to bring light to the new day.
>   Léon-Gontran Damas, "Qui pourrait dire"[7]

Thus was born the poet Césaire, in the dazzling coherence of his jour-
neys between past and future, the wild harvest of quills scattered since
Gore for the flight of the Caribbean bird initiated to its own reawakening
far from the ashes of nostalgia and resentment, the essence of a free language hidden under a disguise of languages, the fierce "we" illuminating
the "I":

> Trophey head lacerated limbs
> deadly sting beautiful spurted blood
> lost warblings ravished shores
> childhoods a tale too stirred up
> dawn on its chain ferocious snapping to be born
>   oh belated assassin
> the bird with feathers once more beautiful than the past
> demands an accounting for its scattered plumes
>   Aimé Césaire, "Beau sang giclé" (1983, 307)

So here you are today, Antillean Désirade, rich from this inheritance.
Less exiled within yourself since an overused and oppressive language—
French, English, Spanish—has supplied this writing with a dignity conquered by a transmutation of defeat into victory, the magic of poetry teaching you to steal victory from the victors' demons. Less exiled, since in you
the Creole language reclaims the original oral version of the familial narrative that your writing wishes to translate.

And here you are, upright and free, stripped heiress, challenging those who manage and exploit the spoils of colonial ruins, who trade on their fear of the "other," and who offer both the affliction and the vaccine. You defy those who see only alienation and a scorched landscape as their trajectory, and who think themselves absolute masters of the "I" of the "Other," under the illusion that their imperialist languages and cultures keep in check peoples who are supposedly powerless to bring together their dispersed languages. The wise can be blinded by those who know how to keep a balanced alterity, free of the crutches of good or bad conscience, good feelings or resentments. But Rimbaud, Char, Michaux, and Leiris have already given you the keys to these wild parades. And Frantz Fanon leaped to save your skin from the mask of colors.

Yes, you are a native of two or three languages. Your mother tongues: music, Creole, French. Married in the melodies of nursery rhymes: *Choubouloute* and *Chère Elise*. Married in the violence of anger expressed in Creole, as in the formal brutality of reprimands spoken in French. Married in the landscape endowed with an endless richness of words to pay homage to all those who, since the Caribs, journeyed forth. For the names of islands: *Madinina, Karukda;* for the names of flowers and birds: *Manz-Marie* the sensitive, and *Colibri Foufou.* And always honor and respect for all speech. As far as you can remember, even as far as your illiterate ancestors, no one has taught you to despise a language, in spite of forbidding circumstances. Scorning all censure, and wise to the cost of silence and to their right of speech, Caribbean nations relish any language that their music has turned to honey: Creole, Spanish, French, English.

You are also born of a people for whom dance is a reflection of balance. Never forget to dance with your languages, following the poet's command, far enough from yourself so that your style cannot follow you. And allow the rhythm of the *laghia,* of the Antillean *bel-air* and of the Afro-Cuban *guajira* to draw in your mind a space where you can more freely translate the resonant alliance of your delight and your grief.

Yes, your island, losing her nakedness in the archipelago's richness, has managed to turn the seed of violation into creative delight and to quench her thirst with those who share that thirst:

> The size of a man's country often varies according to his heart: small if the heart is small, vast if the heart is big. I have never suffered from my country's smallness, which is not to say that I have a big heart. And given a choice, it is here in Guadeloupe that I would rather be born again, suffer and die. Yet not long ago my ancestors were slaves on this volcanic, hurricane-swept,

mosquito-ridden, narrow-minded island. But I did not come to the world to assume the weight of the world's grief. I prefer to dream, standing in my garden, like all old women my age, until death takes me as I dream, in all my joy. (Schwarz-Bart 1972, 11)[8]

So, Antillean Désirade, you dare to write that your love for your island is not a reflection of the foreigner's gaze. And if you dare to write it and describe yourself in the present, without guilt and without recourse to courts of the past nor to juries of the future, listening to your vital "why?" without denying the detours of the "how," then you will dare to let your writing body lovingly mold its wayward path to the future, as its uprooted sap nourishes your store of spirit:

> Exile thus goes into the feeder made of stars
> bearing clumsy grains to the birds born of time
> which never fall asleep
> in the fertile spaces of stirred up childhoods.
>   Aimé Césaire, "Birds" (1983, 275)

Part One
~ ~ ~

Creolization and
the Creative Imagination

Most of these essays take a personal perspective on creolization and its embodiment in Caribbean culture and literature. Starting with Wilson Harris's search of a mythological/metaphysical expression, they address the search for the cultural meanings of creolization, as devastating as some of their aspects may seem. The essays reveal the reality of creolization as the unceasing process of transformation of political, religious, social, and cultural elements constantly acting upon one another or humanizing one another, as Harris shows in his discussion of Legba and Hephaestus. In some cases, as in Brodber's "Where Are All the Others?" these explorations grow into a search for cultural inheritance, for a return to a beginning that can yield a collective memory. In these essays, as in Harris's imagined genesis, creolization is indeed at the crossroads of forgetting and remembering, but most importantly, Harris points out, it is at the crossroads of an elusive past to be re-imagined and a future yet to be imagined.

In "'Creoleness'—The Crossroads of a Civilization?" Wilson Harris creates a mythological genesis of creolization which, in his use of the Haitian Loa Legba and the Greek god Hephaestus, explores the complex metaphysical linkages and mixed traditions that nurture emotions and passions within individuals and in society. Harris goes back to his personal experience as a Guyanese Creole to trace how creoleness applies to the genesis of the imagination in South America and the Caribbean. In a multifaceted meditation, Harris examines the paradoxes of creoleness through what he calls "the creolization of the chasm," which is the appropriation of one cultural artifact by another culture through involuntary associations. Harris's conception of creolization as the humanization of extra-human faculties and as a transcendence of black and white is balanced by Carlos Guillermo Wilson's essay, which reminds us of forms of racism that survive in the mestizaje cultures of Hispanic nations of the Caribbean and Central America. Starting from the creolization that produced the Garifuna culture and language of Central Americans of African descent, Wilson, himself a *Chombo* or Black Panamanian, denounces the imperative to "whiten the race" that has dominated the national agenda in Cuba, Puerto Rico, the Dominican Republic, and Panama.

In "Who Is Afraid of the Winti Spirit?" Astrid H. Roemer explores the many aspects of Surinamese Creole culture in her native Suriname and in Holland, and she analyzes its African presence in Winti religion. Roemer argues that African Winti practice is at the heart of creolization in Suriname, just as it is the heartbeat of Surinamese Creoles in the Netherlands.

In "Three Words toward Creolization," Antonio Benítez-Rojo presents creolization as a discontinuous series of recurrences in which the dynamics of the plantation repeats itself in the Carnival of language and music, dance and literature, food and theater. Sherezada (Chiqui) Vicioso explores the world of her childhood in the Dominican Republic and the development of her awareness of people's skin color. In "Dominicanyorkness: A Metropolitan Discovery of the Triangle," Vicioso retraces the world of her childhood when she discovers how skin color limits women's destinies. Her journey to consciousness culminates in New York, where she is confronted with institutional racism. There, and at the university that she attends, she becomes aware of the elements of her American creolization: she is a mulatto, a Latina Caribbean woman, and a social construct of U.S. capitalism. In a similar tone, Brodber in "Where Are All the Others?" searches for the connections between African American and Barbadian manners and speech. Her recollections of Miss Manda serve as the foundation for her meditations on the politics of language and its impact on Caribbean culture and literature. In "A Brief History of My Country," Lourdes Vázquez interweaves the history of Puerto Rico with that of her ancestors to examine the manifold dimensions of mestizo literature as manifestations of Puerto Rican creolization.

1

~

Creoleness

The Crossroads of a Civilization?

Wilson Harris

There are, I am sure, many approaches to the ideas, themes, and concepts embodied in what is called "creoleness." My main interest in writing this essay is to seek to trace how creoleness may apply to fiction, indeed to the genesis of the imagination in the living soil of South America and the Caribbean. May I say at the outset that such genesis for me is ceaselessly unfinished and that this sensation of *unfinished genesis*—in worlds of space and nature and psyche—has its roots as much in Old Worlds as in New, in the crossroads of a civilization upon which we may have arrived in subtle and complex and involuntary ways that are altering conventional linearity and conventional frameworks.

I do not wish in doing so—in tracing the application of creoleness to fiction and to the nature of our potential to change our responses to reality—to engage in purely intellectual argument or theory. Indeed this is not my intention at all. What I hope to do is to touch chords of deep-seated emotion and passion which lie within shared layers of experience in person and society: layers that are native to the embattled, philosophic core of universality, universal crisis, within creoleness.

My mother and her middle-class family in British Guiana in the 1930s were called Creoles. Our ancestry was mixed: Amerindian; European; African; and, on my father's side, perhaps Asian as well. (Because of a family rift, I have never properly known his antecedents.)

Sometimes the term *Creole* was implicitly or covertly hurled at us like a metaphoric brick (designed to alert us to our impure lineage and mixed race) by the pure-blooded tenants, so to speak, of a property that my father—who died when I was two years old—had left me in his will. I occasionally visited this property when I was at school—perhaps first when I was eight or nine—and it imprinted upon me unforgettable unease if not guilt or terror. Such properties were, in their tenement order, slices of a plantation world. They existed sometimes cheek by jowl with beautiful colonial residences and houses which prompted the guidebooks to speak of "the garden city of Georgetown"; as if to cement an involuntary treaty of sensibility or insensibility between the *inferno* and the *paradiso* in South American soil. Infernal plantation age, paradisean garden city!

From childhood, therefore, creoleness made me aware of the complex labyrinth of the family of humankind into which I was born in the twentieth century. I felt myself peculiarly involved with the tenants who threw their fictional stone at the Creole landlord—involved in their deprivations and disadvantages. They were African Guyanese, East Indian Guyanese, sometimes poor white Portuguese Guyanese. The label *Indian* possesses half-static, half-kaleidoscopic proportions in the mind of the folk as if to bring the paradox of mixtures, of creoleness, into Carnival play. *East Indian* was a label applicable to the descendants of Indians who arrived from India into Guyana under a system of indenture in the nineteenth century. The label tended to run at the edges into American "Indian" or Amerindian tribes, who formed a small but legendary proportion of the Guyanese population.

It is contended in some quarters that Creoles were the pure, lineal descendants of early settlers in South America and the Guyanas. But my experience is different. The wounds, the vulnerability of the Creole bring a different emphasis into the human comedy. I found myself on the edges or margins of a world, the estate of the world, that were shifting into numinous disorder in order paradoxically to alert us to shared responsibilities within the unfinished genesis of arts of survival. This numinous paradox was largely masked from us by ghetto-fixated habit.

As a consequence, therefore, in the eyes of the depraved tenant of the New World creoleness was so internalized yet suppressed that scapegoats became the order of the day. Creoleness became a form of self-deceptive division even as it harbored within itself a potential for the renascence of community. Such renascence could not be easily stilled, and thus it engendered patterns of nemesis in its suppression.

A perverse, yet apparently natural, order of political fiction tended to grip the populace. Creoleness was a badge of blood and mixed descent from wicked plantation owners who had made astronomical fortunes by sweated labor or by slaves in previous generations. Whatever historical truth lay in this, the tragedy was in reinforcing a fixation with protest, a suppression of profoundest creativity to throw bridges across chasms, to open an architecture of space within closed worlds of race and culture. A mind-set came into play that was to bedevil, I believe, the arts and the sciences. For without complex revisionary bridges between art and science, conscience is paralyzed by dogma; and freedom, in my view, grows increasingly susceptible to a hidden mafia or ruthless establishment within civilization.

I use the term *mafia* not in any political or national context (such as Italian mafia, American mafia, or any other aspect of a hegemonic underworld), but in order to illumine a perverse commitment to privileged frame or family, a hidden authoritarianism that cements its vested interest in the preservation of ruling convention by fostering an incestuous realism or comedy of manners in fiction, fashion, and the like. Although one may argue that fashions in the arts may incline toward rebellious extremes, nevertheless they are underpinned, it seems to me, by the logic of consensus or conditioned, short-term responses to reality in consumer societies, the logic of materialism; a logic that sustains, however unwittingly, an invariant code or fate. The body politic grafts into itself considerable skills in the sophisticated manipulation of bias and prejudice, even within those who protest against the rule of things. Such protest is fated to be conditioned by the very thing it targets. One merely has to glance at the rise of authoritarian, rigged elections in newly independent states once under British, French, Dutch, Spanish, or Portuguese rule.

This is a crucial matter of form that, it seems to me, is rarely considered by cultural and political vested interests on the right (so-called) or the left (so-called). There is virtuosity of form or skill or talent in playing upon, or within, an invariant model or frame. There is originality of form that taps caches of imagery and possibility in a state of eclipse through/beyond/within apparently invariant but *partial* models.

We need, I am sure, to consider all this with the greatest care to arrive within the immeasurable but curiously concrete ground of *involuntary* association between invariance (unchanging premise or frame or story line of art) and complex chasms that may offer resources of transubstantial dimensionality and change, transfigurative bridges between apparently closed orders still susceptible to conquistadorial habit.

The word *chasm* is adopted therefore in this exploratory essay to imply that within the gulfs that divide cultures—gulfs which some societies seek to bypass by the logic of an institutional self-division of humanity or by the practice of ethnic cleansing—there exists, I feel, a storage of creative possibility that, once tapped, may energize the unfinished genesis of the imagination. In that energy eclipsed bridges and potential bridges exist between divorced or separated or closed orders and worlds, bridges that are sometimes precarious, never absolute, but which I think engender a profound awareness of the numinous solidity of space, inner space/outer space, space as the womb of simultaneous densities and transparencies in the language of originality.

I shall endeavor to further illumine by degrees what I mean by *chasm* and also what I mean by *involuntary association* (a term I employed a little earlier in this essay) and their pertinence to the paradoxes of creoleness. Clearly, one must confess, *creoleness* is a peculiar term. It may sustain a conservative if not reactionary purist logic. It may give a privileged aura to (so-called) pure-blooded settlers in the New World. In fact, not only may the descendants of Europeans in the New World wear the mask of the Creole, but so do Africans, East Indians, Chinese, and others. Indeed, as in my family experience, *creoleness* signifies mixed race and a cross-cultural nemesis capable of becoming a saving nemesis. *Saving nemesis* may also be a peculiar expression, but it implies recuperative powers and vision within a scale of violence that is dismembering societies around the globe.

One may well ask therefore: Does creoleness sanction New World tribes (unrelated to Carib, Arawak, Apache, Blackfoot, or other Native American peoples) who designate themselves now *African* Americans, *Irish* Americans, *Italian* Americans, *German* Americans, and so forth? I recall on a visit to Yale University in 1972 I was addressed by an African American poet of a pale color (brown pigmentation). I was sure he was an American of European and African descent, but the advertising for his reading and address emphasized solely his African ancestry. It gave me a curious feeling of a public-relations trap into which it is fashionable to fall. By the same token one reads of *black* fiction, *black* poetry, the *black* arts, *black* painting, and the like.

On the other hand does creoleness complexly, hiddenly, overturn tribal bias; does it involve a spiritual subversion of idols through symbolic portraitures of *blackness*? Does *black* hint at an involuntary association of many cultures? Does *black* reach beyond mere pigmentation along racial and tribal lines into densities and transparencies of tone, a layered wealth of tone—musical, rhythmic, poetic—in which diverse cultures may share? Does *black* puncture prescriptions of blandness masquerading as light?

Quite honestly I do not know the answer to these questions, but in my own work as an imaginative writer, across many decades since the end of World War II, I have encountered an eruption of intuitive clues within unconscious into subconscious into conscious layers of dialogue with the past that indicate for me *numinous perhaps nonsensational changes in human nature itself* (so subtle are these changes that they are easily smothered by a sensational world), changes therefore within the genesis of imagination in nature and space and psyche.

I say all this, of course, with caution, without dogma, without a desire in any way to promote a theory. The issues that confront us (whatever insights of hope one may have garnered from one's work) are incredibly grave. And yet I do not underestimate the personal vision in the teeth of a mass-media world. It is through such deeply intuitive insights drawn from hard work and concentration that one may reflect in new ways upon areas of history that are replete with ironies of involuntary association between cultures. Such ironies highlight an addiction to invariance, closed minds, and divided cultures, even as they disclose, I think, the mystery of cross-cultural wholeness steeped in the freedom of diversity to cross boundaries that restrict our vision of therapeutic and evolving reality.

It is said that when the ancient Caribs appeared in pre-Columbian times upon what is now known as the Caribbean Sea, they came without women and chose their wives from the Arawaks whom they seized and overcame. There are parallels in history which lead us to believe that their choice was influenced by criteria of kinship resemblances to be perceived even in a foreign people, clanship resemblances to be analyzed even in conquered peoples, and a family code or criterion to be plucked from the body of a stranger. This is natural—natural choice, let us say; but it also possesses sinister implications. The ancient alchemists coined the term *opus contra naturam* to alert us to the trickster faces of nature, one of which may easily beguile us so that we absolutize it, by apparently natural choice, into a status of such privilege that, by degrees, we come to deceive ourselves about our powers or capacities to seize and institutionalize the purity of nature. We are tricked by nature, as it were, into consolidating partiality, partial appearance, into an absolute frame, an absolute good.

When the Nazis invaded Poland, they separated Polish families, selecting children from among their Polish brothers, sisters, or cousins because they conformed to an Aryan model. They shipped these children to Germany, where they were taken into German families. A sinister question mark attached to those who, for one reason or another, were mixed or dubbed non-Aryan. There was nothing new in such implicit ethnic cleansing. In the flux of cultures and civilizations across the centuries—cultures at war one with another—the recruitment of children who appeared to conform to a standard elevated by a victor or invader, was established practice. When the Ottoman Turks conquered Constantinople, they treated Christian children who matched favored criteria of purity and likeness in a manner similar to the Nazi treatment of Polish children centuries later.

Let us return now to the theme of the "chasm" within humanity and to *involuntary associations*. It is possible to gain new insights into fiction and creativity through what one may call the "creolization of the chasm" within illuminations drawn from, or nursed from, the fabric of involuntary associations embedded in humanity.

In the selection of a thread upon which to string likenesses that are consolidated into the status of a privileged ruling family, clearly cultures reject others who remain nevertheless the hidden or unacknowledged kith and kin, let us say, of the chosen ones. The rejection constitutes both a chasm or a divide in humanity and a context of involuntary association between the chosen ones and the outcast ones. The relationship is involuntary in that, though, on one hand, it is plain and obvious, privileged status within that relationship endorses by degrees, on the other hand, a callous upon humanity. And that callous becomes so apparently normal that a blindness develops, a blindness that negates relationship between the privileged caste and the outcast. That negation cannot absolutely cut the thread of relationship, but it throws a shroud of habit upon it until it virtually fades and remains an involuntary association. The relationship becomes less and less an active ingredient in the multifaceted integrity and flexibility of nature and psyche.

A bias grows which may profit from that hidden relationship in purely formal experimentation (Picasso's formal, let us say, appropriation of facets in the African mask); but unless a genuine cross-cultural apprehension occurs of the unfinished genesis of the imagination affecting past and present civilizations, an innermost apprehension of changing, cross-cultural content within frames we take for granted, the involuntary ground of association to which I have referred, remains between privileged and afflicted cultures.

The creolization of the chasm in humanity should alert us to a series of caveats. What is at stake are the gifts one culture offers another, gifts that imply new and changing ways of reading innermost vulnerability within civilizations and cultures. Formal experimentation is important, but conquistadorial habit may employ sensational color and tone in its intercourse with others, to eclipse the nonsensational or unfathomable ground of cross-cultural astonishment when models of involuntary association break cultures, though such continuities never can be structured absolutely.

Needless to say, this essay sets out my personal view within a continuing exploratory capacity that bears on my apprehension of imaginative truth. Perhaps it may help if I look, once again in a personal and undogmatic way, beyond and through the appropriation of facets in one cultural artifact by another culture, such as I implied with the Spanish painter Picasso and the African mask. To do so, to look through and beyond sophisticated patterns of appropriation, which are implicitly cross-cultural, we need to raise the issue of gifts—born of unconscious momentum within the chasm of humanity—that one culture unselfconsciously (it follows from what I have just said) offers to another culture, to raise also the issues of partiality and vulnerability in all models we may perceive fallaciously, I believe, as social, cultural, or technological absolutes.

The differentiation in content within diverse cultural models—content that may seem opaque to one culture viewing another—needs to be translated and transfigured in fictions that give simultaneous representation to densities and transparencies. All languages are subtly, hiddenly connected, and the live, fossil particularities in the language of fiction—arising from variables of the unconscious/subconscious/conscious in the chasm of humanity—help us to arrive upon unsuspected bridges, bridges of innermost content that have a deeper, stranger luminosity and incandescence than the purely formal appropriation by one culture of another's artifacts.

I am saying that such luminosity, such incandescence, exacts a price. The simultaneity of densities and transparencies is a "depth phenomenon" of the language of fiction which throws up, brings up, in ways we scarcely understand and tend to overlook, continuities between cultures: continuities that open diverse content (once deemed opaque) into unsuspected capacities for the renewal of an inner dynamic of universal civilization.

Who would suspect, for example, a link between Legba (the Haitian loa who stands at the crossroads of the Caribbean and the South/Central Americas) and Hephaestus (the inimitable craftsman of the ancient Greek Olympian gods)? The key to such a link lies in paradoxes of vulnerability in civilizations apparently remote from one another. Legba's vulnerability is manifest in his one-legged frame. He is also aged: the years, the generations, centuries perhaps, clothe him. *Yet he brings the gift of agelessness.* What is agelessness? Agelessness, I would suggest, is not to be equated with the hubris of immortal identity, though the desire to do so remains virtually incorrigible and strong. Yet we may combat such seductive but fallacious strength when we begin to perceive that Legba is consumed by the poverty, the dire predicament, the hunger of the Haitian people, in whose pantheon he is a god. He is being consumed, yes, but a paradox links him to the dire predicament of his people and to immortal identity or privileged family. The consumption of his body by the soil and the fire of time is so protracted—the fire is so invisible in its long, drawn-out persistence—that a living residue grows up again and again upon the crossroads of a society to make him appear invulnerable and strong, whereas what is at stake is the issue of vulnerable soil, vulnerable resources, vulnerable capacities, that need to be read and understood differently, differently from prescriptions of political and cultural habit, by original, human imaginations.

An invisible fire, as it were, lives agelessly within him as if to offset the terminal malaise of a civilization. That offset is paradoxical, for it postpones a necessity to read reality differently. It cultivates hubris and fallacies of strength. And yet within that cultivation one may still, however glimmeringly, perceive an incandescence, a luminosity, a transfiguration of resources that may break by creative degrees (to match the protracted ritual of invisible conflagration within the institutions of society) a hidden linkage of catastrophe to authoritarian and hierarchical habit.

Within that breakage, an immortal god such as Legba is wounded, appears crippled, to bring his gift to civilization. The caveat or warning inserted into the gift tends to be overlooked because such a crippled one may mesmerize society in having virtually arisen from the grave of a doomed order, a doomed Haiti—a doomed Caribbean, some would say—in the light of the perilous conditions that prevail there.

It is easy to assume that Legba's wound is an irrelevant window through the frame of privileged hierarchy and that he invites us to cement a longing for absolute dynasty or power. But the caveat remains; it may brighten, it may flicker, to tell us that the capacity for non-consumerable proportion in Legba is not endless. It is ageless only in the sense that originality invokes a compression of times in creative fictions and that a *transfiguration* may run out of the past into the present and the future to turn invisible fire around into a therapeutic signal.

Legba has his roots in Africa. However, his creolization in Haiti is a signal of mixed resources born of Haiti's relationship to conservative, tribal Africa as well as to confused legacies of slave-owning French landlords cheek by jowl, so to speak, with revolutionary, counterrevolutionary politics in France and the rise of Napoleonic dictatorship. Haiti's Africanness was embroiled, therefore, in the contradictions of a classical Europe in that the classics were taught to the ruling, educated, political classes. Indeed, in this scenario we come abreast of the self-deceptions in a purely formulaic (some would say Cartesian) education, in which a so-called dialogue with the past rests on *descriptions of, not numinous arrival in,* the complex, disturbing life of tradition. I have mentioned it before, but let me stress it again: a purely formal appropriation of the material of the past reduces the past to a passive creature to be manipulated as an ornament of fashion or protest or experimentation in postmodernist styles, post-modernist games. Such games are rooted, I believe, in a one-sided modernism which takes us back to defects in the enlightenment associated with the Renaissance, an enlightenment that aborted a profound cross-culturalism between science and art, as among the diverse cultures of humanity around the globe.

To arrive in tradition involves an appreciation of profound tension between originality and tradition; it involves a breach in formidable prepossessions of a materialist mind-set, a mind-set that has exploited nature, exploited landscapes/riverscapes/skyscapes over the past two hundred years since the Industrial Revolution, a mind-set that takes for granted the exploitation of others through technological innovation.

There can be no perfect or absolute arrival in tradition, and some measure of descriptive logic is necessary; but we need a narrative that helps us to sense the partiality of linear progression and brings home to us in genuine stages of creativity (rather than purely intellectual experimentation) the simultaneity of the past, the present, and the future in the unfinished genesis of the imagination.

Legba's creolization makes visible, I would suggest, an insecurity in the pantheons of the gods around the globe. Such insecurity is a kind of arrival in tradition: it runs counter to secure ideologies or dogmas in which immortality is described as the grain and blood of hierarchical privilege.

Legba's numinosity and insecurity revolve around two strands drawn from the tapestry of civilization. One strand is the fallacy of invulnerability, of supernatural strength despite eroding environments and institutions, of complacent declarations of strength with every return from the grave of his diseased society. He is pinned, as it were, again and again as an ambiguous godlike Creole (aged and ageless, weak and strong) to be questioned deeply in his apparent passivity and complacency in our new and original visualization of him in this essay. The other strand, therefore (in our original address to him now), is to raise the specter of transfigurative repudiation of fate which he may conceal, invisible fire that consumes remorselessly yet is not absolute, fire that consumes yet may turn around into a resource of evolutionary change and complex transfiguration of the prison house and frame of cultural habit.

This brings us to the enigma of the gifts that the gods bestow upon humanity. We come to the edge of technologies; we accept at our peril in their purely formulaic transparency. The gift of every advance in technology is fraught with ambiguity in its innermost content.

Even the exploding furnace of the atom remains opaque in its application as a therapeutic tool in our civilization. Its dangers, its horrendous mushroom, are all apparent. Its terrifying beauty is apparent. Yet it remains dense within a civilization that is still blind to an innermost incandescence of evolving and changing alphabet of the psyche.

Legba's peculiar cousinship to ancient Greek Hephaestus may help us with regard to the issue of technology that I have raised. Hephaestus was maimed, and the other immortal gods saw him sometimes as a figure to be ridiculed. It is difficult to establish precisely what injury he endured; it may have been his legs, or it may have been obscurely genital. Whatever it was, it incited in him a cunning and jealousy less characteristic of gods, one would think, than of mortal humanity. His status as a visibly maimed immortal may seem absurd. Such paradox undermines yet confirms, in ultimate and unfathomable essence, an immunity of soul. Immune self or soul or paradox of genius is other than the masquerade of brute refinements of power or mechanics of potency to which the Olympian family is addicted.

The distinction between an immune system (in a therapeutic or medical sense), an elusive self or soul (in numinous immunity), and a fallacious immunity, or exemption from the torments of creative conscience; the distinction between inner fire that threatens to consume but may heal, and brute refinement that disenfranchises the soul, is the thread that runs through Haitian Legba and Olympian Hephaestus.

This is a distinction of great stress, and, as a consequence, Hephaestus appears at times to resort to base traps and trickery to compensate his pain and his jealousy of others who gain the prize of love in cheating and robbing him. His masterly skills—technology, artisanship—degenerate into glittering nets and machineries of hate, spite, venom with which to wage war. A tragic precedent is set. Yet one needs to remember that Hephaestus was driven by a sense of loss and grief in the face of others whose behavior was rooted in Olympian vanity; at times, ruling utterances and precepts that seemed one-sided and biased, reflective as well of caprice and prejudice, whatever heights in the exercise of justice in the affairs of humanity they claimed for themselves. Was it not Plato who expressed a degree of loathing and foreboding at the behavior of the lofty family of the immortals?

It is necessary to see, at this stage, that immortality may consolidate itself into a facade for regimes that lose their capacity for self-critical, self-judgmental momentum into dimensions of the reformation of the heart and the mind of an age. One such dimension is the chasm in humanity to which I referred earlier in this essay, the "creolization of the chasm." Legba and Hephaestus are symbols of the chasm raised onto a plane of maimed immortality to strike an uneasy, perhaps terrifying, balance between abnormal stress within the body of a civilization and creative/re-creative genius.

That balance requires a penetration of the opacity of immortal regimes, an opacity rich with involuntary counterpoint between the powerless (who are deemed irrelevant and cast aside) and the powerful, a counterpoint as well between the numinosity of weak species (ingrained nevertheless with the unfathomable integrity of nature) and brute tyranny masquerading as the survival of the fittest.

Hephaestus' maimed and cunning sexuality, for instance, raises—as I have already implied—the chasm of humanity into the pantheon of the gods. At one level, Hephaestus seems to us little more than a puppet or a clown, and he appears to remain blind to his own genius which is darkened and conscripted to aid and abet technologies of trickery, waste, or war. We who scan him through Haitian, Creole, Legba may arrive in the past and bring him upon the crossroads of a present civilization. There we may scan, in new fictions of philosophic myth, an *involuntary* counterpoint, let us say, which he brings into play against the hubris of sex—so much a part of the malaise of late twentieth-century civilization. We may unravel the opacity of immortal regimes—regimes of ruling fashion, regimes of sophisticated exploitation of species—to illumine, in some degree, a cruel addiction to uniform orders of rape disguised within the phallic, invented masks of bulls, or the sculpture of sharks, the horn of deer, that the immortals may wear to execute a perverse Carnival which throws its long, pointed shadow into the symbolic vivisection of the animal kingdom.

Is it absurd to suggest that Legba's shield in old age (weak yet strong old age) is implicit in a comedy of overturned, Hephaestian armor that Achilles wore? The seed of that armor is the conflagration of Troy—perhaps a measure of conflagration that fascist Haiti may well bring upon its head in the foreseeable future. Yet time—within that overturned, Hephaestian shield Legba unconsciously bears—is still on the side of the Caribbean and Central and South America.

When we seek to make a distinction between the opaque content of ancient symbolizations or legends and purely formal innovation employing characteristics borrowed by one culture from another (as Picasso, let us say, borrowed characteristics from the African mask to create a new formal style), we need, I think, to address an *involuntary* ground of association which is native to the arts of humanity.

That involuntary ground reaches subconsciously, unconsciously, *through* the *humanization* of nature that we set up into ruling models in our places of learning and in the humanities, the universities, reaches *through* such models into nature(s) which, I repeat, are *extrahuman* even as they (such natures) bear on humankind, even as they bring gifts to humankind. Such gifts are akin to quantum fire of soul (*anima mundi*), quantum oceans, quantum landscapes, quantum riverscapes, which imply minuscule linkages between being and nonbeing, psyche and pebble or leaf or wood or cloud or tide or rock.

The quantum imagination, in my view, may be curiously visualized as a revisionary epic which seeks to reclaim extrahuman faculties in incandescent equations between being and nonbeing. The subtle, complex rhythms of nonbeing, the intricate fiber and dimensionalities of space, have been so blocked away that living landscapes become theaters of brute conquest, media to be exploited and manipulated.

Let us put this in another way: Extrahuman faculties may be eclipsed in a hubris that governs models built on an assumption of the domination of nature(s) within institutions that claim to humanize the world even as they entrench biases that may imperil the future of humankind. This is a supreme irony, that arts of imagination have scarcely, it seems to me, ventured into in modern times.

The reasons for such neglect are clear: Extrahuman faculties are so eclipsed, by and large, that their content within legend or sculpture or mask or word or painting, becomes apparently opaque. Yet these extrahuman faculties continue to subsist on inescapable truth within an involuntary ground of association which I would describe as involuntary genius.

Genius in this subconscious, unconscious theater of psyche (acting within, yet beneath, layers of logical awareness) is a phenomenon of the extra-human (what is beyond the arrogant humanization of natures) acting upon the human susceptibility to what is other than absolute, individual logic, what is attuned to a capacity in which we need to *read* ourselves in the book of reality—in fictions of reality—as *partial* creatures. It is within such numinous partiality that one-legged Legba and maimed Hephaestus reach through and beyond themselves (however unwittingly) into architectures of space that are relevant to chasms in humanity and to a multidimensional cosmos.

Let me close this essay by returning to Legba's Hephaestian shield. As I implied earlier, that shield is an extrapolation from the armor that Hephaestus built for Achilles at the request of Achilles' immortal mother. That armor was to topple Troy. Its panoramic motifs are of profound interest. It pictured *self-deceptive* (I would say) and *peaceful occupations and environments*—sheep rearing, woods, gentle fields, and the like—*for it was dedicated to war.* Within such panoramic clarity an *invisible* seed smoldered that would erupt into a flower of all-consuming fire and war. One needs more than a formal appropriation of Achilles' armor if one is to arrive within a capacity to lift an invisible seed of fire, within Hephaestian technology, into a trigger of simultaneous densities and transparencies.

The creolization of Legba, therefore, within a tormented Haiti and Caribbean, is an issue of complex linkages and mixed traditions—transcending *black,* transcending *white*—in which the seed of all-consuming fire turns around into an incandescent imagination that may so balance shadow and light, age and youth, strength and weakness, poverty and wealth, that it throws a ceaseless bridge across the chasm of worlds, an apparently doomed world of materialism and conflict and another real (however apparently unreal) world buried in the content of imaginations history seeks to exploit, for purely formal, stylistic reasons, rather than as an immersion in creative difficulty, in a true, far-reaching, evolving cross-cultural regeneration of the heart and mind of an age.

2

The Caribbean

Marvelous Cradle-Hammock and Painful Cornucopia

Carlos Guillermo Wilson

Translated by Elba D. Birmingham-Pokorny and Luis A. Jiménez

In 1492, the three caravels—the *Santa María*, the *Pinta*, and the *Niña*—landed on the coast of the island of Quisqueya, where later Santo Domingo, the oldest Spanish colony in the New World, was founded. This event was the beginning of an impressive historical Caribbean phenomenon: a marvelous cradle-hammock and painful cornucopia.

The ceremonies of the quincentennial (1492–1992) of that historic October 12, jubilantly celebrated the marvel born in that cradle, or better yet, Caribbean "cradle-hammock." In the fifteenth century, the legends of El Dorado and the Fountain of Youth called attention to the marvelous and obsessive search which started in the Caribbean, and consequently caused much interest in Spain in the news about Tenochtitlán, the great center of the Aztecs; Chichen Itza, a great center of the Mayas; Darién and the Pacific Ocean (then known as the South Sea); and Cuzco, the great center of the Incas. One of the most important legacies of the marvelous cradle-hammock is the Spanish spoken in the Caribbean.

In 1492 Antonio de Nebrija published the *Castilian Grammar*, the first grammar of any European language. Curiously, Nebrija's *Grammar* was published in the same year as the Catholic monarchs' soldiers finally took the Alhambra, the last Moorish fortress, thus ending almost eight centuries of Moorish domination of the Iberian Peninsula—a domination initiated in the year 711 by the African general Tarik in Gibraltar and later supported by another African general, Júsuf.

The Moorish conquest had enriched the Spanish language with Arabic words, but it was in the Caribbean that Spanish quickly accumulated indigenous Caribbean and African words. Referring to the enrichment of the Spanish language in the Caribbean, Jorge E. Porras writes: "Spanish is believed not to exhibit significant substractal influence from Indoamerican or African languages in its phonological, morphological, or syntactic components but it certainly exhibits much of an influence in its lexicon. Just as in Medieval times, when Castilian [borrowed] words from other languages Latin American Spanish enriched its lexical stock with Native American languages such as Arawak (Taíno), Nahuatl, Mayan, Quechua, Tupí-Guaraní, Mapuche, and from African languages such as Kikongo, Kishigongo, Kimbundu, Ewe, and Yoruba" ("Spanish Language in the Americas" 181).

Some Arawakan words like canoe, hammock, cacique, bohio, tebooron, barbacoah, batata, hurricane, and maize are now part of Latin American Spanish, as the result of linguistic syncretism, or mixing. Equally important are some examples of Africanisms: bomba, babalao, bilongo, bongó, conga, cumbia, chéchere, gahngah, guandú, geenay, lucumí, malembe, mambí, marimba, motete, ñame, ñinga, samba, tumba (see Mosonyi; also see Megenny).

The mixing of indigenous, European, and African languages in Caribbean Spanish and other developments such as the Palenquero spoken in San Basilio de Palenque in Colombia, the Palenquero spoken among the descendants of maroon runaway Congo slaves of Portobelo in Panama, and the Papiamento spoken in Curaçao are very much like the religious syncretisms of Santería, Regla, Abakuá, Palo Mayombé, Ñañiguismo, Baquiné, Voodoo, Macumba, Candomblé, as well as the musical syncretisms of Rumba, Samba, Plena, Bomba, Mambo, Bamba, Huapango, Bamboula, Cumacos, Chibángueles, Quichimba, Carángano, Quitiplás, Tango, Milonga, Beguine, Merengue, Cumbia, and Tamborito. They are also like the mixing that takes place in food: rice with chick peas, ajiaco, mondongo with lima beans.

This important syncretism or mixing of languages, religions, music, and cuisine are all original developments of the marvelous Caribbean cradle-hammock, but one of the most extraordinary telluric developments of Caribbean syncretism is the Garifuna culture. According to the research of direct descendants of the Garifuna people, this culture dates back to the mid-seventeenth century, when a hurricane in the Caribbean Sea caused slave ships coming from Africa to crash on the coast of the island of Yurumei, known today as Saint Vincent, near the coast of Venezuela. The shipwrecked Africans' odyssey had started with the abduction of children stolen from their cradles and forced to board the slave ships anchored off the Atlantic coast of Africa. Those who survived this odyssey shared food and huts with the Arawakans and Caribs when they alighted on the island of Yurumei.

There, the African children learned to communicate with their neighbors in a language that was a curious mixture of two indigenous languages: Arawakan and Carib. This Arawakan-Carib syncretism was born when the bellicose Caribs invaded the Caribbean islands and sentenced to death the Arawakan men on the island of Yurumei. The descendants of Carib fathers and Arawakan mothers taught Carib to their male offspring and Arawakan to their female offspring. In the manner of their Arawakan-Carib neighbors, the shipwrecked Africans progressively became Garifunas in an interesting process of syncretism, in which they not only adopted the basic staples of the Indians on the island of Yurumei—yucca and cassava bread—but also contributed to the Arawakan-Carib language with French, English, and Spanish words (the result of their contact with Africans and slave traders, pirates, corsairs, and *flibustiers*). Above all, the intonation of African languages also influenced the Arawakan-Carib language, which later became the Garifuna language.

Scholars of Garifuna culture have pointed out that the British settlers in Yurumei—in an attempt to match the prosperity that the French settlers of Haiti gained from their fruitful sugar cane fields—tried to enslave the Garifunas who had, thanks to their shipwreck, escaped the yoke of slavery. When these settlers tried to capture the Garifunas—as free labor for the sugar cane fields and for the mills for the production of highly coveted sugar, the Garifunas launched a revolt under the leadership of Satuyé—the greatest Garifuna hero. When the Garifuna warriors—armed primarily with machetes—were defeated by the firearms of the British, as punishment for defending their dignity and rejecting the yoke of slavery, Satuyé was executed on March 14, 1795. Five thousand Garifuna followers of Satuyé were captured in the Palenques (Indian ranches) of the island of Yurumei. Two years later, on March 11, 1797, the Garifunas who didn't accept enslavement were deported in eleven ships headed for Jamaica. More than a thousand of them died aboard the British ships, and after painful sailing in the Caribbean, the surviving Garifunas were abandoned by the captains on April 12, 1797, on the island of Roatán near the coast of Honduras. In Honduras the Arawakan-Carib-African syncretism or mixing continued, and there the Garifunas established their capital in Trujillo. Later they established Garifuna settlements in the Caribbean coast of Honduras: Ciriboya, Carozal, Sambuco, San Juan, Tornabé, Triunfo de la Cruz, Saraguaina, Masca, and other communities. Garifuna communities were also established in Livingston, Guatemala; in Orinoco and La Fe in Nicaragua; and in Stann Creek, Hopkins, Dangriga, and Punta Gorda in Belize.[1]

The Garifuna language is the main patrimony of the Garifuna culture. And this Arawakan-Carib-African linguistic syncretism demands attention because although the phonetics of the language are African, unlike other Palenquero languages (such as the Palenquero spoken in San Basilio de Palenque in Colombia or the Lucumí which is sung in the ceremonies of Santería in Cuba and Candomblé in Brazil), the base of its vocabulary is not African. According to Professor Salvador Suazo, "The linguistic structure of the Garifuna language is made up of 45 percent Arawakan words, 25 percent Kallina or Carib words, 15 percent French words, and 10 percent English words. The remaining 5 percent is made up of technical Spanish words [for the Garifunas-speakers in Honduras, Guatemala, and Nicaragua] and of English [in the Garifunas communities of Belize and among residents of the United States of America]" (Suazo 1991, 6).

Suazo offers some examples of the Carib contributions to the Garifuna language: wuguri (man), wuri (woman), arutubu (hammock), yagana (canoe), fágayu (oar); Gallicisms: weru (verre), músue (mouchoir), gulíeri (cuiller), búnedu (bonnet), mariei (maríe); Anglicisms: súgara (sugar), wachi (watch), machi (matches), haiwata (high water), giali (girl).

Garifuna culture is an important development of Caribbean syncretism which can counter both the images generated through a colonial educational system and—more devastatingly—through the popular images that we, in some nations of Central America and the Caribbean, have of Africa and of Africans in the New World. These popular images are still those of the films of Tarzan, King of the Jungle and Great Savior, who in Africa constantly defeats the dangerous Africans (the majority of whom are Pygmies and cannibals) who supposedly were the ancestors of the slaves in the Caribbean. Unfortunately, our public-school textbooks continue to present the African aspects of our culture and history through an emphasis on the African slaves who were happy because Christianity saved or delivered them from pagan and dangerous Africa. Emphasis is also placed on the "ungrateful" African slaves, who, instead of loving their masters for the salvation of their souls, dedicated themselves to marooning activities or to fighting the yoke of slavery, rescuing their human dignity, and obtaining their freedom. Thus, our students never learn from their textbooks that Africans participated in the great Pharaonic civilization in Egypt, as well as in other rich and powerful kingdoms in Nubia, Ethiopia, Mali, Shongay, Ghana, and Zimbabwe. Nor do they learn from official textbooks about the heroic deeds of conquistadors, explorers, and maroon chiefs of African ancestry such as Juan Garrido, Nuflo Olano, Juan Valiente, Estebanico, Yanga, Bayano, Ganga Zumba, Benkos, Satuyé, Fillipa Maria Aranha, Fabulé, Chirinos, Coba, Felipillo, and José Antonio Aponte (see Rout).

Garifuna culture is indeed an outstandingly positive example of Caribbean syncretism, underscoring the pride and courage of Africans in the New World who rejected the yoke of slavery (and, when necessary, defended their dignity with their lives), but this syncretism has also been a painful cornucopia. Painful are the almost four centuries of African slavery in the New World. The yoke of African slavery in the Caribbean began in 1517, when Bartolomé de las Casas, petitioned Carlos V to concede licenses to Spanish settlers to import to Santo Domingo black slaves directly from Africa, a solution to the genocide of the Indians, and as a substitute for Indian slave labor.[2]

The unquestionable and undeniably important African contributions to the Creole cultures of the Spanish Caribbean stand out in Santería, in Ñañiguismo, in Merengue, in Bembé, in Bongó, in Rumba, in Ajiaco, and in the Garifunas, etc. However, as far as a Hispanic Caribbean identity is concerned, the African heritage is not only rejected (as in the obsessive preoccupation with racist sayings such as: "the race must be improved" and "your grandmother, where is she?"), it is also denied. Aside from being a fanatic illusion, this obsession is also an example of the profound and hateful racism that many Cubans show when they affirm that the "true Cuban" is white; that many Puerto Ricans exhibit when they proudly proclaim that Puerto Rico is "the whitest island" of the Antilles; that many Dominicans demonstrate when they swear to be "Dark Indians" and not black like the Haitians; and that many Panamanians manifest in their passionate hatred of Chombos.

In Panama the best example of the negative consequence of creolization is the separation and national hatred that exists among the so-called colonial Blacks (descendants of African slaves dating back to Vasco Núñez de Balboa) and the black West-Indians (disrespectfully called "Chombos"). This latter group is composed of the descendants of two waves of English- and French-speaking West-Indian workers from Barbados, Haiti, Grenada, Jamaica, Martinique, St. Lucia, and other islands. The first wave emigrated in 1850 to participate in the construction of the trans-Atlantic railroad—a project financed by the North Americans during the California gold rush. The second wave of West-Indian workers emigrated to participate in the construction of the failed sea-level canal (under the direction of the French), as well as in the construction of the lock-canal, 1904–1914 (under the direction of the North Americans).

Many Panamanians hate the Chombos because they are not all Catholics (since their grandparents were originally from the West Indies, many of them practice other religions); because they prefer to speak French and English in their homes; and finally because, according to racist Panamanians, too many Chombos have failed to participate sufficiently in the process of ethnic whitening in order to "better the race"—or to put it more frankly, to erase all that is African. As a result, all traces of an African gene or phenotype is hated and rejected: the woolen hair; the flat, broad nose; the thick lips; and above all, the black skin of the Chombos.[3]

The Cuban poet Gabriel de la Concepción Valdés, Plácido, was one of the first in the Caribbean to denounce the racist obsession with whitening the race:

> Don Longuino always claims
> with a passion stronger than bacon skin,
> and with his sallow complexion
> which African lineage betrays,
> "I come from pure and noble blood."
> Deluded, he proclaims to be
> from sublime kinship!
> Let him tell it to his grandmother!
> *Jorge Castellanos, Placido, 48*

On the island where many are proud to be natives of "the whitest island" of the Caribbean, the Puerto Rican writer José Luis González has stated: "As far as the African roots of Puerto Rico popular culture are concerned, I am convinced that the essential racism of the island's ruling class has done everything possible—at times in brutal ways and at times with subtlety worthy of a better cause—to avoid, to conceal, and to distort its importance" (74).

This Cuban, Puerto Rican, and Dominican obsession with whitening have been synthesized and have become in Panama the cornerstone of both the "Panameñista" concept and the Constitution of 1941. The latter solely welcomes those immigrants who are "capable of contributing to the improvement of the race" and calls for the denationalization of the Panamanian [Chombos] descendants of grandparents and parents of illegal immigration who are "members of the black race whose original language was not Spanish" (Constiticion de la Republica de Panama, 5–7).

In my own essays, poems, short stories, and novels, I have denounced and condemned the aspects of creolization that have as their sole goal and intention to erase the African heritage in Caribbean culture and identity.[4]

In other words, I denounce the rejection of the African in the process of creolization which initially began with the rape of young African slave girls and which still persists today in the hatred concealed in the edict: "It is necessary to better or improve the race." For example, in *Chombo* I display that rejection:

> Abena Mansa Adesimbo vehemently opposed the name that had been given to her child. She argued that they should forget the African traditions because it was important to keep in mind that they weren't in Haiti, Jamaica, Barbados, and even less, in Africa. She recalled that during the short time that she was able to attend public school, the teacher severely criticized her name for being so African and asked her daily why West-Indian blacks did not adopt Panamanian last names such as Chiari, Wong, Heurtemate, Ghandi, Tagaropoulos. (59)

In a poem entitled "In Exilium" (1977, 8), I protest against any form of syncretism that has as its only intent the erasure and destruction of the heritage and pride of my African ancestors:

> How disgraceful!
> I am ASHANTI
> and they address me as
> Carlos
> How insulting!
> I am a CONGOLESE
> and they call me
> Guillermo
> How base!
> I am YORUBA
> and they name me
> Wilson.

Another poem, "Desarraigado" (or "Uprooted" [1977], 9) articulates the psychological conflict produced by the erasure of the African heritage in the Caribbean identity:

> African grandmother,
> Do you not recognize me?
> My language is Gongoric.

My litany is Nazarene.
My dance is Andalusian.
African grandmother,
why don't you recognize me?

Finally, in the novel *Los nietos de Felicidad Dolores* (1991) I also portray characters of African descent who absurdly surrender to and become accomplices of the ideology of whitening:

> Blaaaaack woman of the devil. I have already told you a thousand times not to get involved in my business. If I want to give my telephone number to all the American soldiers, of course, to the whitest with blue eyes, it's my business and au contraire, it should not matter to you nor to anyone else. And don't remind me that I have five illegitimate petits enfants because I don't feel ashamed of it. In fact, I am very happy and, yes, very proud that there were five blond soldiers, yes, very blond with blue eyes, the ones that made me pregnant. All of them white. Well, I did as my Godmother Karafula Barrescoba advised me: "Look for a white husband in order to improve the race." Fortunately, my five children don't have woolen hair like those chombo boys with so much African blood. Neither are they thick lipped. Nor snub nosed. Neither are they. . . . (75)

Creolization was indeed the inevitable result of the initial violent clash among the Indians who lived in such places as Quisqueya, Xaymaca, Borinquén, and Cuba; the European conquistadors who invaded these territories of the Caribbean Sea; and the African slaves brought to the New World to excavate gold mines, cultivate sugar cane fields, work in sugar mills, and build fortresses and ports. The ensuing mixing of the languages, religions, music, and food was indeed positive and admirable. Sadly, this creolization has not defeated the absurd, repugnant, and above all, insulting attitude that is an affront to the pride and dignity of the African heritage of our Caribbean cultures.

3

~

Who's Afraid of the Winti Spirit?

Astrid H. Roemer
Translated by Wanda Boeke

A taki, fosi mi ai opo,
dan mi ede jere joe!
Fo'fosi m' ai opo,
dan m' ede bari joe!
. . . Nomo f' Aisa Goron,
babaloetoe Mama!

Even before my eyes had opened,
I already heard your voice.
Before my eyes were opened,
I was already bewitched by you.
. . . You, Aisa! Mother of
all the Earth's Creatures!
    Edgar Cairo (trans. W. Boeke)

With this song-poem from the masterful family saga *Jeje Disi* (*Character Forces*) by the Surinamese man of letters Edgar Cairo, I wish to pay respect to the unspoken narrative element that will always transcend by far the theorizing and thematics of Winti—the topic of this essay. But this song-poem is also the after-scent of the secret bearing the name *Winti*, the secret which more or less breaks up our Creole families. Secrets evoke fear. A subculture that is nurtured on feelings of fear is sometimes violently oppressed and silenced—actions that evoke even more fear.

This essay is my attempt to intellectualize the phenomenon of Winti through two lines of approach—one historical, the other personal. Though for both approaches I use the same language, Dutch (the language of the colonizer that legally prohibited this subculture, this way of life, this religion, and regulated it into the underworld) to deconstruct the fear surrounding Winti.

I will try to establish the relationship between a particular aspect of Winti religion's metaphorical codes and a particular aspect of Surinamese literature—namely, my own literary work and its poetic sources.

My first postulate in this context is that a large part of the metaphors from the remnants of the Winti religion are based on or point to classic African myths as well as to survival myths that originated in the times of slavery outside Africa, in the African diaspora. In addition, due to a confluence of circumstances, specific metaphorical images have become a vital part of what Creole folklore and mythology still are today.

Literature carries in a society the tradition of making myths, but generally literature also runs parallel to history. In addition to the larger historical traditions of a country, a nation, a people, literature presents us with documents belonging to smaller social categories such as class, sex, family, clan, and tribe; literature thus gives us an insight into the cultural eccentricities of all kinds of subcultures.

This myth-making bears characteristics that Lévi-Strauss calls *bricolage,* because it indicates a method of piecing together a concept from fragments that are active in a culture at a particular moment. Metaphors manage to express in language the notion that subject and object have a certain strength in common. The most social aspect of a metaphor is expressed by a "god"—the being that unifies an aspect of a person with an aspect of nature.

My first line of approach, "His Story—Or, the Wind Cannot Be Grasped," tries to situate Winti as an African phenomenon in the culture of Surinamese Creoles. At the same time, I will try to provide particular notions about moral and humanitarian values that link Winti to the vestiges of our African heritage. Since Winti has been described and explained (to make it comprehensible to outsiders) as a religion, a way of life, a healing model, with sacred and profane rituals, a kind of communications infrastructure has come about; it has a body of systematically organized concepts and geometric signs that point to recognizable and symbolic matters.

This infrastructure provides the codes for metaphors of personification and transformation, for instance. Moreover, popular myths become logically convertible and reveal the origins from which modern or new myths and metaphors draw their strength and form.

My second line of approach, "Bricolage—Or, My Stories," is an effort to clarify my own condition as a Surinamese Creole writer, with reference also to the form, content, and inspirational sources of my own work—and life.

Perhaps the two sections are paradoxically related. Be that as it may, the one derived from the other, and my language forces me to bring the one and the other to light in chronological relation.

His Story—Or, the Wind Cannot Be Grasped

The historical creolization that is specific and unique to my birthplace, Suriname, the heterogeneity of its population, the multiculturalism and the polyglot use of our language, as well as the diffuse colonial and post-colonial history of each ethnoreligious group separately and together, all form the basis of our emotional and intellectual consciousness. It is this basis that, via points of identification, finds articulation in Surinamese literature. Every literature has a reconciliatory function—a certain degree of recognizability for everyone. However, communication systems, under which metaphors find themselves, can be so unique to the (sub)culture, and so integral that they do not function as points of identification. Winti metaphors are a good example of this.

Our (Surinamese) Creoles descend primarily from various tribes from West Africa who were, from the fifteenth to the nineteenth centuries, forcibly and violently embarked and shipped to the Americas and the Caribbean. The romanticized narratives of novels, films, and documentaries as well as the factual material produced from archives and scientific research have provided us with important and lasting information on the historical aspects of the diaspora of the so-called black race.

Men and women who had, as a matter of course, preserved ancient collective values and norms, who had maintained living networks of kinship, especially blood relations, were torn from their vital and long-standing reality, violently dislodged, and made to live in loose social bonds with no recognizable (sub)culture, no understandable language or signs, no reliable or permanent contractual kinship relations, no own ground under their feet. Slaves were burdened with an unbearable inventory of duties, and their status—whether they be men, women, or children—was absolutely beyond the pale of the law. Anything formulated against any form of oppression, anything that developed into relations, patterns or subcultures, was immediately punished. Each slave's life was typically characterized by a series of relations—to human beings, nature, and culture—that were violently shattered.

Of course, developing and consolidating significant family relations was out of the question. The marks that two hundred years of such experience etched into the collective and individual soul and psyche of these disinherited Africans display and disguise themselves in the twentieth century in numerous and complex variants of behavior. Even the notion of "Creole" that the free African-Surinamese claimed more and more fervently as a name for their own people—following both the abolition of slavery in the Americas in 1863 and the state control system that ended in 1873—is burdened with a very painful historical conflict of loyalties. However, in postslavery society, these "freed" people formed the underclass—propertyless, stateless, outlawed, ignorant of the world, and dependent. Afflicted by these traumas, they concentrated on gathering all their forces of survival in order to migrate "upwards." The Dutch, on the other hand, caused and consolidated all that non-Western-European pain as they represented a model, outlining explicit requirements for success, delineating (endless) norms for upward social mobility.

In Suriname, it is evident that religion as well as immense fear that the past should repeat itself continued to produce a "mobile survival force" principle. Nonetheless, this trauma-laden way of life remained full of conflict and is the most characteristic reflection of the new Surinamese citizens' general feeling about life. They overcame the conflicts inherent in this essential state of consciousness, which gradually organized itself politically and which expressed itself destructively (and sometimes convulsively) against the established European order. Each individual citizen of Suriname internalized a profound sense of his or her new rights and duties and knew how to trace and/or imagine that his or her roots reached farther back than the postslavery society.

The experience of broken kinships and other intimate relations for two centuries had traumatic consequences for the family structure of the Creoles, whose vitality and drive to survive (necessary if parents are to bring up their children) had been paralyzed. For two centuries they lacked confidence, security, and a positive perspective on the future. Creoles were structurally denied the responsibility for others in both the immediate- and extended-family context.

The post–1863 reality of most Surinamese families entailed the absence of fathers, who were often forced to earn a living in the country's interior and who were therefore often away from home for months. Mothers were left behind to shoulder responsibility for the children, and they never knew whether their spouses would come back. A network of women (blood relatives and neighbors) who shared the responsibility for one another's children (sometimes also sharing money and property) was thus developed. Within this context, slowly but steadily, new educational concepts and objectives began to form themselves. These evolved into patterns of education and expectation in which the directive for a future perspective arose not from the constructive relationship between the parents but from the political contingencies of the day.

The "mobile force of survival" among both female and male Creoles manifested itself in a variety of conflicts which can be understood as profound, radical, and complex matters of loyalty. One of the most outstanding survival methods for Creoles has been Winti, a so-called Afro-Surinamese religion.

In 1972 a Surinamese, Charles Wooding, presented a doctoral dissertation on the "phenomenon" that he called an Afro-American religion in Suriname. In Wooding's cultural-historical analysis, this "phenomenon" received—for the first time—scientific attention from a native Surinamese. According to Wooding, this religion focuses on the belief in personified supernatural beings that can both possess and disconnect an individual's consciousness. In doing so, these beings can disclose the past, the present, and the future, and cure illnesses that are understood to have supernatural origins.

The word *Winti* literally means wind; metaphorically, it stands for breath or spiritual force. That is, Winti is an invisible substance—in paradoxical relation to the Greek concept of *pneuma:* wind or spirit. Most Creoles interpret Winti to be the personification of a host of supernatural beings who can enter earthly creatures, plants, and all manner of substances in both positive and negative ways. In most extreme cases, Winti spirits will possess and identify directly with living creatures and humans, and even speak through them.[1]

A Surinamese Winti therapist of Creole origin practicing in the Netherlands, Henry J. M. Stephen, calls Winti an "Afro-American religion with magic or spiritual rituals." Stephen stresses, above all, the world view of this religion. This, in Western terms, means that everything is filled with God. The gods can manifest themselves and, depending on their intentions and restrictions, they can choose aspects of creation: wind (for example, a rotating wind), water (such as a whirlpool), fire, trees (*kankantri*), animals (for instance, serpents or anthills) and individual humans (mostly adults). According to the Winti communications structure, the four elements—air, earth, water, and fire—are dominated by a hierarchical series of air, earth, water, and fire gods. All of these gods, whether female or male, are to a greater or lesser degree in contact with each individual, because humans "live" in these elements. The relation or interaction be-

tween individuals and gods enhances the way in which human individuals and collectives use the four elements; this determines whether a positive (rewarding) or negative (punitive) relationship will be created between god(s) and human(s).

Eschewing further technical distinctions,[2] I will simply note that there
are at least three clear variables which determine the Winti consciousness
of a person and/or family: ethnic consciousness, class consciousness, and
Christianization. All of these variables influence the making of myth, for
example, in literature. In this light, as I mentioned earlier, only through
metaphors is language capable of expressing the notion that subject and
object have a certain force in common. In metaphorical language, the unity
of human thinking and imagination is achieved in the central idea of a
multitude of gods, or the embodiments of the identity of a person with
nature. The essence of the metaphor is expressed by the "god"—the being
that identifies an aspect of the person with an aspect of nature. Winti religion offers a rich and vivid example of such metaphorical language.

In daily practice, devotion to Winti has been both a way of life, one
comparable to Holism, and a therapy, a system for curing illness. It is not
possible to separate Winti from the cultural and historical context of the
Creoles—a term that mostly refers to the urban blacks of Suriname. In the
city of Paramaribo, for instance, Winti has become a phenomenon of a
"spiritual sort" among Creoles who have a certain affinity with it. In the
forests of the interior of Suriname, where the so-called bush Negroes live,
this belief system is the dominant religious code, a recognizable and visible way of life.

For all who practice it, Winti is, first and foremost, a survival strategy
with a militant—political and revolutionary—value. During the initial and
mortifying times of the evolution of the diaspora in the Caribbean, Africans could "organize" themselves through their Winti practice and communicate meaningfully with one another. An indication that in those times
Winti gave a "revolutionary impulse" to society is that the Winti religion
was rigorously forbidden in the colonies.

But if Winti, the only African-rooted way of life, was forbidden, what
was left for the Creoles to base their humanity?

In the multiethnic society of Suriname, other ethnic groups were able
to ground their communities in their religions—Islam, Hinduism, and Buddhism, for instance. It is no wonder that those communities are not in as
much despair as the Creole community, whose way of life is influenced by
the order of the day—be it Christianity, Winti, pure Western or non-West-
ern patterns, or personal pragmatism. Somehow this flexibility helps us to

overcome our daily troubles, but it does not help us to construct a stable way of life that might construct either a vision or a practical lifestyle for our future generations.

When the first major migration to the Netherlands took place—first incidentally from 1950 to 1970 and then massively and structurally from the latter 1970s to the present—it was only the concrete or actualized perspective regarding the Creoles' future that changed, not our passionate intention to "migrate upwards." Creoles may have been able to rationalize the "historical traumas" that shaped our lives, but we had not been able to cope with them. And, over time, confrontations with Dutch society—issues of welfare, possibilities for development versus xenophobia and discrimination—revived the raw memory of this collective pain.

How, then, can we integrate Winti religion into our way of life today as we had consciously integrated certain aspects of Winti into our cultural attitudes of the past? One way to do so is to neither suppress Winti nor to approach it with shame as if it were some peculiar "sentiment" from our ancient past. In Winti we can try to find the sources of our humanity, the sources of moral and ethical views. People from Asia (the Hindustani and the Indonesians, the Chinese, and the Jews, for example) have their religions (Islam, Hinduism, Buddhism, Judaism), and our plight as Creoles is that we do not have anything beyond what Christianity offers us.

As long as some Creoles remain fearful of our African heritage and ashamed of our Winti-rooted mind, we will be unable to use our full capacity to (re)gain a coherent sense of our humanity or contribute to society in a more actualized, structural, and theoretical way.

Bricolage—Or, My Stories

There is, for me, only one "I," and that is my self: the person I am, who is increasingly easy to be made operational in quality and conditions.

This "I" is the only thing that I really know about existence in general, that I respect and love completely and without reservations.

This "I"—the "my self"—is the life force, the feeling force, the dream force, the thinking force behind everything that flows out of me as material product: for instance, the work that I publish. This "writing self" is not merely a component of "my self" but the total self that I give to the process of writing.

This process takes place, as far as I know, under specific conditions: stipulations that are based on years of experience; that have been well thought out; that all have my character, the facts of my life, and my ideas as a point of departure. Since I have lived longer in Holland than in Suriname, my daily experiences have made me aware of my "otherness"— my so-called diaspora status—and my powerlessness within. Only by not lamenting this powerlessness do I find another way of thinking, just as at sea a swimmer incapable of opposing the current relies on drifting to remain afloat.

So my writing—a contrapuntal writing or writing back—against colonial violence is a heavy job: I have to force myself to reorder and re-create the stream of chaotic information from my inner world and the outside world. My autobiographical reality helps me to "reconstruct" reality in metaphorical or literary ways, because in my own personal truth I find ideas, feelings, dreams—and the longing to rebuild reality. This autobiographical reality has an extremely important function in recreating and reordering. This reality provides the "I" with the ideas, the feelings, and the dreams—in other words, the building blocks with which to practice the art form of literary writing.

Still, autobiographical facts in this context do not belong to the purely personal. The autobiographical is the totality of what enters into the "I," and there is actually nothing that can avoid this in "confrontation" with me, since this "I" is equipped with a perceptual sensitivity that extends far beyond the reach of the purely personal. This sensitivity can be called talent, training, or a psychic constellation. I call it my political engagement.

It must immediately be noted that the "I" must gather incredible strength in order to succeed in re-creating and reordering from the chaotic flow of information from the internal and external worlds. For this re-creating and reordering, I make use of diverse forms and metaphors. This choice is carefully weighed.

Forms (novel, short story, poem, song, theater piece, radio play, column, essay, etc.) relate to the scope of the work, and moreso to the time, the space, and the action which the theme requires to enter into the internal and external world of others; in this sense, form also relates to the communications structure. My forms are therefore, in fact, communications structures.

Metaphors are also communications structures, although on a more content-oriented level. The "I" metaphor represents center, concentration, confrontation—heart, soul, reason. It is an unequivocal image and for "my self" the most valuable, since the "I" becomes self-conscious by being in relation to an "other." This is interesting because in a literary sense, the "other" presents itself in metaphors. In the relationship between the metaphorical "I" and the metaphorical "other," the truth can reveal itself. Truth, however, is never unequivocal and also requires metaphors in order to be revealed or made operational.

The misunderstanding among diverse cultures, religions, ethnicities, and sexes would immediately be resolved if one could see past the metaphors. We can enjoy metaphors the way we enjoy natural phenomena; the way we enjoy melodic lines and rhythmic motifs performed in the discrete color and sound registers of each instrument; the way I recently enjoyed the outspoken hues of a Karel Appel exhibit in the Community Museum of The Hague. If we understand these metaphorical structures, then a space opens up to enjoyment, wonder, and admiration. Then every type of cultural conditioning melts away and lets the "self" remain as an unequivocal "I" which can be even more open perceptually to information from the internal and external worlds.

Science, technology, and democracy—the so-called civil rights and all kinds of emancipation—did not really liberate the human race; on the contrary, violence is increasing. There was a time when I knew what caused this mess: the man/woman relationship, the black/white problem, and the North/South imbalance. But what is my part in this whole violence context—I mean that women, Blacks, and people from the Third World continue to have relations with men, whites, and the so-called rich countries? Am I, a black woman from Suriname, supporting this worldwide violence and racism in a certain way? My writing rages in the silence that follows this question—my writing against a violent world!

4

Three Words toward Creolization

Antonio Benítez-Rojo
Translated by James Maraniss

In this brief essay, I examine the notion of creolization through three words: plantation, rhythm, and performance. I ought to add that I don't mean these remarks to be taken as objective; they come simply out of my desire to see myself as a person with a Caribbean identity, as I understand it.

Of course, the use of these three words in Caribbean discourse is hardly new; they have been the subject of much writing, from both inside and outside the area, since the sixteenth century. In his critique of the plantation, seen as a macrosystem that functions in the world, Fray Bartolomé de Las Casas wrote, around 1520:

> As the sugar mills [of Hispaniola] grew every day, so grew the need to put Negroes to work in them. Seeing that we [Portuguese] have such a need and that we pay well for them, go out every day to capture them, through any vile and iniquitous means. . . . As they themselves see that they are looked for and desired, they make unjust wars upon each other, and in other illicit ways they steal one another to be sold to the Portuguese, so that we ourselves are the cause of the sins that one and another commits, as well as those that we ourselves commit in buying them. . . . Formerly, when there were no sugar mills . . . we had never seen a Negroe dead from disease . . . but after they were put into the sugar mills . . . they found their death and their sickness . . . and for that reason bands of them run away whenever they can, and they rise up and inflict death and cruelty upon the Spaniards, in order to get out of their captivity. (3:273–76)

Regarding the other two words—rhythm and performance—we note that, in 1573, the town government of Havana ordered that the free Blacks should be included, with their songs and dances, in the festivals with which Corpus Christi was celebrated. These Creole manifestations, emerging from an interplay of European and African elements, reached Spain in the third quarter of the sixteenth century—particularly the so-called zarabanda— and were commented on by Cervantes, Lope de Vega, Quevedo, and other writers. In fact, they were so popular in Spain that the Inquisition censured them more than once as indecent. I mention these cases to reinforce the fact that, from the earliest moments of colonization, the plantation system, as well as the Creole rhythms and performances, have been subjects of extensive commentary. And the use of the word criollo (Creole), as both noun and adjective, also dates from these early periods, as we know.[1]

Of course, what the plantation represented to Las Casas was quite different from what it represents to me. For Las Casas, the plantation was an immediate problem; it was a machine with no past that generated violence and sin in Hispaniola, Spain, and Portugal, as well as on the western coast of Africa. As he wrote the paragraph that I have quoted, Las Casas never imagined that the complex dynamics unleashed by the growing demand for sugar and other plantation products would begin to figure in a new discourse—to which his words now belong—that would refer not just to the sixteenth century but also to future centuries and to large parts of America, Europe, Africa, and Asia. But if Las Casas never saw the plantation as other than a problem of his time, to me, four centuries later, it is the womb of my otherness—and of my globality, if you will allow me this world. It is the bifurcated center that exists inside and outside at the same time, near to and distant from all things that I can understand as my own: race, nationality, language, and religion.

Yes, I repeat, the plantation is my old and paradoxical homeland. It is the machine that Las Casas described, but it is also much more: the hollow center of the minuscule galaxy that gives shape to my identity. There are no organized history or family trees in that center; its tremendous and prolonged explosion has projected everything outward. There, as a child of the plantation, I am a mere fragment, or an idea that spins around my own absence, just as a drop of rain spins around the empty eye of the hurricane that set it going.

Well then, what relation do I find between the plantation and the process of creolization? Naturally, first of all, a relation of cause and effect; without the one we would not have the other. But I also see other relations. From my perspective, our cultural manifestations are not creolized, but are rather in a state of creolization. Creolization does not transform literature or music or language into a synthesis or anything that could be taken in essentialist terms, nor does it lead these expressions into a predictable state of creolization. Rather, creolization is a term with which we attempt to explain the unstable states that a Caribbean cultural object presents over time. In other words, creolization is not merely a process (a word that implies forward movement) but a discontinuous series of recurrences, of happenings, whose sole law is change. Where does this instability come from? It is the product of the plantation (the big bang of the Caribbean universe), whose slow explosion throughout modern history threw out billions and billions of cultural fragments in all directions—fragments of diverse kinds that, in their endless voyage, come together in an instant to form a dance step, a linguistic trope, the line of a poem, and afterward repel each other to re-form and pull apart once more, and so on.

In the coming together and pulling apart of those fragments, many kinds of forces are at work. In my country, Cuba, for instance, the arrival of the radio, the Victrola, the recording industry, and the cinema contributed to the popularity of the *son*, the *rumba*, and the *conga* in the decade of the 1920s. Previously, this kind of music existed only among the black population and was not accepted as a national music. However, once the majority of Cubans had internalized these rhythms, they in turn contributed to the formation of what was known then as Afro-Cuban culture, a culture that produced the symphonic music of Amadeo Roldán and Alejandro García Caturla, the *negrista* poetry of Nicolás Guillén, the magic realism of Alejo Carpentier, the essays of Fernando Ortiz and Lydia Cabrera, and the painting of Wilfredo Lam.

Something else was happening simultaneously. In 1916, a group of distinguished black veterans of the War with Spain (1895–98) had asked the pope to designate as Cuba's patron saint the Virgin of la Caridad, a dark-skinned virgin. The pope granted this request immediately, perhaps not knowing that to many black Cubans, the Virgin of La Caridad was also the Oshun of Santería. While the so-called black music made its influence known in other cultural forms, Santería legitimized itself along with Catholicism as a national religion, influencing music, painting, dance, theater, literature, and even language—for example, words of African origin such as chévere, ashé, mayombe, bembé, ebbó, ekobio, babalawo, asere, íreme, orisha, and bilongo started being used extensively during those years.

In Cuba now, nobody speaks of Afro-Cuban manifestations: what was once something concerning Blacks before 1920 became Afro-Cuban and is now simply Cuban. One might think that all this happened because Cuban culture has been subject to an accelerated process of Africanization. But that is not the case: the public practice of Afro-Cuban religions was prohibited by the Cuban government until quite recently, negrista litera-ture and negrista symphonic music stopped being produced many years ago, and the painting of Wilfredo Lam is made now for tourists alone. In fact, Cuban culture, like any other culture born on the plantation, has for many years had African, European, Asian, and American components; and these components, in a state of creolization, approach or withdraw from one another according to situations created by unpredictable forces. If it is true that Cuba serves as an example here, it is also true that this paradigm repeats itself throughout the Caribbean. For example, both the First and Second World Wars played a part in foregrounding the African compo-nents of Caribbean culture. This seemed then to be a new thing, but in fact these components always were there and always will be there.

In short, the certainty about creolization is that it inevitably refers to the plantation. To borrow the jargon of Chaos here, I would say that the plantation is the strange attractor of all of the possible states of creoli-zation, given that all of them, in their disorder, hide forms of order that look for their guiding model in the black hole of the plantation. And so it could be said that the plantation repeats itself endlessly in the different states of creolization that come out here and there in language and music, dance and literature, food and theater. These elements are summed up in the Carnival.

Now, with regard to Caribbean performance and rhythm, I shall take examples from contemporary Caribbean fiction to illustrate my points. Of course, I could use the works of Wilson Harris, Alejo Carpentier, Gabriel García Márquez, or Maryse Condé, but I prefer to cite more recent writers, such as Caryl Phillips, of St. Kitts, who writes in his novel, *Crossing the River:*

> A long way from home. . . . For two hundred and fifty years I have listened. To the haunting voices. Singing: Mercy, Mercy. . . . Listened to voices hoping for Freedom. Democracy. Sing-ing: Baby baby. Where did our love go? Samba. Calypso. Jazz. Sketches of Spain in Harlem. . . . I have listened to the voice that cried: I have a dream that one day on the red hills of Geor-gia, the sons of former slaves and the sons of former slave-owners will be able to sit down together at the table of broth-

erhood. I have listened to the sounds of an African Carnival in Trinidad. In Rio. In New Orleans. On the far bank of the river, a drum continues to be beaten. . . . A guilty father. Always listening. There are no paths in water. No signposts. There is no return. A desperate foolishness. The crops failed. I sold my beloved children. *Bought two strong man-boys, and a proud girl.* But they arrived on the far bank of the river, loved. (236–37)

How would I define this novel's performance? In the first place, I would say that the praise that English critics gave to *Crossing the River* was deserved—the critic in the *Times Literary Supplement* said that the novel was "a triumphant piece of writing." But I also look in these reviews for judgments about its performance. For example, praise that the novel's "beauty lies in its very ellipses and suppressions," that "Phillips has a fine ironic sense of time," or that the novel "is dense with event and ingeniously structured" curiously leave out any reference to rhythm, which is one of Phillips's preoccupations. Says Phillips, "Where did our love go? Samba. Calypso. Jazz. Sketches of Spain in Harlem. . . . I have listened to an African Carnival in Trinidad. In Rio. In New Orleans. On the far bank of the river, a drum continues to be beaten" (236).

It is obvious that Phillips, as a son of the plantation, performs his own literature to the rhythms of the samba, the calypso, and jazz. And that's not all: his choice of punctuation—along with the number of syllables in his words and the syntax that connects them—gives a rhythmic meaning to his narrative discourse. Where does this rhythm come from? From within Phillips. So we might say that the performance of his literary language—what the critics see as ellipses and suppressions, and so forth—is dictated by the writer's interior rhythms. And though these rhythms might seem African, they are, in fact, not entirely so. Africa, as Phillips says, is irrecoverable: "There are no paths in water. No signposts. There is no return" (237). It is true that the rhythms of the samba and of calypso have their origin in Africa, but only if we understand rhythm to be a sequence of internal pulsations. For these pulsations to become rhythms, they must be wrapped in sounds. The pulsations that the rhythm of the samba follows are of African origin (we know that they belong to Bantu culture) but the sound of the samba is not a totally African one, just as it is not completely a European one. One could think, then, that it is Brazilian, but I would say that that is so only superficially. If we were to try to determine the origin of these rhythmic sounds, sounds that include many instruments along with the human voice and the rubbing of shoes against the floor (the way it is danced), we would find that this complex polyrhythmic system began to take shape on the plantation.

Natalio Galán, a Cuban musicologist, once said that within every rhythmic motif there lies a centuries-old mystery. I think that he was right; hidden within the samba there are the ancient pulsations brought by the African diaspora, the memory of sacred drums and the words of the griot. But there are also the rhythms of the sugar mill's machines, the machete stroke that cuts the cane, the overseer's lash, and the planter's language, music, and dance. Later there came other rhythms, from India, from China, and from Java. And finally, all these rhythms mixed with one another to form a network of rhythmic flows whose most notable expressions today are salsa, Latin jazz, and West Coast African music. This complex polyrhythmic orchestration was born on the plantation and now lies within the memory of the people of the Caribbean. It is what inspires Phillips's performance; that is, the way the novel is written and the way it sounds. "On the far bank of the river, a drum continues to be beaten" (237) marks *Crossing the River* as a novel in a state of creolization.

Let's take another example from a recent novel, also praised by the critics. In *The Longest Memory* by Fred D'Aguiar of Guyana, we read: "You do not want to know my past nor do you want to know my name for the simple reason that I have none and would have to make it up to please you. . . . I just was boy, mule, nigger, slave or whatever else anyone chose to call me" (1). Here, first of all, we have the reproduction of the plantation's void. Of course the slave in the novel has a name: Whitechapel, his master's name. But is this his real name? In my own case, do I see myself as Spanish simply because my name is Spanish? Then what is my real name, the one that corresponds to my real identity? Needless to say, had I been born in Spain with the same name, my name would reflect my identity without conflict. However, no Caribbean person—that is, no person with a truly Caribbean identity—carries his or her own true name, just as his or her skin pertains to no fixed race. The same observations pertain to language. The novels of Phillips and D'Aguiar, like others I will mention, are written in English, but none of them is totally English: they are Caribbean because of their poetics—structure, theme, character, conflict, technique, language—which I call performance.

More specifically, the stylistic performance of *The Longest Memory* is manifest in the difference between its chapters: the first is formed by a monologue spoken by a slave who has betrayed his son; the second by a planter's monologue; the third is an overseer's diary; the fourth is the words of a slave woman; the fifth, a poem; and the sixth, a dialogue among planters.

Another chapter is formed by the words of a white woman who teaches a slave to read, and still another by an editorial in a Virginia newspaper, and so on. What adjectives did the critics use to describe this brilliant performance? They used terms such as dense, intense, compact, and controversial. No European critic said of *The Longest Memory* that it was a novel of great rhythmic complexity. Nevertheless, in his attempt to describe the plantation, D'Aguiar wrote a text for a symphony for percussion, in which each character interprets a different rhythm; that is, a work of polyrhythmic density that gathers rhythms from the whole world.

It is precisely because of these performances that I believe Caribbean literature to be the most universal of all. I will go a step further and argue that the more Caribbean a text is—the more complex and artistic its state of creolization—the more readers it will find in the world. Some publishing houses have already understood this reality, and they are going to do a good business.

Obviously, one cannot say that all Caribbean fiction has the historic character of the examples I present here. Nevertheless, even when the action of a Caribbean novel takes place in the twentieth century, it always refers back to the plantation through its rhythm and its performance. Take, for instance, "Children of the Sea," a story by Haitian-American writer Edwidge Danticat. She writes:

> Do you want to know how people go to the bathroom on the boat? Probably the same way they did on those slave ships years ago. They set aside a little corner for that. When I have to pee, I just pull it, lean over the rail, and do it very quickly. When I have to do the other thing, I rip a piece of something, squat down and do it, and throw the waste into the sea. I am always embarrassed by the smell. It is so demeaning having to squat in front of so many people. People turn away, but not always. At times I wonder if there is really land on the other side of the sea. Maybe the sea is endless. Like my love for you. (1995, 15)

These are the words of a revolutionary student who, to avoid dying at the hands of the Tonton-Macoutes, has decided to flee to the United States in a little boat. As we see, in his voyage he relives the middle passage that connects Africa with America in the plantation's macrosystem. Later, when the boat takes in water, the humiliated passengers are forced to throw all of their belongings into the sea, including the clothes that they are wearing. Finally, they all drown, and their naked bodies keep company with the innumerable children of the sea who have disappeared beneath the waters of the black Atlantic. This story's narrative discourse, like those of *Crossing the River* and *The Longest Memory,* is fragmented: in a series of fragments we read the words of the man in the boat; in another series the words of his sweetheart in Haiti, who tells a story that is no less painful. Each of the individual narratives has its own typography and its own rhythm. The title of Danticat's book is *Krik? Krak!,* written in Creole, and it alludes to the peasant custom in which the story teller says "Krik?" to which the one who wants to hear a story answers "Krak!" We must then associate the dialogic structure of the story with the book's title, just as the boat's passengers tell stories according to the rules of *Krik? Krak!* But it is also obvious that, through this double game, Danticat puts herself in contact with the reader. Though her text is written in American English, it is deliberately connected to Haitian Creole oral traditions. According to the silly labels that we use in the United States, Danticat is a Haitian-American; in fact her identity is in the hyphen, that is, in neither place: Danticat is a Caribbean writer.

Finally, taking another recent novel, *Divina Trace,* by Robert Antoni of Trinidad, let us consider the following sentence:

> . . . *oy oy oy yo-yuga, yo-yuga da-bamba da-bamba oy* benedictus que venit in nomine Domini *oy* lumen de lumine de Deum verum de Deo vero *oy* Marie conçue sans péché priez por nous qui avons recours à vous Sainte Catherine del Carmen purísima hermosa azucena maravilla ayúdame cuídame fortaléceme socorredme favoréceme fuente de bondad de gracia y de misericordia *silverfish flying starpetals* exploding bursting out sudden silent from below the bow. (231)

What kind of language is this? The language of the plantation, including Latin, the language in which the Catholic Mass was said. The *Washington Post* reviewer of *Divina Trace* referred to the novel's magical realism with an avant-garde twist, but we can express this same opinion in other words: the magic realism of the Caribbean and the experiment of the modernist European novel come together here in a chaotic performance. The result is a bifurcated novel, fractal, gaseous; a novel whose performance can be placed quite near the big bang of the plantation.

Actually, *Divina Trace* offers a touch of real genius. Pages 203 and 204 are blank. Instead, a metal page performs as a mirror through which readers look at themselves and see a grotesquely disfigured face. This, naturally, is part of the novel's double performance: in the mirror, the western reader will read a joke or an irony or a mystery, but the Caribbean reader will see any one of his/her multiple masks. However, the mirror in *Divina Trace* functions at another level. The novel's plot develops around a monstrous character, half child and half frog, conceived by a mysterious woman named Magdalena, half saint and half whore. As the novel progresses, we see that nobody knows much about this child. A character says,

> Some called him the jabjab heself, son of Manfrog, the folktale devil-sprite who waits on a tree to rape young virgins at dusk. Others saw nothing peculiar in the child a-tall. Some even said the child was beautiful, perfect: that the child was the reflection of the viewer. Some argued the hex of an obeah spell. Others the curse of Magdalena's obsession with swamp Maraval. . . . Still others said he was the result of a congenital abnormality which caused him to appear like a frog. . . . Son, we can resign weselves to only this: there is no logical explanation. We will never know. (Antoni, 58–59)

With these words Antoni pushes the reader to a site of polemics: each reader projects in the mirror not just his/her face but also his/her ideology—every mirror is a text in which the observer reads him/herself. For some the reflected image will be that of the Creole; for others it will be a native of some country in the Caribbean; for others it will be the reflection of his/her own race. These reflections, invested with the political and social ideas of the observer, will never be coherent images, but rather distorted ones; they will be images in flux or, rather, images in search of their own images. Therefore, the mirror of *Divina Trace* reflects the many faces of Caribbean readers, but in the end it reflects an identity in a state of creolization, a reflection that oscillates between history and myth; that is, a paradoxical mask launched into the distance by the explosion of the plantation.

In the end, the performances of Phillips, D'Aguiar, Danticat, and Antoni can be seen as attempts to represent the trip to the origins of Caribbeanness. Or, if you prefer, they trace the journey of the fragmented Caribbean self in search of its hidden unity. Can this unity be found within the black hole of the plantation? My answer is both yes and no. A performer, through his or her performance, can resolve the paradox of his or her identity. But only poetically. As the character in *Divina Trace* says, for a paradox there is no logical explanation.

5

Dominicanyorkness

A Metropolitan Discovery of the Triangle

Sherezada (Chiqui) Vicioso
Translated by Maria Cristina Canales

I discovered the geographic limits of my world when I was very small. One, two, three, four, five vertical streets before reaching the main street, El Sol Street, with its sunny and inaccessible shop windows. Six horizontal streets, one street up, contiguous to the ravine, five streets down, almost touching the fortress's brown and gray wall.

I also discovered the limits of my grandmother's house which stretched out like a long, thin worm devouring bit by bit all that was green. Like bees, everyone had his or her own space. I was lucky to discover that there was room under the bed. It was a tall, metal bed, which, if pushed forward a bit, allowed the light to enter through the blinds. There, I set up my own house and arranged my own furniture, the type that Luis Marmita used to make and my grandmother used to buy because she "felt sorry for him." Small, cheap furniture typical of a small-town Christmas. Sad miniature imitations of American modernist furniture. I also used to keep my dolls there (what became of them?) and the set of toy cups that Doña Estela gave me for Three Kings Day. Only Loby would disrupt the perfect order in which I kept my things, for I had even measured that space to be broom-proof. That was my make-believe, my doll world, as the song goes. I think it was a Mexican song, or was it a children's T.V. program I saw in Miami, or was it on New York's Spanish-speaking channel?

I had also discovered the backyard's limits. My instinct for agriculture once prompted me to grow corn and sugar cane, but my grandmother stopped me short with one question: "Don't you see that there is not enough

62

space?" I tried to argue, but it was true. There was not enough space for the corn and the sugar cane among the begonias, the ginger, the red poppies, the *campanas*,[1] and the cherry tree. I discovered then that a person cannot be a farmer without land.

We still had Canaima! Not Rómulo Gallegos's Canaima (we did not know then that others existed, nor had they assigned the book in school) but our Canaima—the ravine. There were truly places to be discovered there, "mines" we used to call them. "We have a little mine there," and that was a big thing. Some, like Colón, had discovered a place and had claimed ownership of it in front of the others, I don't know, maybe because of some incipient tendency toward private property, or because it was the only way to hold fast to a space in this world owned by others.

> "Grandma, let me go to Canaima!"
> "That's not for girls!"
> "But, please, Grandma!"
> "I said, no!"
> "But, GRANDMA!"
> "Who did you take after, such a tomboy?"

Saturdays were always synonymous with expectation and envy. But then, dusk would come and so would the boys, with plenty of fish, filled with the hills and full of stories and adventures. They would talk about snakes and spirits. About fishes and crossroads. About strangely shaped clouds. They would talk about birds. Male birds, I imagine, or used to.

The universe seemed to be male then. Boys could go fishing. Boys could stay playing in the streets until eleven—we, until nine. Boys could go out alone. Boys could have all kinds of friends—though not always from every social class. Boys could play baseball and marbles. Boys could swear and talk about forbidden things. At night, I would always see them under the lightposts at the corners telling stories and making jokes. They would talk about mules and, I guess, also about women.

> "I always do everything wrong. You should have looked
> like Juan, and Antonia like Luis. . . ."
> "But, Mother!"
> "But what? Can you imagine yourself white and with Juan's
> green eyes? And Antonia, with Luis's blue eyes and blond curls?
> It would have been a knockout!"
> "But, Mother!"

"No buts! If you want to go to that party, you must have your hair straightened. . . ."

"But, MOTHER!"

"To have you take after your father! It's not that I didn't love him just as he was, don't get me wrong, but the boys should have taken after him, and you and Antonia, after me."

"Your passport. . . ."[2]

"Here."

"What is this business of 'india clara'?"

"Excuse me?"

"No but's. . . ."

"That is my color. In the Dominican Republic we are classified by skin color. I am 'india clara', that means 'light Indian'. . . ."

"Indian is not a color. . . ."

"But,"

"No but's. . . . Look, I don't have time for this kind of business. . . ."

And in fact, nobody seemed to have time to explain to me this "kind of business," which I was made to internalize by dint of hair straighteners and of Perlina cream to "lighten" my skin color; by being told that I had to marry a white man to "improve the race" because, by some awful genetic error or secret revenge, my sister and I had come out "india clara" like my father. Rather than "Indian," he was really *"Jabao,"* that is, white, rather ruddy, freckled but with "bad" hair.

"But, there are no Indians left in the Dominican Republic!," my "Indian" friends from Central and South America would tell me, astonished.

"I know but that's how we are classified over there. I am a light Indian. If I were darker, I would be an Indian-Indian, and if I were "beyond help," I would be a cinnamon-Indian."

"What about Blacks?"

"Well, they usually pay the guy preparing the I.D. card to put "cinnamon-Indian" where it asks for skin color."

"Oh!"

"But everything became complicated when we moved to a New York neighborhood where there were black Americans who looked like us."

New York—in the words and deeds of Lady Macbeth, best friend of the doll-house owner who had tried to win her over to a militant Christianity (the armchair type has never interested me except for its rituals: Gregorian chants and incense), soon began tearing down all my paradigms.

And so I went from *The Life and Works of the Saints* and the mystics Jacques and Raisa Maritain to Theilard de Chardin and Gabriel Marcel, from Gabriel Marcel to Sartre. When I was ready to believe that life was an absurdity unworthy of continuance, Camilo Torres appeared. His symbiosis allowed us—those of us who were Christians—to refrain from suicide when faced, in our twenties, with the loss of meaning of life.

From Camilo, I luckily moved on to study young Marx, like all of us, a poet at age twenty. It was a Marx then taught at the universities, which was, of course, consistent with North American eclecticism and its disqualifications. From young Marx, I progressed to the writings of Ernesto Guevara, the man most admired by the Latin American and Caribbean generation of the sixties, and then on to a more serious study of *The Capital*, Engels, Hegel, Fromm, Weber, Marcuse, Gunder Frank, Paulo Freire, and other visionaries of social restructure.

The journey from "buts" to consciousness turned into stubborn determination against the racism of American universities. It was articulated with my brothers and sisters from the English- and French-speaking Caribbean in the face of a sexist society, where to be woman, Latina, and intelligent was an insult.

Frantz Fanon, Marcus Garvey, C. L. R. James, Archie Singham, and, later on, Amilcar Cabral made me search in Africa for the lost links of my identity and that of an entire generation who, like me, had never considered the term *light Indian,* the hair straighteners, and the Perlina cream as evidences of the underlying racism, transmitted from generation to generation, that exists in the Dominican Republic.

But the Caribbean was missing, that other humanity, subjugated by fire and sword, whose identity quest had gradually reduced it to folklore, to anthropology, or to a collection of stories.

The double triangle needed completion. There is the one Eric Williams described in his explanation of slavery as the axis of the triangular trade— among the Caribbean islands, the colony that was then the United States, and England—which allowed an incipient capitalism to develop and forever made us unequal. And then, there is mine: as a woman in a culture which, in Getrudis Gomez de Avellaneda's words, neither holds us captive nor sets us free; as a mulatto in a society where you do not go to a party unless you straighten your hair; and, as a Caribbean woman on a half-island where the Caribbean is limited to Cuba and Puerto Rico and where Spanish is not a bridge but a wall.

Trapped in this parallelogram, divided Star of David, unable to be polished until it reaches the diamond's perfect harmony, I have returned to the circular origin of my nothingness, knowing that I am a social construct, a mulatto and a Caribbean woman.

Having been reduced to the local stigma of Dominicanyork but without the skyscraper's immense verticality, I ask myself, what now?

How do you go up to the *basement*?

> ". . . BASE-MENT."
> "I know, Grandma. . . ."
> "How can a daughter of mine write in Spanglish!"
> "*But. . . .*"
> "I told you that, once beyond ideologies, language would suffer the Berlin Wall's fate," smiles Lady Macbeth, with her usual cynicism. . . ."
> "BUT!"

New York, 1987

The odor of grapes, of fish, ascends
Deco antiques parade
there, a balcony between the steel
and a small, red geranium plant,
which, precocious, dares to peep out
the traffic, black and immune to the
crowds waiting to pounce
the traffic light's con
versation defies the aggressive trucks
beautiful and tempting rises
the Fifty-ninth Street bridge.

It is East New York, this New
York which ignores *cuchifritos*[3]
fried plantain and pork rinds,
alcapurria,[4] Ruben Blades,
drums transforming rooftops
into summer nights, *Areitos*[5]
Feasts, altars, rum, cocaine
Shango, Oggun,[6] razors, guns
Anaisa and orange blossom bouquets

yellow, white, purple flowers
to avert the evils of hatred.

Passageway, tunnel, excursion to
Dante's seven hells, not
the Italian but that Argentinian
bongo player surviving in
Manhattan Avenue's Viet-Nam
Ho Chi Ming washed dishes in your bars
Juan Isidro, Bosch, Maximo Gomez[7]
the whole exile of ideas, poetry
agonizing in every Julia.[8]
Oh! New York, my naked pain!
Oh! New York, humanity lying-under!
through you I came to understand that the first
definition of Homeland
                              is nostalgia.

6

Where Are All the Others?

Erna Brodber

A dummi rolls for the roldaldo
A dummi rolls for the roldaldo
. . . .
Laughing away to her heart's delight
Mr. Fine-young man you've got to pay
My Mama for her crockeryware
A dummi rolls for the roldaldo
A dummi rolls for the roldaldo

There were two Miss Mandas. There was Mrs. Bean, Mr. Bean's wife. No matter what happened, she smiled; Mr. Bean smiled too. This to my four-year-old mind was the epitome of marriage—two people looking at the same thing at the same time, seeing the same points at the same time, smiling at the same thing at the same time. You did things for the Beans. I certainly approved of them and wanted to preserve them. I remember running to catch up with them to give them a piece of paper. They were so happy and grateful to receive it. It was the wrapper from the weekly Jamaica Times, which came through the mail to us. The Beans had come to my father for a "paper" to get some help after the hurricane of 1944. Papa had turned them away. He had given out all the "papers" that the government had given to him. I felt they deserved a "paper," they were so lovely. All I could find was that discarded wrapper. And they took it so graciously. It was only when they tried to cash it in at the government office that they learnt the truth about my gift to them, for the Beans were totally illiterate. The Beans begged. They were even willing to stand around and ask for a taste of our kindergarten attempts at cooking. I loved them. We all loved them. They were "them." I don't even know now how I came to know that Mrs. Bean was Miss Manda, for nobody called her anything but Mrs.

Bean—though in our village surnames and Mrs. were things written, not said. The Beans did cutlass work for my father occasionally. You can see that they must have been dirt poor. Indeed, if my father was their casual employer, for in the social class index as I was to learn twenty years later, a man with less than ten acres of land was not a planter or a farmer but a cultivator, a peasant, poor and mistrustful. Mrs. Manda Bean and her husband were poor, illiterate, hard-working, begging people. They were normal.

The other Miss Manda was the real Miss Manda. She was married to Joe Chiss. Chiss was his nickname. Did Joe Chiss, called "Chiss" sometimes but more often "Joe Chiss," have a surname? I don't think I ever heard it, but I do know that to call him either of those two names could bring you a shower of abuse. And I do know that on one of those days when my cousins came from all over the island to visit, they had instructed my four-year-old self, the youngest cousin then, to call out "Chiss" when he appeared, and my father had felt it necessary to apologize to him. The proper way of addressing this gentleman was "Mass Joe." His Miss Manda was, without a doubt, poor. He drove my uncle's cart and must have been paid, yet in my mind he was poor—poorer than the Beans who sought casual labor from my father, who had less land than my uncle had and who seriously needed the little bits of yam seed that we cooked in our Ovaltine pans. Joe Chiss stands out in my mind as poor because (so the story went, and I believed it) he sold his land by the banana roots, two shilling and six pence per piece, when in need. He must really have done so, for the size of the land on which he and his wife lived was no bigger than a sixpence. When I look back at it now, I see that Joe Chiss was poor in the village mind not so much because he did not have money but because he didn't have the will to hold on to his heritage. No one— but no one— sells his land. Weeds may grow on it; the grass may die; you may plant nothing viable on it; but you do not sell your land. It is the evidence that your forebears lived; to sell it is to sell not just yourself but your dead. His Miss Manda was Solomon's lily. She neither toiled nor spun. Naturally she shared Joe's status.

There was a son. Whether he was Miss Manda's son, or Joe Chiss's son, or the product of the two is something I don't know. I don't think anyone knew. I certainly know that it didn't matter. Who produced whom was irrelevant in those days. Who grew whom was what was important. "Right" names, the names in pen in the government's book was nobody's business, so Mass Joe and his Miss Manda grew a son and his name was Parson. He did no regular work. Though he was, of course, younger than the

two, he was the one bent from the waist. Much, much later in life, someone who came into the district to live enlightened me concerning Parson's
bent back. He had V.D. The evidence? She had seen him boiling bushes. I
don't know that V.D. bends you from the waist. All I know is that I was
afraid of Parson. He smiled like the Beans. Always smiled. But while the
Beans smiled together, Parson had no set body with whom to smile. His
specialty was smiling at. He would look at you intensely, smile and sing:

> Pe, Papa, Pe Papa,
> I love no one but you.

That's all he sang. Love choruses. The singer of the family was Miss Manda.
   Unlike Manda Bean, Joe Chiss's Miss Manda was a nonworking wife
who was not known to seek or to have sought work. She was rumored to
steal. Corn and coco. Teacher taught us the so-called Negro song:

> Down in the cornfields
> Hear their mournful cry
> All the darkies am a crying
> Crying cause he leave them behind.

Every jack man and child sang that when Miss Manda was sighted, editing
the lyrics to read:

> Down in the corn and coco fields.

Miss Manda was called "drake." I don't know why. Mandrake? I don't
know why, but call her "drake" when she was within earshot and blue
light would fly. And that was as often as anybody wished, for Miss Manda's
anger was a village pleasure. Miss Manda was poised to fight; she would
start battles that she couldn't win and never won, and that was part of the
pleasure Miss Manda brought. She was the unhero. I personally witnessed
one of Miss Manda's fights. I remember it well for it was the first time I
had seen adults—and women at that—getting ready to spar. Joe material-
ized from wherever he had been and, as her opponent advanced to what
everyone knew from experience or rumor would be the kill, he yanked
his wife away, pushed her behind him still holding her hand, and set about
making peace with her opponent, while Miss Manda shouted in her most
excellent English, a thing unheard of in day-to-day life, much less in spar-
ring bouts. "Let me go, let me go, Joe, I say let me go," Miss Manda said
loudly—I heard that—meaning to say, "Let me go so that I can finish off

this miserable offender." Joe did not let her go. There are those who heard an additional imperative, this time in the local language, "Hole mi, Joe, hole mi," meaning to say, "Protect me from this person. You know I cannot fight and will not win this battle." Whether that was said or not is not the point. What people took from that event was that once more Miss Manda had instigated a fight that she couldn't manage. "Let me go, Joe, I say let me go. Hole mi, hole mi, hole mi," was a scene anyone who wished to, reenacted to make Miss Manda even madder.

I know now that one of the things that made Miss Manda such a sore thumb in the village was her inability or her refusal to merge two cultural orientations in a manner pleasing to the village. Whoever heard of a fighter saying, "Let me go"? What was required at a time such as this was huffing and puffing, no words at all. Much railing. Body language only. And when words finally came, they should be in the local language. The trouble with Miss Manda was that she knew another language. Another quote that followed her around like a curse was, "Don't follow those fools. Drake is an animal." Miss Manda said those words. The new headmaster's child, on the instigation of settled peers, had called Miss Manda "Drake," and Miss Manda said those words. A poor, workless, fighting, bad-word-speaking, thieving woman like Miss Manda had no right to speak the English language in the normal course of daily interaction. For some reason, Miss Manda did not know that. She was inadequately socialized. But I have no doubt that it was this glimpse of another orientation that made her husband so protective of her. Joe Chiss wanted, needed, and protected that part of Manda that could speak the English language.

I have said that Miss Manda could sing. She could sing. She never sang at any village concert. Nobody invited her. Nobody would. Miss Manda was too given to quarrels, bad words, and such lower-class behavior to be invited to participate in decent people's things. It was Cindy who sang for her. Now, in the village eyes, Cindy was as good as Miss Manda was bad. Cindy cried on her twelfth birthday. Why? She didn't want to grow up. People said this was a sign of goodness. Cindy was in the choir. Whenever the hymn "By Cool Shilom's Shady Rills, How Sweet the Lilies Bloom" was sung, you could expect a wash of tears from Cindy. There was a bit of mournfulness in the tune, I admit, but the words had nothing at all to do with sadness. Yet Cindy cried, and everyone said this was a sign of her innocence and that the Lord loved her.

I have never seen Cindy as much as talk to Miss Manda, but I know and I am sure that everyone else knew that Miss Manda instructed Cindy in singing. How else could Cindy know the words to those songs? Miss Manda was my neighbor, not Cindy's, and I could only catch the tune, not the words of the songs that came over to our house from Miss Manda's sixpence yard; yet these were the ones that Cindy sang, in the same voice, with lyrics fairly understandable, at village concerts. "A Dummi Rolls for the Roldaldo" usually took the house down. This was a song about a wild girl whose parents had found a "nice" young man to marry her and settle her down. She knew, though, that he was not so "nice" and set about to prove it. He was allowed to sleep in her house one night, and she moved her mother's crockery cabinet close to her room. Groping toward her door, "Mr. Fine-young man" accidentally pulled this piece of furniture down and with it her mother's fine china. She sings:

> Mr. Fine-young man
> You've got to pay
> My Mama for her
> Crockeryware

And then the chorus:

> A dummi rolls for the roldaldo
> A dummi rolls for the roldaldo

Where did sweet, innocent Cindy get the phrasing of that song such that all could get its meaning? Even I at four or five. And the calypsoesque gleam in her eyes was that of the mischief-making Miss Manda. So too was the body language.

Miss Manda and Miss Manda's songs have been bothering me lately. We all know about code-switching. In the Caribbean setting in which we have been reared, where there is an African cultural orientation and a European cultural orientation and several gradations between, a person is socialized into the ability to match occasion with form. To get the fit wrong, as in the case of Joe Chiss's wife, Miss Manda, is a social sin which could have psychiatric proportions. Everyone knows the different styles of behavior and the class position associated with each. To be socially sick is to use a form that is not consonant with one's social class. If you are poor, a thief, use bad words, live in a sixpence yard, you should not speak English. You do understand it, but you should never communicate in it. Miss Manda sinned twice: she got the match between form and occasion wrong, and she spoke in a tone and language that were not befitting her class. Miss Manda did not know her place.

In our Caribbean—where race, color, and material wealth intersect with cultural orientation to form grids into which people are placed and into which they place themselves—it is important for social and psychological peace that one know one's place. Miss Manda's feet were not just too big for her shoes, she hadn't even caught on that there were shoes; so she was diseased, made others diseased, and was therefore mad. Until I began to consider Miss Manda, I did not realize the extent of the mental and psychological gymnastics that the so-called lower class in the creolized and creolizing Caribbean go through daily in order to be socially correct. So much work, "scientific work," has been done on the lower class in the Caribbean, on the concept of plurality, on the notion of class, on creolization, but we don't know Miss Manda's pain. She is suffering from incomplete creolization. How many others are there?

Miss Manda's songs—they had not a drop of Africa in them. No Jamaican English either, nor did they describe Jamaican situations. Who did we know who had fine crockeryware and a place to put it—much less a bedroom in which one girl slept by herself? And those songs were not "Sweet Afton" flowing gently and taught at school. They were too risqué for the formal education system.

Lately as I sit here in Virginia, I have been mulling over one of my rare triumphs which is circuitously related to Miss Manda's songs. Barbados has never interested me. I have sat time and time again in the airport there for the mandatory half-hour, waiting to be called back into my plane to continue my journey from Trinidad or Guyana to Jamaica—or the other way around—and never so much as felt curious about what went on beyond the in-transit lounge. This I have been doing since 1961, when my family extended itself into the Eastern Caribbean and I became financially mature enough to fund my travel there. It was not until 1980 that I got into Barbados. I went there not on my own steam but at the dictates of those who paid me then. Someone invited me to a jazz club, and I swear I felt that I had been lifted out of the Caribbean and into one of Baldwin's novels.

It was not so much the music that transported me out of the region but the interaction between the piano player and the others around him—the club's staff and the patrons. The piano player was the band. There were only a few of us patrons there, so I could see very well the way people held their bodies to talk to one another. I couldn't hear what they said above the music, but I could hear the sound of their voices interfacing with the music. I asked a linguist about my sense that there was a connection between Barbadians and the people who appeared in Baldwin's works. He said he had always thought there was a relationship between the Barbadian and the African American dialect. I described to my African American girlfriend the resemblance in communication styles that I saw. She said "Nah" in just the way a Barbadian would.

Here comes my triumph.

I continued to visit Barbados and chose to focus on Barbadian women. Although I had never consciously thought of listening to or looking at the relative styles of African American females, I certainly had been listening to a lot of them on tape and had been reading their creative works, for in the period of which I speak, I had been devoting my recreation time solely to black American female singers and writers. As I watched Barbadian women at bus stops, in stores, in offices, everywhere, and shamelessly eavesdropped on their conversations, I became more and more convinced that there was a connection between these two parts of the African diaspora that others—Jamaica, Guyana, and Trinidad, for instance—did not share. I put this to two male American historians on one of my visits to the island when I attended a cocktail party following a conference. One of the men was black, the other was white. "Nah," they said. No resemblance. No special connection. "Call that waitress over for me," I said, "and then consider what I have said." They called her over and then began between themselves to talk with great passion about women they had known with that self-same way of 'coming on' to men. "I bet you she. . . ." "She reminds me of a girl I used to. . . ." "Them, those women. . . ." I couldn't decipher the passion, and therefore could not follow them, because I am not a man; but I knew that I had won. They were men enough to admit that.

That is my triumph, and I relate it to say that I have kept my ears and my mind open since then for leads to the nature of that which connects Barbados to the Africans of the United States. It came to me later that Barbados and the early American colonies—Virginia, for instance—were settled at about the same time by the same kinds of people and did not change hands. The mix of Britishers had been the same; the mix of African, very likely the same; and unlike Jamaica, Trinidad, and Guyana, these early colonies had had no Dutch, Spanish, or French influences, no maroon societies to disturb the particular African-British Creole content. It was no great mystery then, that Barbadian Blacks and U.S. Blacks should share some special qualities. My mind refused to let the issue go at that and remained open and waiting.

Paul Robeson entered it. While teaching in Pennsylvania, I encountered his autobiography and saw him crediting the Irish for their influence on African American music. A year later, I went to teach in Virginia and there attended an exhibition, "Away, I'll Fly Away," in which a notice regarding a runaway African American slave described him as speaking in an Irish dialect. Closeness contributes to the transfer of culture; the Irish were among the secondary whites. They tended to be the overseers in British-held territories; they were the indentured laborers and the prisoners banished to the colonies. That the Irish and the African cultures should become mixed and produce Blacks in the United States who were like Blacks in Barbados was perfectly reasonable, then.

I had—before this understanding came to me—been in Jamaica quietly opening my ears for leads when I went to a talk by an Australian professor of English who introduced us, among other things, to the Australian song:

> I wish I had someone to love me
> And someone to call me his own

"How on earth could that be Australian," I said to myself, "when my mother sang it to us?" When I next saw her and asked her about it, she remembered neither the song nor the talk but offered, "The Irish would have brought it to us both." There they were again, the Irish.

So here I am in Virginia, sitting down and thinking about these things. Asking questions here and there, meeting this colleague who can't get over the way the music, the dancing, and the preaching styles of African Americans remind him of the Irish community in deep rural Virginia from which he hails, and I am forced to go back to Miss Manda's songs. Which of the secondary whites, living so close to slave, ex-slave, and peasant-class African Jamaicans passed on those ribald songs to Miss Manda? Which of them gave us those children's games which survive in indisputable English? I want to know what the Irish, the Scottish, the Welsh gave to the Creole mix as much as I want to know: "Is it Ibo, Fulani, what particular part of Africa is my heritage?" I have no doubt that with the kind of work being done by Kamau Brathwaite and Maureen Lewis-Warner—to mention those whom I know best—I will solve the African riddle, but who will tell me about the others? Where are the others?

It is May 15, 1994, and I am listening to "Weekend Edition" on National Public Radio in Ashland, Virginia. Did I really hear someone authoritatively say that Irish music is derived from West African music of the seventeenth century? The plot thickens. Will anybody be able to disentangle this creolized and creolizing mess?

1

A Brief History of My Country

Lourdes Vázquez
Translated by Robert M. Fedorchek

History That Invents Itself

We began to invent a homemade Creole manner of expression when the Tainos left us an island with a few gods perched atop the tallest mountain, a list of words that continue to form an active part of our vocabulary, and a territory organized by regions and towns with clearly and fully identified names. All of this before the colonists killed them off.

The thirty or forty ethnic groups represented in the slaves who arrived in the island and intermixed with the rest of the population brought us more of the same thing—a culture and a rich, colorful, forceful language which we have incorporated into food, dance, music, religion, and death—in other words, into life itself. Words like *cocolo*, which refers to a black native of the West Indies, and *culipandear*, which is a way of swinging the hips (especially when women move them so slowly it's as though time stood still between each movement) are just two examples of our rich colloquial language. If we add the proverbs and idioms and customs, then we can testify to the profound dimensions of this cross-breeding.

From the Moors we inherited a number of musical and baroque words like *alberca*, which is more than a swimming pool since it has hand-painted tiles on the inside and a garden with flowers and fruit trees; or the word *aldaba*, which does not mean lock since it is an iron or bronze device affixed to doors to knock on them. To this list we can add Basques and Catalans along with their contributions; South Americans, who take refuge in our country every time there is a row in theirs; and, naturally, our

76

own people, Antilleans, from the rest of the Caribbean basin, who move back and forth from one island to another in a constant ebb and flow. And let's also add to this list all the pirates, buccaneers, and freebooters who tired of roaming the seas and decided to remain on the island—aged men with weary bones, but accompanied by wide-hipped Creole girls. The population continued to intermix, producing lovely mestizo sons and daughters, while it kept on developing a language of its own, one foreign to Old Castile. I am a product of that mixture.

My great-grandmother came from Venezuela, a direct descendant of that region's last viceroy. My great-grandfather was an Eastern European Jew who arrived in America on a ship loaded with slaves and started a business on the Caribbean seaboard. Fleeing from an act of revenge taken by other slaves, my great-grandfather sent my great-grandmother and all their children to Puerto Rico on a boat. The children scattered throughout the island, mixing with the population. My sweet-faced paternal grandfather, Juan Vázquez, was an artisan who, after traveling on foot from Humacao to San Juan in search of a better life, reached a barrio in Santurce. Along the way he worked as a baker, a farm hand, a carpenter, and a cabinetmaker. He met and married María Pérez, my grandmother, with pretensions to royalty, with whom he started a business of homemade pineapple wine.

When I make the journey from San Juan to Humacao on the turnpike, which nowadays only takes an hour, I often think about my grandfather, about the straitened conditions in which he had to have made the journey from Humacao to San Juan. How long did it take him? Do you suppose he had shoes? Where did he spend the night? How many days did he spend walking? How many snakes, scorpions, and toads did he have to crush on the way? How many roadside whores taught him the horizontal laws of life? I never knew my maternal grandmother, Francisca, but I imagine her as Rubén Darío's mistress since her name was Francisca Sánchez and there could only have been one Francisca Sánchez. People tell me that she was a tall, beautiful woman, a laundress who washed the shit-soiled shorts of all the males of the Carrión family, the bank owners who lived in the wealthy section of Santurce. My maternal grandfather, Cristóbal, became a street vendor after his small grocery store was leveled by a hurricane, wiping out his savings, his property, and his stock. He liked to ride horseback over to Upper Trujillo and would sneak away from his wife, Francisca Sánchez, and every time that he did so, she had to go and record the birth of another child in the registry office. My grandfather would ride over there, to the tallest mountain, to sit under a tree and get drunk of a broken heart from so much green grass and so much rain. And there he fathered sons and daughters who eventually became my uncles and aunts.

What Were They Writing on That Island and for What Reason?

Literature in my country was always monitored by the government. What were the inhabitants of that colony writing and for whom? With what objective? Spain used to watch over its colonies with the keen eye of a despotic monarch, but in one way or another, my ancestors, availing themselves of irony and double entendre, managed to write and, with considerable difficulty, publish an occasional piece. Already, in the middle of the last century, a group of Puerto Rican students studying in Spain (all males of course) devoted themselves to writing sketches of customs and manners. One of those students, Manuel Alonso, published *El Jíbaro*, one of our first books of political satire, in which he included sketches, Creole poetry, and notes in the form of edicts on Puerto Rican issues as a way of poking fun at the Spanish government's censorship.

When I was a girl I used to read and reread Manuel Alonso, without understanding half of the things that I came across. The following edict, however, sticks in my mind: "Don Tintinábulo Caralampio of the Nocturnal Lepidopterous Insects, Lord of the Carambímbolas of the Big River Rock, Pasha of the Balearic Islands, President of the Senate of China and of the Cochinchiniana, Count of the Martín Peña Mangrove Swamp, of the Shakers of Loíza. . . ." (Alonso 26). The edict openly ridicules the number of personages with a royal title who would turn up on the island and infest it, as they continue to infest it, Spain, and the whole of Europe. I found out about all of this afterward. Coming as I did from a Santurce barrio—which was precisely where the great number of swamps and marshes near the Martín Peña mangrove swamp originated—I used to picture the Count of the latter all smelly and with his skin green from the vegetation and dung. I imagined him with deep red lips and violet eyes, a Bohemian with a black cape like the ones worn by the student music groups who used to come from Spain at Christmastime, and I would imagine that he was flying through the neighborhoods of the wealthy in Miramar. When I read this edict, I also learned of the place where my grandmother would order us when she was angry—to Cochinchina. In other words, Cochinchina lay considerably beyond China, on the farthest side, the one that has not yet been explored. Even today Cochinchina is an area that cannot be pinpointed on the map, but everybody on my island knows where it is.

The Implications of Bilingualism

Then the gringos came, and apparently they came to stay. As a matter of fact, we'll soon mark one hundred years of sheer gringo suffocation. Censorship continued to such an extent that in the 1940s a number of writers were imprisoned in the United States, leaders in the fight for independence, along with the head (Don Pedro Albizu Campos) of the nationalist movement, who was jailed because he had made a series of speeches against the regime. On the other hand, from the time the gringos set foot on the island the imposed language of instruction was English, until a wonderful Puerto Rican attorney named Doña Nilita Vientós Gastón took the matter to court in the 1930s and it was ruled that instruction would be given in Spanish. Obviously, in my country Spanish is spoken; so evident is this fact that the current governor, who is more American-minded than the gringos themselves, has taken it into his head to assure us that when Puerto Rico becomes an American state, my island will be one that maintains its native ways—in other words, we will continue to speak Spanish. And this drives the gringos crazy, since in the United States itself there is at the moment an intense campaign to make the country "English-only."

As a result of the early years of gringo colonization we still have the custom of addressing primary- and secondary-school teachers as "misis" and "mister." If you visit a government office, you will also find "mister" and "misis" everywhere you go. "Good morning, Mister Rivera," says the secretary. "Did you prepare that letter for me, Misis Santiago?" he replies. If you go to a hospital, all the nurses are "misis." "Misis, it hurts me here." I have three aunts who are nurses, and even though they're elderly now, they continue to be misis. "Misis, how are you?" their ex-patients ask when they see them in the street. All in a spirit of distinctive, island usage.

I don't think that we're a bilingual nation. Creoles are terrified of English, but the upper class, the former landowners, who nowadays run the businesses and are the owners of the great corporate law offices and the big banks, know English perfectly and take care to ensure that their children know it. This pseudo-bourgeoisie set up, a few years ago, a number of private schools for their children, with special emphasis on gringo culture and the English language; and from there it's on to the United States, which is the finishing school that in another era Madrid or Paris was. That's the way things are.

The great majority of us Puerto Rican writers write in just one language, although there are two or three who have been able to go from one language to another with a certain amount of success. To be a bilingual writer is one of the most complex aspects of bilingualism, but within the tradition of Hispanics in the United States, it is one that dates back to the end of the last century. On the one hand, we Puerto Ricans fight for dear life in defense of our language. It's a matter of country or death, as Che used to say. Or was it Fidel? For many, to write in English signifies a betrayal of the native country. "What native country?" I sometimes wonder as I search for a native country that sometimes slips through my fingers.

Furthermore, there exists in the United States the strange custom of categorizing writers according to their origin, thereby creating a kind of literary apartheid. Like all apartheids, this one consists of a segregation, a literary segregation in which everyone's writing is categorized by race and sex—either because the establishment never made room for minorities and this is the way to get it, or precisely because that very establishment determined that the writings of the so-called social minorities would be organized in accordance with secret norms based on origin. It's a phenomenon very similar to the one known during the days of the British Empire as "commonwealth literature." I've decided that it's the manner in which imperialist countries view the rest of the world, especially if the rest of the world was colonized by them or because that rest of the world lives in their territory.

The anecdote that I'm going to relate here has left me with a number of questions. I recently attended a conference on Caribbean literature, and the numerous references on the part of conferees from the English- and French-speaking Caribbean to the willingness of London and Paris publishing houses to support the literature of both regions surprised me. Our situation is not the same. We Puerto Ricans scarcely have ties to two or three publishing houses in Spain, ties which have been forged through very personal efforts. In fact, the situation is that we Puerto Rican writers cannot look to Madrid or New York as outlets that provide us with a springboard to success.

I reside in New York, which complicates matters even more. The special consequences of being a Puerto Rican writer who writes in Spanish and lives in New York means, in essence, that although I'm a U.S. citizen, my writings are better known in the Caribbean and in Latin America. Still, I don't consider myself a bilingual writer. To be a bilingual writer is to enter a suspect category, even though there are numerous bilingual writers throughout the world. Then again, I feel no pressing need to write in English, even though from time to time I'll insert an English word into my work, something that would not have happened were I not living here.

Magic Realism

We've been working on magic realism since the Tainos decided that the region of the dead was called Coaybay. Here in Coaybay the dead come out to take a walk and eat guava at night. In order to recognize the other dead, one touches the area around the navel, as a dead person lacks a navel. The lack of a navel was the countersign to that more transparent region. About the Blacks, I remember the drum playing from three in the afternoon until sunset on the streets of lower Santurce. The drum playing was mixed with rhythms like guaguancó, mambo, son, and danzón. My escapades with my male cousins to listen to the stories told by those people who would sit down to explain the world according to the laws of Eleguá, taught me from an early age what the world was all about.

Through a few Frenchmen who fled the Haitian revolution, we obtained an anonymous translation of Allan Kardec's *The Gospel According to Spiritualism,* which contains the explanation of the moral maxims of Christ and their concordance with spiritualism as well as their application to the various stations in life. My grandparents took possession of *The Gospel According to Spiritualism* and made it their own.

My paternal grandparents were mediums and, moreover, founded a temple for spiritualist solace in the living room of their home. But much more than this, they were instrumental figures in establishing on the island the House of Spirits, a pretty respectable center for spiritualist study in Santurce. For as long as we can remember, our grandparents visualized with their powers the characteristics and sex of their grandchildren, as well as the problems that they would confront in their earthly lives. They've done it with every one of us and have not erred in their prophecies. That's why to this day the house is not only full of children, grandchildren, and sons-in-law, but of exalted spirits like Madama, the Indian, and Rosendo Matienzo Cintrón, who today is found in history books and is the wisest spirit of them all.

Madama usually appears at the outset of a spiritualist session or when some obsessed soul makes its entrance. She is, moreover, the announcer-spirit, the one who brings good and bad tidings. The Indian, on the other hand, is more than four thousand years old and has existed since the time of the first settlers in remote China. On account of his ethereal condition and his considerably advanced age, he has traveled over the entire planet and meets with the witch doctors of the Amazon and the gypsies of ancient Slovakia. He possesses the wisdom of Chinese medicine and is one of the few who knows the secret of the lotus flower. People say that his work is guaranteed. Rosendo Matienzo Cintrón, henceforth referred to as R. M. C., is the most advanced spirit and is besides a fighter for the just things in life. In spiritualist sessions R. M. C. gives instructions to the family regarding the steps to be followed in national emergencies, which are constant. This spirit is in great demand, summoned as he is by masons and secret lodges, legislators and government bureaucrats, the unemployed, workers, servants, and whores. The family holds him in high esteem. Occasionally a backward spirit appears, but my grandmother, who is a clairvoyant medium, sees it and helps it to break loose from its earthly weaknesses by sending it to the infinite so that it can better itself.

With the intention of purifying clairvoyant faculties, my grandmother has pitchers of clean water carefully placed throughout the house. The problem is that the water attracts the mosquito Aedes Aegiptis, which is why it occurred to my grandmother to cover the pitchers with a small piece of silk cloth. The worms that work the silk have a spiritualist property which is studied by oriental mediums, and in such a way that the flowback of clairvoyant faculties is not affected. This explains the certainty that these spirits exhibit.

We've always had to be accustomed to the comings and goings of people, to the crowds of unemployed, to musicians and bolero dancers who came in search of relief; to the cures, the smells of herbs and tonics; and to the lilies and the vase of clean water on the table. Life, say the spiritualist manuals, is a cycle. Life and death or life-death is one and the same, and the only thing that separates them is a physical body full of infirmities that ends up eaten by worms.

About how we embraced our nationalism, about the constant censorship and the years of persecuting liberal and pro-independence families, there are bulging archives in Spain, France, Denmark, the Dominican Republic, Cuba, and the U.S. Pentagon, and still others in the Masonic lodges of Europe and America. Our adaptation to the Creole world of *The Gospel According to Spiritualism,* about which I am writing at this moment, is explained by the need to be able to fight back and ease somewhat our tribulations. And this is why R. M. C.'s spirit is so important.

From the Other Side of the Ocean

One day my father decided, like thousands of other Puerto Ricans, that we had to go to New York. I was about five, and New York for me at that time consisted of a dark apartment in Ramona's house in the Puerto Rican barrio. A lot of people were in and out of that apartment, among them a few of my aunts and uncles who had also crossed the water. The kitchen had a big table where Ramona, a Puerto Rican immigrant, used to serve hot chocolate to the multitude of people who passed through her apartment, because it also served as a boarding house for dozens of Puerto Rican families that wanted to settle there in the barrio. The hot chocolate and a tall, skinny Ramona are all that I remember, because my mother decided that the cold wasn't for her and returned to the island, leaving her husband dumbfounded and working in a hat factory.

The first time that I saw a "Nuyorican" it was a girl who was chasing after a cousin of mine. That summer when she came to the island changed my knowledge of the basic things in life. The facts: (1) she had immaculately pale skin and lips painted red like a fireman's helmet; (2) she had a daring way of dressing, with half of her breasts hanging out; (3) her family had allowed her to travel alone and visit her fiancé; (4) she went into my cousin's room and stayed there alone with him, with the door closed, the light out, in silence before the whole world; (5) and she expressed herself better in English than in Spanish, and basically spoke "Spanglish."

My mind filled with questions, and I didn't consider anyone in my family capable of giving me the right answers. And there was more: I felt that I had been the butt of a joke, the object of a secret shared only by adults. What kind of culture was it that allowed you to do everything that was forbidden by ours? In no way did I associate that New York with Ramona's house and her steaming chocolate. Therefore the questions kept coming. Who are those equals of ours, and where do they live? Why did they leave? What do they do? On the other hand, I always knew that I had several aunts and uncles in New York, but New York could have been Cochinchina, and I would have time when I became an adult to learn the exact location of Cochinchina in the geography of our world. When I met my cousin's fiancée I realized that New York belonged to a more tangible place, hence more accessible to our spirit. So I pestered my parents until they gave me a trip to New York as a birthday present, and I went to stay with an uncle in Brooklyn.

I arrived in New York accompanied by a cousin who had a very simple agenda: acquire a boyfriend. I only wanted to clear up the mystery of the lips painted red like a fireman's helmet. Within a week, my cousin had her boyfriend, and he was one of the handsomest guys in the barrio. He had a languid expression, which is so characteristic of the youths of my country, and a sleek body. I secretly fell in love with him. The first time that I heard the word *boricua* was one afternoon when my cousins and I went up on the roof to wait for a summer eclipse. From there you could see the entire barrio and all the Puerto Rican young people of both sexes who were also anxiously waiting for the eclipse. The immaculately pale girls, all of them with their lips painted red. Red like the envy that I felt at not being able to appropriate their independent body language and daring ways without being overwhelmed by guilt and Muslim shame. It was a very hot, brilliant afternoon, and my cousin's boyfriend with his languid expression saw us and shouted from the sidewalk: "Boricua, do you see Puertorro from there?" The words came in through my ears, nose and mouth and reached as far as my chest. I was speechless. Intuitively I understood that to be boricua is to be Puerto Rican and that Puertorro was a diminutive of Puerto Rico. That's what it was about. To assume your Puerto Ricanness without reproach, on that rooftop and anywhere else. I was around fourteen and swore that I would love that man until I died. Today his languid expression continues to be mirrored in all the boricua youths of this city.

As a result I believe that the most important city for Puerto Ricans is not our capital, San Juan, but New York. Puerto Ricans came here along with Cubans at the end of the last century and wrote the first Puerto Rican literature in newspaper and magazine articles, diaries, and manifestoes which have yet to be collected in a volume.

Since then there have been generations of working-class and unemployed Puerto Ricans who, inspired by our music and the various musical forms of Afro-Americans and Afro-Caribs, have developed one of the most sophisticated expressions of our music: the salsa, but not without first having passed through the experience of Afro-Cuban jazz, Latin jazz, Latin bugalú and the Latin soul. Starting in the 1960s a group of Puerto Rican and Nuyorican writers developed one of the most intense and rich of literatures. Fiction as well as Nuyorican poetry have, in short, enlarged our vision of the world with its broken language. When the *azotea* is no longer "roof" but rufo, when the *balcón* is no longer "porch" but porche, the manner of thinking in the language is transformed.

About Our Irreverence

In the last twenty or thirty years, our literature has been irreverent. There is no school that concerns us, and much less a style or idiomatic appropriateness. Here is where my writing comes in. To depict the life of the urban working class and the lumpen proletariat in the manner of Marx is our obsession. To record their speech patterns and their particular grammar, all the jargon of street words and their users; to interweave true stories with fiction; to mix our social classes in all kinds of Creole scandals, has been a means of reaffirming our mestizo ancestry. It is moreover a way of attacking, deconstructing, and demythologizing the values of lower-middle-class culture. It is for this reason that our writing is filled with the tales of men and he-men, women and broads, workers of both sexes, homosexuals, lesbians, transvestites, and whores.

Erotic and occasionally pornographic language may appear in a natural way in any text. As Foucault has said, sex becomes a prop and a spearhead for denouncing social hypocrisy. Because aesthetic conventionalisms are being called into question and because we live in a constant bombardment from English, as much in the media as in private education, we have created one of the richest literatures in the Caribbean, particularly the literature written by women.

We Women, Period

Chroniclers relate that Taino women not only danced the *areytos*[1] but that they also led and sang the songs. It seems that we Puerto Rican women writers have inherited this tradition and made it a part of our task. That orality is what I try to express on the written page. Perhaps because the ones who have watched over a large part of our oral history have been our women as they expressed many of our concerns through stories, gossip, forbidden tales, and what we have read in the newspapers, what happened years ago and today, causes grave misfortunes. They're stories that on occasion seem like television soap operas told effectively and without chauvinism.

Just in case, I hunt down all the stories out there that I can and devote myself to testimonials as a way of getting to the bottom of the loneliness, grief, and emotional mistreatment of so many of our women. I wrote a biography, based on testimonials, of a little-known Puerto Rican poet, Marina Arzola, who died in the 1970s. I dug out the meanings of her death, of her everyday life, which was so similar to that of many other brilliant women on our island. In this biography there are serpents that abduct women, winged horses that carry messages of madness, and even sorcerers who dispossess a princess of her treasure. While I was transcribing the testimonials, I would envision the tales from my barrio in Santurce when the neighbor women together with those of my family would gather on my grandmother's porch to amuse themselves by telling true stories. As they talked they created images, sounds, and new variants in the language and its form, and the mysteries of the origin of speech would be resolved in no time at all. My own experience with so many troublesome spirits in my grandparents' and parents' homes, the drum playing two blocks from my home, the salsa orchestras, and the comings and goings of so many bolero dancers and musicians in my grandparents' house, made it very easy for me to write this account and all the others to come.

This brief history of my country compels me to look at the future and observe my children: my daughter, a Latina with a porcelainlike face and lips painted red like our desire to live; my son, a boy with languid eyes and a body like the trunk of a cypress tree; both of whom speak both English and Spanish with perfect ease, both of whom search for their identity in the salsa nightclubs and the hip-hop rap of this, our great city.

\

Part Two
~ ~ ~

Creolization, Literature,
and the Politics of Language

The essays collected in this second part explore more directly the role of Creole languages in the production of consciousness and literature, and focus more specifically on the linguistic terrain that Caribbean literature explores. The question of language is at the core of these explorations of the Caribbean imaginary, because in the Caribbean—as in many other parts of the world with a colonial past—many literary texts reflect a struggle with the imposed language of the colonizer in which they are often produced. While several essays discuss the specific history and development of the Creole languages—and explore their meaning in literary production in general, and on the author's own creativity in particular—all articulate, directly or indirectly, the subversive process of appropriating and transforming the inherited "master" language. These essays show how, through a transformed language and the creation of new techniques, styles, syntaxes, images, rhythms, and meanings, Caribbean writers have overcome cultural displacement and exerted control over their own creation.

In the last essays of Part One, Brodber and Vázquez already introduced the social and personal politics of language in Jamaica and Puerto Rico. In "Creolization and Caribbean Literature—the Politics of the Word," Merle Collins continues this exploration of how the history of the Caribbean has shaped the development of various forms of bilingualism. More specifically, Collins examines how this history has influenced her own language choices. Collins explores the concept of creoleness, examines its transforming power in shaping a "new" Caribbean literature, and tracks its representation in her own writing.

In "The Stakes of Créolité" Ernest Pépin and Raphaël Confiant take on some of the critiques recently leveled on their use of créolité. Reaffirming the roots of créolité in Césaire's and Glissant's views of a subversive "decolonized" aesthetics, Pépin and Confiant argue here that what is at stake in the literary notion of créolité is nothing less than the culture's imaginary. In "'Créolité' without Creole Language," Maryse Condé unravels the history of the word *Créole* and the concept of créolité. She shows how Creole languages have served as the instruments of linguistic subversion as well as resistance to colonial oppression. Though Condé claims her Guadeloupean roots, she refutes the manifesto of the Martinican "school of créolité," with its rigid linguistic rules and restricting canon, and refuses to be creatively confined to her native land. Pulling along in her wake other French Antillean writers, Condé claims the need for and right to unrestricted individualism.

In "The Victory of the Nannies and the Concubines," Frank Martinus Arion takes the Papiamento trail into the past to explain how it has become the dominating national language of his native Curaçao, in the Netherlands Antilles. Arion explores the politics of this Afro-Portuguese Creole, which penetrated into the "big houses" as early as the beginning of the nineteenth century.

In "The Process of Creolization in Haiti and the Traps of Creole Writing," the poet, novelist, linguist, and neurologist Jean Métellus sounds a note of dissent; he dismisses the numerous theories that for a century have defined Haitian Creole as the result of the slow blending of African, European, and native languages. According to Métellus, however, recent research demonstrates that Haitian Creole stems from the grammatically unstructured vernacular French of the seventeenth century. Used by the French colonists in their daily communications, this simplified French was passed to the black slaves who internalized it as their own. This, Métellus argues, resulted in the complete erasure of all African languages. For Métellus the current half-phonetic, half-phonologic orthography imposed on Haitian Creole is another form of colonization, because it transforms Creole into an international anglicized language.

In "Race, Space, and the Poetics of Moving," M. Nourbese Philip recreates the liberating Creole gaiety of the Trinidad Carnival displaced in Toronto, Canada. Her text testifies to the linguistic resilience and resistance to power structures of creolization in her native island. Through the metaphor of Caribbean people carnivalling and "moving" through the streets of Toronto, Philip tells the story of the long and painful "moving" of Blacks into history. Philip shows how cultural, social, and linguistic realities are shaped by the politics and ideologies of a community at a given time, and how these in turn shape her own literary creativity.

8

Writing and Creole Language Politics
Voice and Story

Merle Collins

I will begin my discussion of Creole language politics and its influence on my writing where my language experience first started. Certainly Creole words must have been among the first that I heard. The voices that made an early impact on my consciousness spoke to me in Creole, shaping, correcting, advising, scolding, chastising, loving. When I listened to people talking about their life experiences, they spoke in Creole. When they didn't want me to understand and spoke among themselves, they spoke what I came to know of as *Patwa*, the lexicon which the Folk Research Centre in St. Lucia is now researching and referring to as *Kriol*.[1] These were the voices of my socialization.

Early in my existence, however, I knew that some people talked "bad," deep Creole, and some talked "good," a lighter Creole or even English. When I entered pre-primary school, my teacher spoke English, although she also communicated in Creole sometimes. Whatever language she chose to communicate in, she made us young people aware that there was such a thing as "proper" English, which wasn't the same as home English. That was the beginning of my formal education and of my understanding that there was an English to be aimed for, something more prestigious than the "tear-up" English I spoke at home and with my friends on the street. This English to be aimed for was close to the language the doctor spoke when he came on his weekly visits to the surgery. The nurse in the visiting station spoke that too, sometimes, although she mixed it with Creole. Later on, I knew that the estate owner spoke that English also, even though he spoke Creole because he seemed to like it and also because he wanted everyone to understand him clearly. His wife, however, and another estate owner I knew who was a woman, spoke English consistently. This helped to keep a social distance, apparently particularly necessary for women, because Creole was so familiar. Politicians were expected to be able to speak good English, but it was acceptable for them to speak Creole at meetings, especially around election time. Parents were concerned that children should not concentrate too much on "bad English" but aim at perfection of the "Queen's English" which they learned at school and which was important for social and economic advancement.

Early in my socialization, therefore, I was made conscious of the differing status of English and Creole. It was not called Creole, though. That is a fairly recent, academic formulation. It was just "the way we talk," "we kind o language" or plain old "bad English." It still is usually regarded as such. This "Creole" formulation is a sign of the times, and certainly, in my estimation, represents an advance. The ongoing search for a name and for explanations of the grammar of languages forged in the Caribbean represents a perception that these languages are not dialects of English or French or Dutch but have structural differences related to the history and structure mainly of African languages.[2]

While I did not realize it at the time, my early language experience spoke of politics and society, telling stories of class, race, and also gender. When, at school, I first began to have an interest in writing, I would not have dreamed of presenting to the school magazine a story written in Creole. Where Creole was used in dialogue, my voice, as writer, would certainly have been one purporting to be English. Today, the distinctions are much more blurred. This is not to suggest that the blurring only began with the coming of age of my generation. As early as the 1950s, in London, Samuel Selvon had written *The Lonely Londoners* completely in Trinidadian Creole. Partly because of its linguistic daring, this has become a seminal work in Caribbean literature. Since then, the more widespread use of Creole in literary works reflects changing perceptions and the complexities of language use in the Caribbean.

In Grenada in June 1994, I was asked to comment on an ongoing debate about teaching Creole in schools. Did I think it was a good idea? It is important, I said, to teach how Creoles developed, to put them in context as languages emerging from the particular historical experience of the island and of the wider Caribbean. English is an international language, I observed, and students should be taught English and be made to understand that while Creole is a proper language, it has little international sociopolitical status. When my comments were reported later, it was said that I had encouraged those interested in teaching Creole to take a deeper look at the subject.[3]

A deeper look, certainly, but this does not mean an injunction to forget the teaching of Creole because it has little sociopolitical status. It urges, rather, a teaching at this stage of the history of the development of Caribbean Creoles, using research material already available on the subject. Researchers such as Hubert Devonish and Morgan Dalphinis have begun accumulating the material which would provide information on the history of Caribbean Creoles and make it possible to trace syntactical patterns and structures back to origins in such places as Ghana or Nigeria. In Grenada, there are local people also who have been recording various forms of Creole and whose work, it is to be hoped, will one day become more generally available.[4]

A lot more research needs to be done, and while it is important at this stage to teach the history and structure of Caribbean languages insofar as is possible, I feel that a proper organization of Creole language teaching must await the development of grammar books and/or the results of further research. Otherwise, Creole could be in danger of being taught as exotica, an exciting aberration but still not a proper language. The history of the languages should perhaps be taught in association with the history of the African and Asian communities imported into the region so that, understanding, people will begin to develop a pride in the fact that new languages were forged in what might euphemistically be termed extremely difficult circumstances. If structural differences from the official European languages of the colonizer could be regarded as evidence of resistance and of the "long memory" of which Guyanese writer Grace Nichols speaks, then perhaps the status of Creoles would be enhanced where it matters most—among those who speak consistently what they consider "bad English," even if academics choose to term it Creole or "nation language."[5]

With these few comments, I hope that I begin to touch on some of the controversies and complexities inherent in the situation. Where Grenada is concerned, when I refer to the Creole language, I think of the English-based idiom with rhythms and structures of various African languages, the idiom which is usually referred to as "bad English." But Grenada has another Kriol, the almost moribund idiom locally referred to as "Patwa," which has a more French syntactic base, with rhythms and structures of various African languages. In Grenada now there is talk of revival of this idiom and of teaching Kriol.[6] An excellent idea, one perhaps more easily acceptable to educators because this idiom, more reminiscent of French, is very different from the official English and is more easily recognizable as a different language. While the English-based idiom might still, therefore, be vigorously opposed as "bad English" and be seen to "interfere" with efforts to teach "proper" English, Kriol in this situation would appear to pose no real challenge to official English.

In St. Lucia, the Folk Research Centre has for years been concerned about promoting Kriol, a language more generally spoken there than it is in Grenada. The Folk Research Centre would be unlikely to refer to Kriol as "French-based," claiming its separate language status and being more interested in the African and Caribbean components of its shaping. I am supportive of this view but still have not managed to resolve how to refer to the different language forms in a Grenada language situation which is somewhat different from St. Lucia's. I see this not as a problem but as part of an exciting period of shaping, reclaiming, renaming.

These are only some of the issues that are always on the fringes of my consciousness when I write. Throughout my school and university experience, the language of formal education was always English. In Grenada, teachers spoke a mixture of Creole and English but always demanded essay presentations in English. Correctly so. The all-important examinations had to be written in English. Whatever might be spoken, English was the language of writing, of formal communication. At my first postgraduate university experience in the United States, I found myself having to relearn the spelling of certain words in order to write proper "American." Later on in England, I reverted to the proper "English" spelling. I have never been required to write proper "Caribbean" or proper Creole, because it was never perceived that there was anything "proper" about this statusless language, the medium of expression of a people with little international political and socioeconomic power. The issue about "correct" representation in print arises now, when, as a writer, I try to transfer to the page the Creole syntax and rhythms of my socialization, when I try to transfer to the page the words spoken by the characters who inhabit my imagination and are trying to express themselves without translation into English. It arises, also, because language researchers in the region note my formulations and spelling with varying levels of interest and approach me with interesting critical commentary, making me think more deeply about a language I have spoken all my life without seeing it written.

Some of those who shared my high school experience inform me that they like to hear my work read but don't find it very easy to read it themselves. The voice is familiar in communication, but what they read easily is English, not Creole. I understand that. I come from the same experience myself. I believe that because of my home experience (a mixture of Creole and Kriol), combined with the formal use of English at school, I have developed a facility for being able to hear the unspoken rhythm of Creole when it is presented on the page, so that when I read Creole, the rhythms are immediately apparent. In writing my own work, I sometimes refer to Creole language researchers to advise about spelling since my own base is literature and not linguistics.

I sometimes begin writing a story in English and progressively it becomes more Creolized because when characters begin to speak, English sounds strange in their mouths and my intervention as author sounds too removed from my character-friends if I use English. In such cases there sometimes occurs a shift between what Kenneth Ramchand has referred to as "West Indian Standard," Creole and English (77–114).

When I choose to write Creole, however, it has nothing to do with making a point about what *should* be done. Creole, English, French, Spanish, Dutch, are all a part of the Caribbean shaping, and individual writers use what in their estimation best suits their purpose and what most actively inhabits their imagination.

The problems for someone with an interest in Caribbean literature should be no more than they are for any other literature. The study of Caribbean literature demands the kind of preparation required by any other literary effort. And this is the case whether a Creole piece (story, novel, poem) is being presented in the classrooms of the Caribbean; of North America, Britain, Germany, or another European country; or of Africa, Asia, or Australia. Language use is only one facet of the research, since, as with any other literary piece, context, imagery, and the like are important issues. Caribbean literature reflects Caribbean experience and is written in a variety of languages—for example, Creole, English, Dutch, Spanish, French.

Who are you, reader? An academic with an interest in Caribbean literature? An academic with an interest in Creole languages? An undergraduate student with an interest in, but not much knowledge of, Caribbean literature? A postgraduate student with some previous knowledge of Caribbean literature and interest already stirred, excited by the prospect of a debate? An undergraduate or high school student who believes that most Caribbean writing, especially the poetry, is in Creole? Someone interested in issues of language and literature generally? If you know my work, when you read a story, poem, novel written by me, what language experience do you expect? Creole? English? A mixture of these? Do you expect the novel form to be experimenting with ways of incorporating oral Creole traditions into this written form? Perhaps your answer to each of these is yes. Perhaps not. But when you read this essay, purported to be some type of descriptive and/or academic essay, do you expect Creole? I would guess not. English is the language of my formal education, and if not of yours, at least it is an international language that you probably have learned if you are reading this piece in English. I would be very surprised if you had done a formal, classroom study of the structure and form of Grenadian Creole. I haven't, but I have spoken it all of my life. Therefore, the characters who inhabit my imagination use it regularly, and so my fiction makes use of it along with English, which (like you, probably) I have studied.

Rightly or wrongly, I did not agonize about which language to write this piece in. I moved naturally to English. Perhaps one day this situation will change. Pioneer scholars like Carolyn Cooper at the University of the West Indies are helping with movement in this direction. At the moment, however, I am not unusual, among Caribbean people in that part of the region once colonized by Britain, in thinking of English as the language of formal communication. I agonized more about the form and tone of this essay. An academic essay omitting the subjective "I" and striving for apparent objectivity? Drawn toward the discursive on an issue which is so close to the heart of my creative writing, I opted for the obviously subjective "I" and a feeling of closer communication with you, the reader.

Caribbean Creoles, languages of everyday communication, have little status either in the local formal situation or in an international situation. I feel it is important to research them further and perhaps, as a result of this, the region will move increasingly toward their use in more formal communication. This is certainly not a short-term prospect, since it involves not a disembodied artistic situation but deep and ingrained sociopolitical perceptions. Literary texts perhaps provide an important point of departure for debates of this kind. Creole, in that part of the Caribbean colonized by Britain, is not far removed from English in syntax and certainly can be understood, especially with study. Many Caribbean young people studied and passed Cambridge General Certificate of Education examinations on the work of Geoffrey Chaucer, whose English was far removed from the present-day official variety.

In *Subject to Others*, Moira Ferguson makes some interesting comments in reference to an old debate, on the issue of Creole language use in the Caribbean during the period of Africans' enslavement (103). Creole language use was associated with stupidity and childishness. Africans who were unable to speak English—which was not their native tongue—were considered stupid even if they could speak four or five African languages. These, not known or understood by the colonizers, were deemed insignificant. The use of different African languages would not even be recognized, and what the colonizer did not recognize was, in this sociopolitical situation, not important. Good sense was judged by the ability to speak English. As Africans began to communicate haltingly in an unfamiliar language, using the rhythms and structures of their native languages, their language use confirmed their inferiority in the eyes of the colonizer. According to Ferguson, "Lack of knowledge about slaves' speech, chauvinist ideas about language and so-called grammatical propriety continued to reinforce stereotypes about Africans as childlike people, barely participants in the symbolic order" (103). These ideas about language still affect perceptions of Caribbean Creoles today. Negative attitudes have been embedded in the national psyche.

Still, ongoing debates about Creoles and their importance reflect perceptions of a need for redefinition and a change of perception on these issues. The change of perception may be happening slowly, but *one one cocoa full basket.* Look at that: the Creole proverb to a make a point right at the end—and the whole thing in English!

9

The Stakes of Créolité

Ernest Pépin and Raphaël Confiant
Translated by Marie-Agnès Sourieau

When Jean Bernabé, Patrick Chamoiseau, and Raphaël Confiant published
Éloge de la Créolité (In Praise of "Créolité") in 1989, they stirred quite a
furor.[1]

People cried, "How could they!" "What sort of neologism is that?" Obviously créolité had to be suspected of original sin, indeed of mortal sin,
since the word Créole could only conjure up for the franco-creolophone
Antilleans visions of two realities, both shamefully accepted: Creole language and the descendants of the white settlers, the "békés" or "blanc-
pays."

If it was generally accepted, with no problem at all, that Joséphine de
Beauharnais and Saint-John Perse could claim some sort of créolité, it
seemed particularly offensive that the grandsons of slaves, those Negro-
Africans, Neo-Africans, "Blacks" could also proclaim themselves "Créole."

Was this not an imposture, a fraud, or at the very least a betrayal of
roots; an unseemly denial of origins? Was this not a guilty regression toward the infantile disease of exoticism, against the telluric and volcanic
flashes of an Aimé Césaire as well as against the salutary and therapeutic
analyses of a Frantz Fanon? Furthermore, was not "antillanité" (Caribbeanness), as defined by Edouard Glissant, adequate enough to express
the "inmost depths of ourselves"?

And above all, had not Negritude put forward the definitive theory of
our identity?

That's what it's all about; for us, a hybrid people whose face is blurred by our ongoing *métissage;* a deported people whose mind is chiseled by multiple alienations; a people in gestation whose journey is lost in tortuous combinations—so tortuous and so sinuous that it turns into a forced return to the lost transparency of our native countries.

According to the authors of *Éloge*, it's a matter of reactivating "our creative potential," of recovering a "more precise expression" and "more genuine aesthetics," of surveying "the Caribbean ecology and referential space," of subverting our tropisms of exteriority—the exteriority of aspirations (Africa), the expression of revolt (black people), and self-assertion (We are Africans)—in order to "understand what constitutes a Caribbean person" (1993, 19, 20).

These are generous postulates, meant to unveil a reality covered with all the ashes of our wanderings and all the scars of our marooning!

But how should we do it?

Any thought implies foundations, calls for levers, and suggests steps, procedures, and elucidating processes. So be it. The "interior vision" and "self-acceptance" are just such levers. As for the necessary steps, here they are: "To learn again how to visualize our depths. To learn again to look positively at what revolves around us. . . . Interior vision defeats, first of all, the old French imagery that shrouds us, and restores us to ourselves in a mosaic renewed by the autonomy of its components, their unpredictability, their now mysterious resonances" (24).

Quite simply, it's a matter of reclaiming and decolonizing our imaginary; and of assuming our rich bilingual heritage.

Some will no doubt assert that Negritude said the same thing and, what is more, that it had the indisputable merit of saying it first!

Quite true! The objectives of both movements may be similar, but their perspective is different. The black man's great outcry was to redeem Blacks and black African cultures. It was brilliantly done, despite a few resounding controversies. This corresponded to the necessity of establishing a vast movement of decolonization upon the royal throne of the right to difference. But since then, the colonial empires have broken up into nation-states, and each of them has gone its own way. Therefore, it has been necessary to address the question of cultural identity not from a global perspective but from specific perspectives conveying particular situations.

For a long time the question of identity was defined in the mode of the One: one language, one territory, one religion, one history, one single root. Our multicultural heritage yields a polycentric approach in which the question of identity generates a mosaic identity affirmed by idioms, languages, places, systems of thoughts, histories fertilizing one another and untying the unpredictable. An identity of coexistence is necessary and is an imperative to reject the exclusiveness of the One and its militant isolation. It is from this fertile ground that Créolité stems, not as an antinegritude but as a broadening of the initial breakthrough of our world as it actually is, as a light revealing our heterogeneous reality.

In literature, créolité unearths our buried orality (tales, songs, proverbs, puns), carrier of countervalues and countercultures. It leans on the true memory as a matter of urgency for an itinerary more suitable to our time-space—through the revisiting of the systems of dating, positioning in space, legibility of the obscure—and all this by differing from colonial chronicles.

Créolité spies the tangibility of life (markets, wakes, lewoz, lolos [beliefs], strategies of seduction, and so forth) in order to detect the sign of the thwarted, even smothered, project. Créolité is immersed within the "creolized" modernity of the world and thus supports the creativity of the Creole language: "The Creole poet, the Creole novelist, both writing in Creole, will have to be at once the collectors of ancestral speech, the gatherers of new words, and the discoverers of the créolité of Creole" (45).

This implies that our relationship to language takes into account the spirit of languages within a creative dynamics and beyond all reductive fetishism. Through this relationship to languages, which also applies to cultural relations, créolité rediscovers another history of the world—the history of its multiplicity. These are the past créolités—Egyptian, Greek, Chinese, Eastern Indian, African—that gave birth to our world. These are the créolités of today that are building the world of tomorrow.

How, then, is this reflected in literary creation?

It is important to remember the theoretical framework provided by Edouard Glissant—not only what he contributed as an essayist but also as a novelist, poet, and playwright. Glissant "brought back home" our theory of literature through the exploration of all the hidden, unspoken, and underground textures of our Caribbean milieu. Is it necessary to mention *Le discours antillais* (1981) or his novels *Le Quatrième siècle* (1964) or *Malemort* (1975)? Edouard Glissant's undisputed contribution to both present and future generations is his recentered approach to the reading of Caribbean culture, and especially of Creole literature. Instead of posing Africa as fundamental matrix, Glissant put forward the unfinished and unpredictable creativity of the historical, geographical, and anthropological space of Creole society by focusing our "point of view" as well as releasing a semiology of ourselves. The Caribbean world, perceived as crippled and abnormal, suddenly became comprehensible, if not logical. Our cabins, our hills, our beliefs, our speech, our languages—in other words, our presence in the world inscribed in "the prophetic vision of the past"—regained their eloquence and density.

The literature of créolité can only be understood if we take into account Glissant's contribution. Take, for example, Patrick Chamoiseau's *Texaco,* and it becomes clear that this novel proposes a new reading of history and especially of the organization of space and social sedimentation.

A traditional reading would have concluded that *Texaco* is an outgrowth of a marginal world, an unbearable outgrowth that should be returned to urban norms based on Western concepts—in particular the fixed order where individualism blossoms and the Creole spirit is evacuated. Chamoiseau opposes this vision by unveiling the bottom layers, showing what is at work in the depths of this microsociety and how it uncovers and teaches us about our present historical adaptation: a nonitemized temporality (time of the bois-caisse, of the fibro-ciment, etc.), a new reading of historical filiations from the hills to the heart of town. Chamoiseau reveals an elaborate network of resistance at work, strategies of cohabitation, controlling space and its sociology, from which emerges a creativity or rather a most remarkable human creation. Of course, this calls for a renewed literary style and an original staging of the discourse.

Similarly, Raphaël Confiant's *Le nègre et l'amiral* (1988) encodes and decodes the Martinican real-life experience at the time of Admiral Robert. Here also, through the narrative, Creole culture provides the raw material of the novel.

In *L'homme au bâton* (1992), Pépin attempts to expose the discourse of the Creole imaginary both as a construction that compensates the shortcomings of reality and as a projection of a mosaic identity. Pépin's most recent novels, *Coulée d'or* and *Tambour-Babel,* probe our imaginary, our relationship to the notions of fatality, destiny, reality, surreality, and the supernatural through a complex interplay of coming and going between reality and unreality, tradition and modernity.

The fundamental literary stakes of créolité are to re-vision language, narrative aesthetics, orchestration of events and places from a plural conception of identity; hence the fragile paths traced by the ingenious and subtle architecture born out of the Creole spirit are reasserted.

But all of this is not limited in the least to literature. It is a terrain under construction opened up to multiple economical, social, and political elements. In fact, it is a matter of validating and developing all the strategies crafted by our people in response to the requirements of their specific history.

How can we approach, today, the economy in a Creole way?

How can we approach, today, social relations in a Creole way?

How can we approach, today, politics in a Creole way?

What world should we build while taking into account these facts?

Here are, we think, the stakes of Créolité.

10

Créolité without the Creole Language?

Maryse Condé
Translated by Kathleen M. Balutansky

Our first mistake lies in speaking carelessly of Creole as if it were a linguistic manifestation miraculously limited to a few Caribbean islands—namely Guadeloupe, Martinique, Haiti, St. Lucia, Dominica—their sisters in slavery and colonial history from the Indian Ocean, as well as a small portion of the South American continent: Guyana. Many Creoles have appeared elsewhere in the world, including the English- and Dutch-speaking islands in the Caribbean, in the continental nations such as Belize, Colombia, and Suriname, and in Central and West Africa. It seems to me that a far more accurate description of Creole—and one that would coincide better with reality—is one that speaks of Creole as lexically based in French, English, Portuguese, Dutch, and that names each Creole by way of the island from which it emerged (Guadeloupean Creole, Martinican Creole, Haitian Creole, and so forth).

We may well imagine a time when the appending of the term Creole—which ties the Creole to a dependency on the languages from which it derives—will no longer be necessary as we will refer, instead, to the Guadeloupean, Martinican, or Haitian language, as is already the case in certain militant milieus.

Let us here recall a few elementary but true facts. Loreto Todd, in *Pidgins and Creoles*, gives the meaning—seemingly conveniently forgotten—of the Spanish word *criollo*, Fr. *créole*, as "native to the locality, country" (24). Todd states further that the word is a colonial corruption of criadillo, itself a diminutive of criado, which refers to an educated, or domesticated state as opposed to a savage, or natural state. Other researchers offer a slightly different etymology; according to them, criollo would be the result of the combination of two Spanish words, *criar* and *colono*. In both cases, the meaning is the same. First used in reference to Spaniards born in the colonies, in the seventeenth and eighteenth centuries the term Creole became a designation not only for whites, but also for Africans born on the plantation. From that time, the meaning of the term has expanded to include these people's entire mode of life, including their speech. Lady Maria Nugent, in the *Journal of a Voyage to and Residence in the Islands of Jamaica*, writes, "We breakfasted in the Creole style: Cassada [cassava] cakes, chocolate, coffee, tea, fruits of all sorts, pigeon pies, hams, tongues, rounds of beef, etc. I only wonder there was no turtle" (55).

In the same journal, she refers to Creole language, noting that it is common to both whites and blacks. Marie-Josée Cérol reminds us that in an island like Guadeloupe, the slaves retained for a long time their African languages and that Creole became the language of the entire Guadeloupean society only in the nineteenth century (67). We can conceive that the African languages assumed the function of resistance languages, conveying secret messages and calls for rebellion. On the contrary, Creole was born as a means of communication to be understood by both masters and slaves. It can be seen as the first example of the Caribbean syncretic culture. It goes without saying that when Creole became widespread in each island, at its outset, it was not perceived as a unique linguistic creation, but rather as a distortion, a perversion of the model of the European colonizer's language. Elodie Jourdain, the béké (white Creole) linguist, studying Martinican Creole in 1956, announced her intention "to see what happened to French, the language of high culture, as it came out of black throats" (68).

With the emergence of postcolonial literatures, Caribbean as well as African writers unanimously rebelled against such a concept. They quickly understood that the control of language is one of the primary aspects of colonial oppression—the dependency of the periphery upon the center. Language is a site of power: who names, controls. The politically and economically alienated colonized are first colonized linguistically. In their attempt to gain freedom and self-determination, the colonized must put an end to the preeminence of the colonial language. This is a known fact. Kenyan writer Ngugi wa Thiong'o expresses the need for the writer to reject English and to use, instead, African languages. From his exile in England, then in America, he decided to write his fiction in Kiswahili and in Kikuyu. We need not enter the debate as to whether this position is either revolutionary or simply demagogic. Suffice it to say, it illustrates the need for linguistic subversion that most colonized writers feel, be they francophone or anglophone.

The modes of resistance to linguistic oppression are infinite; because they vary according to the times and the poetic temperaments of the writers, I shall not venture to analyze them in detail within the confines of this essay. A few examples will illustrate my point. In the French-speaking islands, Aimé Césaire was the first to feel the need for this subversion. We know the seeming contradiction in which he found himself; in order to break the domination of the French language he resorted to automatic writing, a technique promoted by none other than a French literary school: the Surrealists. A choice that Ménil's copious justifications, probably conceived a-posteriori, fail to illuminate. The debt to Surrealism remains complete. If, in *Et les chiens se taisaient,* the rebel hails "his gods by dint of disowning them" (37), it would seem that the poet Césaire was much less radical. In the reedition of the journal *Tropiques,* Césaire defends himself with some irritation against those who blamed him for not having written in Creole in his time.[1] In a sense, this displeasure is justified, as the criticism reveals a flagrant unfamiliarity with the Antillean colonial situation during the Second World War. In those years, even a rebellious intellectual could not have conceived a literary production in Creole, the language of nonculture, of nature—the nonlanguage.

Nevertheless, slowly, Creole appeared in literary texts. After Jacques Roumain, who was the first to do violence to the imposed rhythms of the French language, many other anglophone and francophone Caribbean writers (for example, Zobel, D'Costa, and others) chose a simpler strategy of embedding Creole words in their texts, as if by their very presence the words injected the marginalized and despised culture into the heart of the dominant one and in so doing, destroyed the latter's hegemony. Saint-John Perse himself seems to use this approach when he writes: "Smiling, she excuses my streaming face; and raises to my face my hands oily from having touched the Kako kernel, the coffee bean" (1960, 10–11).

More recently other writers, like Earl Lovelace in *The Dragon Can't Dance,* attempt to convey to their rigorously standard English the musical rhythms of their island: "There is dancing in the calypso. Dance! If the words mourn the death of a neighbor, the music insists that you dance; if it tells the trouble of a brother, the music says dance. Dance to the hurt! Dance! If you are catching hell, dance, and the government don't care, dance! Your woman take your money and run with another man, dance. Dance, dance, dance!" (13–14). Yet, others try to blend or simply juxtapose the linguistic structures of vernacular languages to those of the colonial language. In the francophone world, Simone Schwarz-Bart has mastered this technique. "All the rivers," she writes in *Pluie et vent sur Télumée Miracle,* "even the brightest, those that catch the sun in their current, all the rivers run to the sea and drown. And life awaits man like the sea awaits the river. We can meander and wind, turn, dodge, and insert ourselves in the ground, our meanders belong to us, but life is there, patient, without beginning and without end, waiting, like the ocean" (81).

Most of the anglophone writers, including George Lamming and Sam Selvon, make much use of all the resources of the linguistic continuum to create texts that remain faithful to the cultural environment that produced them. Even V. S. Naipaul, in his early novels about Indian society in Trinidad, didn't hesitate to reproduce local speech in his dialogues. In *The Mystic Masseur,* we hear the following exchange:

> It ain't me who make that up, you know.
> How I know you ain't fooling me, just as how you did fool Pa?
> But why for I go want to fool you, girl?
> I ain't the stupid little girl you did married, you know. (79)

Therefore, regardless of what he otherwise thinks, Naipaul, too, participates in the collective project of deconstructing the language of power. Wilson Harris goes even further when he attacks the binary structure—which he believes is the basis of the languages of Europe, constantly engaged in a historical process of conquest and of domination—and attempts to create another language which goes beyond what is already known.[2] Like Edouard Glissant, Harris establishes the relation between history, psychology, and language. He aims at decentering a system, proposing a new architecture of the world, and rupturing the "obsessive opposition," as he puts it, between victor and victim.

In *The Empire Writes Back: Theory and Practice in Post-Colonial Literatures,* Bill Ashcroft, Gareth Griffiths, and Helen Tiffin remind us that this deconstructive impulse is not limited to literary texts and theory. They cite Joseph Owens's study of Jamaican Rastafarians, who have adopted a number of strategies that liberate their language from English hegemony. Their aim is to establish an alternative to the religious discourse of Christianity, which is woven into the dominant socioeconomic, political, and cultural structures, and in doing so liberate the "I." As Owens puts it: "The pronoun 'I' has a special importance for the Rastas and is expressly opposed to the servile 'me.' Whether in the singular ('I') or in the plural ('I and I' or briefly: 'I-n-I') or the reflexive (I-sel', I-n-I-self') the use of this pronoun identifies the Rasta as an individual. . . . Even the possessive 'my' and the objective 'me' are replaced by 'I'" (Ashcroft, Griffiths, and Tiffin 49).

In other words, in spite of all the massive media attention that France has focused on the so-called Martinican school of Créolité, the latter has nothing new to offer. The linguistic problematic has always haunted colonized writers. Their recourse to vernacular languages born within the plantation system seemed like a "miraculous weapon" for their acts of subversion.

"Neither Europeans, nor Africans, nor Asians, we proclaim ourselves Créoles" (13). Thus begins *Éloge de la créolité,* the collective work of two novelists, Raphaël Confiant and Patrick Chamoiseau and of a linguist, Jean Bernabé, which is considered the school's manifesto. In fact, this resounding beginning merely belabors the obvious: ever since the seventeenth and eighteenth centuries, the term Creole has been applied to natives of a country as well as to their lifestyle. What then must we make of this attempt to define the identity of the Creole self? "Créolité," the three authors tell us, "is the unifying or settling aggregate for the Caribbean, European, African, Asian and Arabic cultural elements that the yoke of history has united on the same land" (26).

In simpler terms, as early as 1819, referring to Latin America, Simon Bolivar described similarly "nuestra América mestiza" in his *Message to the Congress of Angostura:* "Let us keep in mind that our people are not European nor North American but rather a composite of Africa and America. . . . [T]he majority of the indigenous peoples have been annihilated; the European element has mixed with the American and the African, and this latter with the Indian and the European" (184).

The process in question is remarkably similar to that of creolization as defined by Edward Kamau Brathwaite in *The Development of Creole Society in Jamaica.* According to Brathwaite, creolization is a "cultural action—material-psychological and spiritual—based upon the stimulus/response of individuals with the society to their environment and—as white/black, culturally discrete groups—to each other" (296). Brathwaite further explains his theory by stating that "the process of creolization is a way of seeing the society, not in terms of white and black, master and slave, in separate nuclear units, but as contributory parts of a whole" (307). It is clear that

Brathwaite's concept of creolization is also the result of a cultural interaction among all the actors of the drama that was played out on the plantation.

In Cuba, once the heresy of the *criollismo blanco* that haunted the nineteenth century died out, the new concept of mestizaje was formulated and promoted by both poets and politicians alike, by both José Martí and Nicolás Guillén. In her study of Guillén, the poet Nancy Morejon explains this notion's revolutionary potential. It is "the constant interaction," she writes, "between two or more cultural components with the unconscious goal to create a third cultural entity; in other words, a new and independent culture, even though rooted in the former elements" (23). Mexican philosopher José Vasconcelos goes even further when speaking of the Chicano community. He envisaged "una raza mestija" which he called a cosmic race, a fifth race embracing the four major races of the world. Such a mixture of races, rather than resulting in an inferior being, provided a hybrid progeny with a rich gene pool.

Interaction, transculturation, reciprocity—the words are similar. The differences between such theories as miscegenation, mestizaje, creolization, créolité are due to the ethnic and sociopolitical configurations of the colonized American world in which they were born and, consequently, to the languages in which they are articulated. As Françoise Lionnet justly points out: "The analysis of French, English, Portuguese or Spanish terms used to define racial categories reveals that those words do not readily translate into one another because they do not cover the same reality; hence have only local significance and are not interchangeable" (12). These theories nonetheless are intended to eradicate the negative images engendered by European supremacy and by the imagined difference between nature and culture, between savage and civilized, between subhuman and human. These theories aim to negate and subvert the dangerous notion of racial and cultural "purity."

The Martinican school of Créolité is singular because it presumes to impose law and order. Créolité is alone in reducing the overall expression of creoleness to the use of the Creole language. *Éloge de la créolité* dictates that literature must be founded on the acquisition of the Creole language "in its grammar, its basilectal lexicon, its orthography, its intonations, its rhythms, its soul . . . its poetics" (44). This implies a notion of "authenticity," which inevitably engenders exclusion, as "authenticity" is based on the very normative ideology that for so long consigned us to the world's periphery. Worse yet, the créolité school is terrorizing in its detailed catalogue of acceptable literary themes. Were the stakes less high, we might smile at the attempt to dictate to the imagination of the writers the quasi-folkloric subjects worthy of inspiration: *djobeurs, dorlis, zombis, chouval-twa-pat, soukliyan, majo, ladja, koudmen,* as if creativity were an inventory summoned at will.

Wilson Harris's statement in *The Four Banks of the River Space* seems the best rebuttal to these impossible demands: "When one dreams, one dreams alone. When one writes a book, one is alone" (4). I maintain that the beauty of creation resides in its refusal of all constraining canonical rules. I maintain that all writers must choose whatever linguistic strategies, narrative techniques, they deem appropriate to express their identity. No exclusions, no dictates.

Vincent Placoly, feigning to write in the sustained French of *Frères Volcans,* the diary of a plantation owner at the end of the nineteenth century, nonetheless creates a profoundly Creole text. In invading the "other"'s—the béké's—imaginary, in appropriating his conscience and magnifying the divide between author and narrator, Placoly achieves a tour de force: he restores the integrity of the world of slavery through a discourse that the reader must subvert. At the same time, the text offers a powerful reflection on history, philosophy, and poetics: "[T]he history of the colonies will be one of trial and error. By day, the silence is shattered by the cries of despair. By night, the islands laugh. Last stop on the march of exploration, these islands are the ultimate frontier of thought, the mist cast upon man's spirit, the heart of phantasmagory, the fountain of true poetry" (30).

Can anyone be more Creole than Xavier Orville? From *Délices et le fromager* to his most accomplished, *Laissez brûler Laventurcia,* his writing weaves deliberately precious images. "To light a fire with words," with his own words, with words freely and subjectively chosen, this is his entire enterprise. His aim is to rekindle the dying flame of the Creole identity. Masterfully, Orville celebrates the resurgence of his island thanks to the spark-woman who will set the country ablaze and cure its inertia. Thanks to her, her people will learn the "secret of great combustions" while she frees the folly of their imagination.

It would be interesting to examine Laventurcia as a character who carries fire and to link her to a distinctly Caribbean metaphor: the volcano. The woman and the volcano preside over a rebellion that will radically transform the Antillean landscape. One could also relate Laventurcia to the omnipresent female divinities of some black African cults as well as to those of the Middle East to show that Orville is engaged in a cultural dialogue that goes well beyond the European/Caribbean or the Caribbean/American relationship.

Freedom of creation? Individuality and subjectivity of the creator? I can already hear the objections of those who claim that I am abandoning the sacrosanct responsibility of the Caribbean writer. I have no intention of arguing, here, for the total disengagement of the Caribbean writer. But maybe it is time for us to welcome the dissolution of the forced marriage between poetics and politics, the consequences of which have been ineffective if not disastrous. Writers as dissimilar as Julio Cortazar and Alain Robbe-Grillet have already reminded us that writers can only rule over words. If they want to make revolutions, writers must concentrate on that domain alone. Regarding the role of the writer and the function of literature, the Martinican school of Créolité offers no innovation but prescribes, instead, variations on the hackneyed theme of engagement. Whatever they may think, these writers have not yet extricated themselves from "the victim stasis" which Wilson Harris has denounced. They cannot conceive of any writing strategy outside of the Creole/French dichotomy that imprisons them. They foresee no thematic or narrative structure that would ignore, circumvent, or even cause the dissolution of the "colonial conventions" of the binary opposition of colonizer and colonized.

As we near the end of the twentieth century, a significant phenomenon emerges which contradicts the pretentious desire to legislate literary creation. The essential characteristic of this end of the century is the massive migration of the peoples of the Caribbean. Aimé Césaire was already writing in 1938:

> Not a corner of this world but carries my thumb-print
> And my heel-mark on the backs of skyscrapers and
> My dirt
> In the glitter of jewels. (25)

Now, by the thousands, they leave their small islands, which seldom yield happiness and are too often doomed by the tyranny or the incompetence of politicians, to settle on the East Coast of the United States, in Canada, in England, or in Germany. Brooklyn-Haitians, Puerto-Ricans from Spanish Harlem, black British from Shepherds Bush. Guadeloupeans or Martinicans baptized "second-generation" by the overstrained French social services. Everywhere colonies of Caribbeans who have lost their land are trying to assimilate foreign languages. The majority of the Haitian as well as Cuban writers live in exile. Already, a segment of Haitian, Dominican, and Cuban literature is written in English. Edwige Danticat and Cristina Garcia, for example, have forgotten their French and their Spanish, respectively, and are on the bestseller list of the *New York Times*. Are we going to exclude them from the field of their national literatures? Are we going to consider as genuine the sole production of writers fortunate enough to live at home? In that case, we would be going against the tide of history as well as against the sociopolitical realities of our time. I believe that we are faced with the need for redefinitions. What is a Caribbean person, and consequently what is a Caribbean writer? Are they always Creole? Where are they born, and where do they live? Cannot the Creole culture—I mean the culture of the Caribbean islands—be transplanted and survive just as well through the use of memory?

In other words, aren't there new and multiple versions of créolité?

11

~

The Victory of the Concubines and the Nannies

Frank Martinus Arion

There is a Dutch saying that "Blood creeps where it cannot walk," and this means that some things are inevitable, even when they happen in spite of insurmountable barriers.

This is very much the case in race relations, where, on the one hand, there are strong official efforts to keep races separated and, on the other hand, a frequent breaking of that rule. Whatever may cause racism to persist in general, the history of West African and Caribbean creolization proves that these causes are not stronger than the biological or, more specifically, the sexual inclinations of human beings, nor are they stronger than the acculturation of children. Hence the victory of the concubines and nannies.

Creolization, in the Caribbean at least, is the process of forging new human and cultural identities primarily out of the white and the black races. The concept derives from the past participle, *criode*, in the Afro-Portuguese Creole language already spoken on the coast of West Africa in the fifteenth century. The Creole verb is *cria*, from the Portuguese verb *criar*, "to breed." The participle means "(locally) bred": standing against that which is foreign and imported. In the early Caribbean, the concept more often had the latter sense—that of becoming native—than the sense of racial mixing. For the European colonists, becoming native in the Caribbean did not connote racial mixing, but rather the adaptation of a new outlook on life, even the adaptation of a complete new culture.

A perfect example of this type of creolization is found in Jean Rhys's novel, *Wide Sargasso Sea*. The main character in the book is a white female, born in the tropics—criode, so to speak. The conflict that leads to the ultimate disaster in the novel hinges on the main character's marriage to a white—noncriode, "pure"—Englishman. The novel, written against Charlotte Brontë's classic novel, *Jane Eyre,* is a very conscious defense of the colored Creole culture against the pure, unmixed—I should even say, barren—English and European culture in general.

Caribbean literature offers many other instances that demonstrate that the Creole white—even when born from only one Creole parent, as in the case of Rhys herself (whose mother was a Creole from Dominica and whose father was a Welshman)—is quite different from the "imported" white. In many cases, the distance between those Creole whites and the imported ones seems to be greater than between the Creole white and the Creoles of color.

In 1936, a full thirty years before *Wide Sargasso Sea,* the Netherlands Antillean writer Cola Debrot wrote a short novel with the totally unambiguous title, *My Sister the Negress,*[1] dealing entirely with the issue of racial creolization.

In Debrot's novel, a young white male, Frits Ruprecht, returns from the European capitals of Paris and Amsterdam with only one goal in mind: to find himself a Negress. He has experienced the behavior of "modern" European women, including open homosexuality, and now he is longing for "true" femininity. On the evening of his arrival, at his father's house where he grew up, he is visited by one of the plantation girls with whom he used to play as a boy. She is a teacher now. His frustration with Europe and his wish to start a new life with a Negress kindle his desire for her. In the dark tropical night, as the realization of this wish seems near, an old field hand bursts into the house to tell Ruprecht that he stands on the brink of committing incest, as his lover-to-be is his half-sister. This novella has remained a literary classic both in the Netherlands Antilles and in Holland. Although the literature of the Netherlands Antilles offers some of the first demonstrations of Caribbean creolization, these islands, ironically, are always neglected in studies about Caribbean literature and culture in general.

Sexual attraction to the opposite gender from the "other" race is demonstrated from the very first days of colonization. In Dutch travelogues we often find evidence of white males cohabiting with black females on the African coast. The most elaborate early description of this phenomenon appears in a travel account of the merchant from Florence, Francesco Carletti, who in 1594 went with his father to the Capeverdean Islands to buy slaves to be brought to Cartagena in Colombia.[2]

Carletti first told his story to the Great Duke of Toscania, Fernando de Medici. In the Dutch translation, the introduction notes that Carletti often assured the Great Duke that he reported only what he saw himself. Carletti's description of the conditions of the Capeverdean island of Santiago is revealing, and bears citing at length:

> On this island there is a small town called Nome di Dio, with a small harbour on its south side. It has a bishop and about fifty houses in which Portuguese live. Some of them are married to white women from Portugal, others to dark African women, others again to mulatto women (these are women that are born there from a white father to a moor, or in other words, black woman). *They prefer the black women to their own Portuguese women, convinced as they are that the relationship with these women is less harmful and more joyful because these women are said to be high spirited and healthier.* But to return to the subject of the married men, the Portuguese living on this island: it is a fact that they prefer a woman of moorish descent from the land more than a white woman from Portugal and it seems that the atmosphere leads to their preference for women from the country itself over those who are imported. *It is, in any case, a true fact that those who are not married to such a woman will try as soon as possible to have such a woman as a concubine.* In the end they get so attached to these women that they marry them and lead a much happier life than with a woman of their own people. It is surely true that there are moorish women that in spiritual power, wit, and appearance leave our European women far behind, leaving aside their color; but even this is, I have to confess, an illusion, for I myself found some of them terribly attractive and that dark color did not turn me off at all. This is the same with other men here that get so accustomed to what they see daily that in the end this doesn't look strange anymore. All those that live on the African continent, at Cape Verde, Congo, Angola, are good witnesses to this. (21–22, my italics)

Such strong transracial attraction is also represented in the classical love affair of the English captain of arms in Suriname, John Stedman, and a slave girl, Johanna,[3] and it is also in ample evidence as an early form of creolization in Brazil. It seems that in the mixed marriages involving Dutch men and women from Pernambuco, the culture of the woman, the criode, was dominant. According to Charles Ralph Boxer, in *Race Relations in the*

Portuguese Colonial Empire, 1415–1825, Dutch men tended to identify with their wives' religion and country rather than with their own (126–27).

Biological creolization is then followed by cultural creolization, which may be very pronounced when the *criode* language—the locally bred language, or Creole—is involved. In most of the Caribbean colonies, mastery of Creole became a sign of identification with the country. In many of the reports on the colonies made by visitors from the mother countries, we find complaints that the children of the Creole whites were rapidly losing both their language and their culture—they were "going native."

These obvious indications of the creolization process notwithstanding, the view that the overbearing influence in the process of creolization resides with the white slave master still persists. According to this "Big-House view"—named in reference to the study entitled *Casa grande e senzala* (The Big House and the Slave Quarters) by the Brazilian sociologist, Gilberto Freyre—it is from the Big House that culture filters down to the slaves.[4] Even in a contemporary Marxist view of culture—which one might consider more progressive than Freyre's view—the slaveowners would still be the ones to generate culture with capital, for as Marxist cultural analysis maintains, it is the economic plantation structure that defines the cultural configuration.

Ironically, this is a view that many blacks and people of color have accepted—namely, the supremacy of the white culture, the culture of the colonizer. The Big-House view demonstrates, in any case, to what extent the academic disciplines known as the human sciences are attached to existing economic relations and to the superficial conclusions derived therefrom. Nonetheless, although the Big-House view has had a great influence on Caribbean and non-Caribbean thinkers alike, it also has been strongly contested over the years—by Aimé Césaire, among others.

Evidence for the opposite view of Caribbean cultural development and reality is perhaps nowhere more amply available than in the Netherlands Antilles, in the existence of the dominant national language: Papiamento. Though specialists are not in total agreement about the linguistic history of Papiamento, most (and I count myself among them) consider it to be a pure case of an Afro-Portuguese Creole brought from Africa by the slaves. However, all agree that it was originally a slave language, despite having become the first language of more than 90 percent of the inhabitants of our country—including the Jewish and white Protestant descendants of slaveowners.

Following this Papiamento trail back to the beginning of the nineteenth century shows that the language moved from the fields into the Big Houses—not the other way around—and reveals that something completely different from the superficially apparent must have taken place in the creolization process of the Netherlands Antilles. That something involved not the adult population, but the children.

Though it looked powerful, the Big House was in reality totally dependent on the small houses surrounding it—for its wealth as well as for the care of its children. For it is through the black women who took care of the white children that the cultural influences of the small houses flooded the Big House. The black or colored house slaves who worked in these Big Houses and fed the white babies (so that their white mothers could keep their firm breasts) could not but feed them also their language and, thus, their stories, customs, and beliefs. White children from the Big House would escape their sad isolation by joining in the loud, joyous games of their black peers in the small houses.

Many Dutch nursery rhymes and some English ones that formerly were believed to be old Germanic relics or nonsensical inventions of children are nothing but specimens of the proto–Afro-Portuguese Creole out of which Papiamento developed.

These songs fall into several categories: personal lyrics; songs for special occasions, like baptisms and weddings; sellers' songs; drinking songs; and loose comments. An elaborate discussion of all these types would take too long, requiring presentation first in their Dutch forms, reduction to their original Afro-Portuguese Creole forms, and translation into English.[5] Here, I will only present three songs in which part of the first line, eene meene, matches one of the most famous nursery rhymes in English. In Dutch this would be written: iene miene, but for simplicity of demonstration, I will maintain the English orthography. The first song is as follows:

> Eene meene mutte,
> tien pond grutte,
> tien pond kaas,
> iene miene mutte,
> is de baas.

The structure eene meene consists of the Creole prepositioned plural marker eene and the word meene, which may stand for child, boy, or girl. Translated to Afro-Portuguese Creole (of Sao Tome), the song looks something like:

> Eene meene mute
> Tempo de gruta

empo de kaza
Eene meene mute
Es debas

In English, this would mean: "Girls/ Boys many/ Time to court/ Time to marry/ Girls/ Boys many/ Down there." The expression "Down there" refers to the fact that, in the middle passage, men were usually transported below deck and women above deck. As Carletti notes in his travel diary, "Up to the moment of departure [the slaves] lived in two separated rooms, the men in one, the women in another. They went on board, the men in the shiphold, one beside the other, so close to each other that they could hardly turn; the women looked for a place on deck as well as they could" (26). This song could have been sung by women slaves on deck as a distraction.

In the second song, only the first line is Creole:

Eene meene melle
wie zal telle
kaatje met de kaaie
Groen Van saaie
groan van smeer.

In Creole, this line reads: "Girls sweet/ Who will count, etc.," and is the expression of a male looking (from below deck?) at many attractive slave girls.

In the third song, the two first lines are Creole and the last one is Dutch. The content of the Dutch line shows without any doubt that the person who made the song knew both languages:

Eene meene marko
franse charko
wie kiest u tot booi?

Which translates to: "Boys I point to/ Tell me if you find anything (of your liking)/ Who do you want as messenger?" This song refers to ship captains' custom of giving young slave boys to one another as gifts.

These Dutch rhymes can offer revealing insights into two American/ English songs. The first is:

Eene meene maine mo
Catch a nigger by the toe
if he hollers let him go.

Reconstructed to its original Creole form, this song would read (in an English orthography): "Eene meene maine mo/ K'e cha ting ke bai deto/ I fi!/ Ole es latigo," which, when properly translated, reveals its slave origins: "Children/ Boys/ Girls calm down/ For you have to go to bed/ It is finished!/ Here's the whip."

The other English rhyme that bears a similar origin is found in *The Oxford Dictionary of Nursery Rhymes:*

> Eena, Meena, Mason, Broke a little bason
> How much will it be?
> Half a crown to half the town;
> Out goes she.

In reconstruction, the entire first sentence, which is Creole, would read: "Eena meena maso broke abaso, etc.," and would mean: "Male children *below the deck!*" [my italics].

These songs may have different origins, but they all reveal their slave roots. The first English song could come from a nanny taking care of the slave children while their slave parents were out working, but it could also have come from a black Creole-speaking nanny taking care of white children. The last song, which has many variants, clearly represents a slave auction, where the different types of slaves are appraised for sale.

I think that in many cases these songs passed into the domain of children—black/slave and white—already in the Creole-speaking environment itself, either as songs adults sang to them or as songs they learned from listening to the adults. Also, white fathers who kept concubines in these environments probably did not understand the songs but took them home as lullabies for their offspring—even in the home country. It may not even be too far-fetched to consider the possibility that some of the more obscure rhymes of Western culture have such origins. For instance, the mysterious "oblady oblada" of the Beatles song may also be a remnant of this creolization process. After all, Liverpool at one time was well known as an auction place for slaves.

It is difficult to observe without disappointment the widespread ignorance of the cultural creolization that emerged from slavery—mostly the ignorance of the very perpetrators of this historic sin. Instead of coming to grips with the magnitude of this historic reality, the creators of the dominant white culture continue to portray themselves as infallible mythical (blond) gods. They benefit from the process of creolization; they appropriate it without recognizing or crediting it, as did one of the most renowned

English poets, Rudyard Kipling. From the just-discussed "Eene meene maine mo," Kipling "created" four mythical—presumably white—characters: "Eenee, Meenee, Mainee and Mo," who "Were the First Big Four of Long Ago"; he does this, of course, without giving the least reference to the Creole nannies who sang the song.

The final irony is that the great purveyor of Western knowledge, the *Encyclopedia Britannica,* describes Kipling for all its readers as having had "a genuine sense of a civilizing mission that required every Englishman, or more broadly, every white man, to bring European culture to the heathen natives of the uncivilized world" (6:883).

12

~

The Process of Creolization in Haiti
and the Pitfalls of the Graphic Form

Jean Métellus

Translated by Marie-Agnès Sourieau

This title defines the scope of my project here, which focuses on the life and use of Creole language in Haiti. The remarkable historical, social, and political nature of my country which, I believe, I know well, prompts me to search for the origins of my maternal language, Haitian Creole. However, this is a large-scale undertaking, and the actual evolution of the language might lead me far away from my native island.

At the present time, there are a dozen or so French Creole languages spoken throughout the world by about ten million people, who are found in Louisiana, Guyana, the Lesser Antilles (Martinique and Guadeloupe) and Haiti. We find also French Creole in places such as the Archipelago of Mascareignes and the Seychelles and Reunion Islands. We know now, thanks to linguists' studies, that these Creole languages were developed in the sixteenth and seventeenth centuries, at the time of colonization.

"Of Spanish and/or Portuguese origin, the word 'Creole' first refers to the Spaniards born in the islands. Therefore the word applied to people well before it referred to the languages that appeared in the same regions," Robert Chaudenson reminds us in his article on Creole languages (1992, 1249).

French Creole languages stemmed from "a popular French marked by 'Oïl' regionalisms—'Oïl' being the language of Northern France; the majority of the settlers came from regions situated north of the line Paris-Bordeaux—and from many dialects. The development of colonial cultures led to the need for a large labor force, hence the massive immigration of slaves; in the American-Caribbean region, the slaves came from West Africa, and in the Indian Ocean region they came from Madagascar, India, and East Africa. These differences in the slaves' origins are, of course, an essential element for assessing the role of the 'substratum' in the genesis of Creoles" (Chaudenson 1992, 1252).

But slaves were not subjected to the same tasks, and therefore they did not learn their masters' language in the same way. The first transplanted slaves, who were less than fifteen years old and far less numerous than the members of the masters' families, lived and worked side by side with their owners. As they were immersed in the linguistic system of the dominant group, they soon forgot their original language and appropriated the "norm" in use, domestic French. Those slaves formed what was called the corps of house slaves. Through their direct contact with the colonists whom they served and cared for, these slaves immediately picked up all the verbal quirks and forms of the families who had enslaved them. When the imperatives of productivity and profitability led to the massive importation of labor onto the plantations, the new slaves, called "Bossales," who were assigned to work in the fields, did not understand their masters, and vice versa. The house slaves became teachers and began to pass on the language that they had learned in the Big House. Therefore, we are faced here with two learning experiences which have borne different fruit.

The mandatory and inevitable learning of the simplified French from France by the house slaves was followed by the imperative learning of the language on the plantations. Therefore, the French Creole languages were born, in the colonies, from the strategies of an appropriation of a very rough French. This historical fact and linguistic scheme resulted in the virtual oblivion of African languages, which were barred from the plantations or deliberately mixed with one another. What we have here is the blurring of the origins—and the total and permanent erasure of identities—and the imposition of a ragged French language to slaves in rags. This very French language became the Creole language, which was willingly spoken by Sonthonax, the several commissioners of the republic, and the first consul's advisers, if not the consul himself.

We are now at a time when non-European languages are less privileged in the study of the formation of French Creole languages. It is understandable that S. Farandjis could celebrate in 1994 the Creole spring of Francophonie. Chaudenson points out that in 1936, S. Sylvain, a Haitian scholar, defined Haitian Creole as an African language with a French vocabulary, a stance that Chaudenson admits generally wins the favor of the

Third World and especially of those who seek to reduce the importance of European contributions to Creole languages and cultures. This trend, which was thought to be losing momentum during the last ten years, is making a comeback, particularly in Canada, at the University of Québec in Montreal, where a team under the direction of C. Lefebvre has attempted to demonstrate that Haitian Creole stems from Fon, a language from Benin, spoken with a French lexicon. We can say that such an undertaking brings back Creole studies to the status they had at the end of the nineteenth century (Chaudenson 1992, 1251).

Other scholarly trends find in Creole the emergence of universal structures inscribed in genetic inheritance. With these theories, we subtly go from objective interaction and causal derivation to mere assumptions. On these trends, Marcel d'Ans aptly comments:

> Chaudenson drew attention to the fact that the mere existence of Creole languages in the Mascareignes islands discredited all speculations regarding the hypothetical action of an "African substratum" in the formation of Creole languages. Because if, on one hand, we can understand that geographical, historical, and above all racial considerations may lead us to think that such a linguistic African substratum is at work in the Antilles, on the other hand it is clear that no possible African substratum can be claimed for Reunion and Mauritius, since the slave and "colored" population shipped to these Indian Ocean islands were essentially of Malagasy origin and thus spoke non-African languages. Furthermore, we have undisputable documentation showing that Creole existed in these islands before the arrival of the first slaves. (Further, everything indicates—although we do not have such undisputable documents—that it was the same in the Antilles, and particularly in Haiti where the Creole languages must have been stabilized in the white population before the arrival of the African slaves [304].)

Therefore, contrary to what some current theories state without evidence, Creole does not spring from a clash between African, European, and Amerindian languages. Creole is not the result of a slow and painful process of growth. It was born from a French language at a time when French itself had not yet been homogenized. And it is this Creole that was instilled into—or rather imposed on—the slaves.

As Robert Chaudenson observed in 1978, social and sociocultural factors played a major role in the rapid appearance and stabilization of Creole, which was not only the language of communication between master and slave but also the "lingua franca" of all different groups in contact with colonial societies. The cultural level of these milieus was rudimentary, and, at the time when Creole was formed, the white population was often numerically greater than that of the slaves. Chaudenson further indicates that "The loosening, indeed the abolition of the pressure of the norm and constraint of the socio-cultural apparatus undoubtedly favored the rapid mutation of the linguistic system, all the more so since the end of the seventeenth century marked precisely the time when in France there were vigorously exerted 'normative' pressures aimed at controlling the popular language" (1978, 78).

In these societies lacking real sociocultural structure, no social group could be normative and serve as cultural or linguistic example. It is, then, as a result of this fluid general linguistic makeup that approximative dialects acquired the status of language.

In his consideration of various linguistic elements, Chaudenson invokes Charles Ferguson's observations about "baby-talk" and "foreigner talk," and the general tendency to simplify speech as soon as communication becomes difficult or hazardous, as is the case for children who are beginning to speak, foreigners who are learning a new idiom, or adults excluded from their language because of illness. We should also point out another set of arguments which draws comparisons between Creole and childlike speech: the substitution of atonic pronouns je, tu, il with tonic pronouns moi, toi, lui, etc. Indeed, in learning the language, children and foreigners use the same process. Chaudenson nonetheless points out:

> The situation of Creole is different; [i]ndeed, as far as children's speech is concerned, the elimination of primitive systems is rapid and carried out under the pressures of the compelling sociolinguistic patterns. But the formation of Creole languages stemmed from the popular or regional French system which was most likely very different from the present standard French. Not only were circumlocutions considerably used, but it seems that verbal themes also clearly tended to be invariable and that verbal inflection was much reduced. . . . If we add to this the Europeans' willingness to simplify their own language in a situation of contact with speakers of different idioms, and the total absence of socio-cultural structure and socio-linguistic "model," it is understandable that under such conditions, not only the

analytical system acted as a substitute to the inflectional system, but also it rapidly evolved to the point of forming a completely different system. (1978, 82)

Thus we understand how we can find in the freely and independently
evolving Creole the tendencies found in the child at the time of speech
acquisition. In the child, the development occurs under the pressure of
the adult's linguistic model; on the plantations, the language in use is not
subjected to any grammatical constraint, it is language at the learning
stage—without inhibitions. As Marcel d'Ans points out, however, it is not
a language "without grammar." "On the contrary," says d'Ans:

[I]t is a kind of "evolutionary meteor" where an entire restruc-
turing universe (normally blocked up by traditionalist education, and only capable of imposing itself progressively and with
great difficulty in particular places of the system) has invaded
all the "critical points" of French grammar, instantaneously giving birth to a new hereditary language which we can only ad-
mire for its vitality and creativity, as well as its unity, stability
and originality. . . . In short, shaking off all at once the almost
fallen layers of a mother-tongue that had become too complicated, a truly new language surged, pearl of orality, stamped
with an energy and effectiveness, at least as praiseworthy as
the diverse archaisms (words, expressions, intonations) that
have managed to remain, reminding us of the old language of
our seventeenth and eighteenth centuries. (308)

Haitian Creole was restructured on the plantations, but was not born
from a dialogue between the white settler and the slave. Our Creole truly
stems from the French language and was first created by whites to simplify their own verbal communications before imposing it upon the slaves.
Creole does not enable any Haitian to legitimate his or her roots since it
does not represent the Haitian's indigenous nature.

Therefore, we can exclude as complete fabrication from our intellectual
horizon the myth of the language born in the sugar cane fields. But this
language "made to measure" could only express limited thoughts and did
not allow speculations on physics, astronomy, philosophy, or other intellectual matters. This language was used for local, direct, and efficient communication. "Do this, do that," said the master, and the slaves in their free
time and in moments of revolt could exclaim: "Take the cannonballs and

toss them onto the next plantation." This was the first use of this bare and oversimplified French language in its transformation into Creole. It was a language for instant use, for speaking of life, sex, and fights in terms as direct and effective as the actions it named. Indeed, this was not the same French that Montesquieu, the author of *De l'esprit des lois,* was speaking in France at the time. Moreover, because Creole languages rapidly indigenized, they gave the impression to those who were assimilating them that they were their native tongues.

Thus, the Creole spoken in the Antilles and the Indian Ocean is a French language, even if it is one stripped of all grammatical constraints and remarkably close to children's speech. Therefore, creolophone Haitians should not claim a simplified system reduced to the simple needs of communication, orders, questions, and answers as their only linguistic universe. They ought to appropriate as well "traditional" French, with all its possibilities for expressing representative, dialectic, and symbolic concepts. Furthermore, this seems to have been the intention of Haiti's founders: the Declaration of Independence was written in French according to Emperor Dessalines's formal wish.

Creole—a utilitarian language for immediate communication—deprived its users of all the possibilities that fully developed languages offer. Every language has its limitations, and those of Creole are great. In Haiti, though, Creole is a factor of national unity; our political leaders have used it and still do so to unsettle the country. They create a cultural gulf—along with the economic gulf—between the peasants who are restricted to their machetes and the upper-middle class who have access to the outside world with the privilege of using an international language. Chaudenson accurately points out the unrealistic nature of treating Creole languages as absolutely equal to European languages. "But it is essential," he points out, "that the citizens may exercise their double right to the languages that are their own: the right to Creole, the language of their daily life, hence of their identity, and the right to French or English, official languages and instruments of communication with the outside world" (1992, 1256).

It is worth noting in passing that, unlike Creole, Vaudou is a purely Haitian product because it was born in Haiti, mixing elements from Africa with the saints of the Catholic religion. Vaudou can constitute a genuine cultural link within the country, a real cement because it is truly African-Haitian: Haitians brought the Vaudou religion with them; it was not imposed on them. Thus, the equation of Vaudou with Creole must be erased from our compatriots' minds.

Today, Haitian Creole is exposed to a new simplification since it is subjected to a half-phonetic, half-phonological spelling system which obliterates the etymology of the French from which it comes. Let's consider the Creole sentence taken from *Ti diksyonnè kreyol-fransé* by Alain Bentolila: "Chak fwa nou bezen kèk ti detay sou yon mo, nou pran on bann tan ap kesyone kèk Ayisyen nou te resi jwenn a Pari" (3). Here, the spelling of the word Paris is quite absurd. If this sentence were to be written with a less specialized spelling, its meaning would be immediately comprehensible to any francophone reader; it would become: "Chaque fois nous besoin quèque ti détail sou ou mot, nou prend ou bann temps ap quesionné quèque Haitien nou te réussi join'n à Paris" (Every time we need a small detail about a word, we waste a lot of time asking some Haitians we managed to find in Paris).

In choosing to make the written form a simple reflection of speech, a simple "visual doublet," an "objective correlation," a mere "representation of speech," or a "simple side point" of speech, Bentolila and his collaborators forget the real goal of writing. As Jean Bazin and Alban Benza explain in their introduction to Jack Goody's *La raison graphique* (26), Jacques Derrida has shown that the science of language is from the beginning closely interdependent upon the "phonology" and "logocentrism" inherited from Western metaphysics; speech is the site of truth, of meaning. Everything happens as if it were first necessary to "exclude," to "lower" writing, to assign it a secondary and derivative role of "supernumery," a simple image of the "living speech," of the "natural" language. This is why only one of the possible usages of writing is taken into account: the transcription of oral discourses "as if writing began and ended with graphic form."

What can we make of the orthography presented by Bentolila and his team in their dictionary? Oiseau pronounced zoiseau becomes zwazo; bois, bwa; éclair, pronounced zéclai, becomes zeklè; voix, pronounced voix, becomes vwa; voile pronounced like the French word becomes vwal; certain pronounced without the "r" is written sèten; loin, lwen; cuisse, kuis or kwis; croix, kwa; coiffeur, kwafè; croissance, kwasance; cafetière, kafetyè; chauffeur, chofè.

It is a Pennsylvania-born American, Charles Laubach, who began to pervert the graphic form of Haitian Creole and created a method which came to bear his name: the Laubach method. As a minister of the Congregational church, Laubach went to Mindanao in the Philippines to learn the country's native language and to evangelize the aborigines of the south. After rapidly learning their idiom, he created a "phonetics" which he mixed with the phonetics of the English language and imposed upon the Filipinos. In 1943–1944 he went to Haiti, where he encountered no obstacle to his imposition of the elements of his experience. Hired by the administration of Elie Lescot to fight illiteracy in the countryside, Laubach and his team studied Creole and set up their Philippine phonetics with the dedicated assistance of the "Committee for the Diffusion of Teaching in Creole."

"The trick was," Marie-Thérèse Archer writes in her book on Haitian creology, "that the expression 'Anglo-Saxon Creole' was never mentioned to refer to and define the invasion of W, K, Y in the word structure of the Creole vocabulary" (341). And what does Jules Faine have to say about the Laubach method? Archer quotes him as saying: "The Laubach Method uses a phonetic alphabet modelled on international phonetics; but even when modified, it is unable to render all the Creole phonemes. Furthermore, this system disconcerts the reader used to Latin graphic forms" (342).

The purpose of writing is to fix, remember, and appropriate knowledge as well as to expand it. But the present writing of Creole corresponds to a new form of domination of the lower classes, a new ruse by the upper-middle class to further enslave nine-tenths of the population and to exclude people not only from Haitian cultural and political life but also to alienate that life from the rest of the world. This orthography contains in itself a new technique of oppression, a true treachery; it illustrates Lévi-Strauss's comment: "the fight against analphabetism is one and the same with the strengthening of the government control on the people" (as quoted by Bazin and Benza, 26). We need a graphic form that opens Haiti to the world—and does not cut off our Creole from its French origins—in order to enable the country to be part of the scientific adventure. As Raphaël Pividal points out, "science uses only writing" (25).

In Haiti, despite the increase in the number of all sorts of schools, illiteracy is as huge a problem as it was at the time of Laubach's arrival. This, of course, is due to several factors. First, there are no good state primary schools; most are private institutions that are not much concerned with student achievement. School premises in the cities are often former bourgeois city mansions bought by the government at the highest possible price and converted into schools with few pedagogical means and materials. Second, in the countryside, whitewashed dilapidated buildings accommodate hungry children taught by poorly paid—thus poorly motivated—teachers. The school system is a shambles. It is a two-tiered system: one kind of school for the capital and the larger cities, another kind of school for the rest of the country. At best, this is a system of exclusion that allows only twenty-six students out of a thousand to pass the second tier of their bac-

calaureate examination, the capstone of their high-school education
(Cozigon 121). The financial burden of education is unbearable for most
parents, who are poor; the teaching methods are unsuitable and the teachers incompetent. Children cannot do their homework in the evening because of the lack of electric power. Finally, behind all this is the government's squandering of public funds and its inability to see the right to
education as a priority.

In 1979–80, under the administration of Jean-Claude Duvalier, the daily
paper *Le Nouveau-Monde* affirmed that for the first time in the history of
Haiti the budget of National Education exceeded that of the Interior. Nonetheless, this failed to reduce the illiteracy rate. Similarly, to underline further the hypocrisy of past governments, we might recall that under the
Pétion administration (soon after Haiti's independence) free public high
schools were created before free public elementary schools. Of course, only
children of well-off parents could first attend a costly private elementary
school before benefiting from this free high-school education.

For decades, political leaders and their accomplices have made a habit
of blaming the French language for all the calamities of the country, including the mediocre intellectual level of those who have been able to
escape illiteracy. French is also held responsible for the low scientific performance of our elites. This is to beg the question and to forget that the
practice of science requires specific conditions, including relations with
the outside world and favorable social conditions. As Jean Dieudonné, a
mathematician who has achieved the greatest distinction awarded to his
discipline, writes: "even today, it is likely that numerous mathematical
talents never emerge for lack of a favorable social atmosphere, so there is
no need to be surprised at the lack of mathematicians of renown in 'un-
der-developed' countries. Even in more developed countries, elementary
education may not be favorable to the emergence of mathematical voca-
tions when it is subjected to religious or political constraints, or to exclusively utilitarian preoccupations, as has been the case in the United States
well into the twentieth century" (27).

Also, the use of French in education was blamed as the principal obstacle to literacy; hence attempts to teach Creole that departs from the
etymology of its vocabulary. However, it is not the French language but
the chronic lack of educational structures that generates illiteracy, a ca-
lamity that strikes peasants and the most destitute—that is to say about 80
percent of the Haitian population. This chronic problem is primarily political, since the concern for literacy has never been on the agenda of our
leaders. With the exception of King Henri Christophe and a few other states-

men like Geffrard, Salomon, and Hippolyte, public education has never represented a priority, let alone a necessity. As early as 1842, Victor Schoelcher, in the March 15 issue of *Le Patriote*, blamed President Boyer, head of Haiti for twenty five years, for "relying on the people's ignorance as a measure of safety" (Barros 611).

In 1905, approximately 1.14 percent of school-age children attended school, and in 1906, 3 percent. From this situation, Anténor Firmin concluded that it was ideal for Haitian ruling classes to carefully preserve the ignorance of the masses in order to "use them as a stepping stone, and squeeze out of them all possible profits as sordid and selfish as they may be" (213). Around 1957, Paul Moral pointed out that one-tenth of the total population was more or less literate, with 25 percent in towns and 7 percent in the country: still the same imbalance. In 1971, 87 percent of Haiti's population was still considered illiterate; from 1955 to 1970, only 12 percent of the total national budget had been devoted to education. In 1987, Marie-Thérèse Archer pointed out that "This dramatic situation goes unchanged in its magnitude. . . . Illiterates amount to 90 percent of the population—or 5,850,000 people of the 6,500,000 population. Culture is homogeneous only at the lowest level" (531). Most of the primary-school teachers have no adequate qualifications, and low salaries discourage the younger generations from entering the profession.

These figures explain the general lack of performance in education. Creole remains practically the only language in the world to be phonetically written. One desperately naive proponent of Creole told me, a few years ago, that it will be necessary for future Haitian generations to go so far as to forget the French etymology of the Creole words for a "real" or graphic form. These extreme attempts to simplify Creole lead, on the one hand, to an underestimation of the ability that Haitian children from illiterate backgrounds may have to adapt to any graphic form, and, on the other hand, to an accentuation of the confusion felt by literate children when they learn English, Spanish, or French. It might be difficult to learn the Cyrillic alphabet or ideographic writing, but the child's future is made particularly complicated when the French origin of his or her Creole language is being eclipsed. Thus, a two-tiered cultural development is created within the country. The economically poor Haitians are taught to read and write a restricted language, while the economically privileged attend schools where an international language is taught—usually French.

In the face of this evidence, should not the need for a language of international communication be evident? Why is there such a willingness— whether it is acknowledged or not—to divorce Creole languages from their true origins? We must not substitute a mythical origin for a real one. Haiti must reach a balanced bilingualism between Haitian Creole and French; otherwise how will peasants—isolated on their land, isolated in their Creole language—survive in this modern world when their European counterparts are transforming themselves into exploiting businessmen and heads of enterprises?

It is not Laubach and Bentolila's system that will free the country from illiteracy: the Haitian middle class must break the chains that keep the Haitian people in slavery and ignorance. The cynicism of linguists on all sides has misled intellectuals and consequently has deprived the country of any opening onto the world. There must come a time when, as creolophile and creolophone Haitian intellectuals, we must take the lead and fight against those researchers who distort and mutilate our language. It is an illusion to believe that the solutions to the problems of literacy have to go though simplification and falsification. We will never tap the potential of our race and the roots of our origins by confusing our lexicon with an eccentric graphic system. We must restore the words to their etymological spelling so that the young child will be able to have easy access to French as well as any other international language. We must acknowledge the rights of the people to their language without its being deprived of its origins. That is indeed the only way for the country to progress and, when orality is truly appreciated by any literate person, to preserve its beauty and charm.

13

~

Race, Space, and the Poetics of Moving

M. Nourbese Philip

Prolegomena

Caribana, the annual festival of the Caribbean community in Toronto, began in 1967 as part of the Canadian Centennial celebrations. The festival events extend over a two- to four-week period culminating in the street "parade" on the first Saturday in August, which is attended by some million people. The prototype for this carnival is the Trinidad Carnival, which has spawned many such carnivals around the world. While celebration is the overt and distinguishing mark of the carnival, from its inception there has been a culture of resistance—to imperialism, colonialism and racism—embedded within it.

That the Trinidad Carnival[1] as we know it is an amalgam of at least two cultures—the European and the African—cannot be disputed. Its timing for instance, the Monday and Tuesday before Ash Wednesday, is clearly wedded to the Christian calendar. But freed Africans in Trinidad also attempted to time their celebrations to coincide with August 1, the date traditionally known as Emancipation Day, thereby rooting it in their own history. Other Caribbean islands such as Antigua and Barbados have also chosen to celebrate their carnivals around this date, linking their celebrations to the annual harvest of the sugar cane crop.

Within the context of Trinidad, Creole culture is seen to stand over from the African (for a long time despised) and the Indian, and connotes more than its denotation of someone born in the West Indies of either European or "Negro" descent. Derek Walcott writes:

> The Creole is the crudest alloy of the Trinidadian sensibility. To
> get to understand them, or it, is the shrillest kind of hedonism,

asserting with almost hysterical self-assurance that Trinidad is a paradise, that it has everything. . . . [I]t is a hedonism which simultaneously imitates and asserts its difference, schizophreni- cally capable of changing complexion, black today and part- white tomorrow, and its apotheosis is still achieved in the Hol- lywood-type gossip columns of our two newspapers, beginning with knighthoods and degenerating into charities, recording the latest orgies of the jet set and the in-crowd. (1975, 14)

The most extravagant display of Creole pleasure, Walcott argues fur- ther, is to be seen at Carnival time. To view Carnival solely as the ultimate expression of Creole culture in Trinidad, however, is to miss the tensions present within any creolization process. The tension in Carnival is to be found in the struggle to control it—first by colonial governors, then by subsequent governments—and the desire on the part of the various peoples making up the populace to express their desire for unrestricted movement and freedom which Carnival has come to symbolize in an almost met- onymic fashion.

These tensions are also visible in linguistic creolization practices—bad English, dialect, patois, nation language, demotic vernaculars—which of- ten parallel cultural creolization. In my discussion of Caribana and its pro- totype, Carnival, I have chosen to make my arguments in a Caribbean demotic of English—the Trinidad Creole which was at one time a French patois. Believing that some experiences demand a faithfulness to the lan- guage in which the experience happens has stimulated this impulse as well as the challenge of trying to make argument in Caribbean demotic English, which traditionally has been used publicly and almost solely for humor, satire, and entertainment.

This segregation of the linguistic space between a language that is privi- leged as the language of order and thought and a "lesser" Creole language is one of the tensions that is always present when creolization takes place The subsuming of Creole (bad English) under standard English for certain privileged linguistic tasks is, in fact, the reverse of the position of Africa and African cultural practices in Carnival. That Africa holds sway in the case of the latter Creole practice is undeniable; that Europe—in this case England—is preeminent in linguistic practices in Creole communities is still the case.

The strength and resource of the Caribbean demotic in which the fol- lowing essay is written lies in what I call its kinetic qualities—its kinopoesis.[2] It is a language that brings over into English the "relationship between the dynamics of speech and the dynamics of action" (Drewal, 228) that is to be found in at least one West African language, Yoruba. It is a language that moves, like the Carnival band, through space rhythmed by time. It is, therefore, eminently suited to capturing the moving at the heart of Carnival.

Race, Space, and the Poetics of Moving

Creole gaiety at its most exuberant can be the most depressing experience in the world. How so when its wildest display is at Carnival, "a Creole bacchanal"? . . . Carnival is all that is claimed for it. It is exultation of the mass will, its hedonism is so sacred that to withdraw from it, not to jump up, to be a contemplative outside of its frenzy is a heresy.
　　Derek Walcott (1975, 22)

Carnival represents an ancient and recurrent rite of passage. It is a festival which occupies a certain space, neuter time. You suspend what you are, what you do, who you are, for a space. Sometimes we perform behind a mask and symbolically become another personality. We put on a ritual mask. It happens in all societies.
　　Gordon Rohlehr (3)

Oh, he danced. He danced pretty. He danced to say, "You are beautiful, Calvary Hill, and John John and Laventille and Shanty Town. Listen to your steel bands how they playing! Look at your children how they dancing! . . . You is people, people. People is you, people!"
　　Earl Lovelace (1981, 36)

Carnivalesque discourse breaks through the laws of a language censored by grammar and semantics and, at the same time, is a social and political protest.
　　Julia Kristeva (36)

sweat and jostle and
jostle and push
jostle and jostle
push and jostle and
and shove and move
to the pulse
riddim pan

riddim and beat
the beat
sweat like a ram goat
sweat for so

And push and shove and jostle and shove and move hip sway hip wine[3] in your wine and look how we enjoying we self—move hip sway hip slap hip big hip fat hip flat bottom big bottom sweet bottom wine-your-waist bottom. Look we nuh, look how we enjoying we self right here in Canada self and Toronto sweet sweet too bad—but look me crosses! Is not Totoben that? Begging your pardon, Mr. Emmanuel Sandiford Jacobs himself, right here in Canada if you please, carrying on as if he don't give a damn blast or shit. Watching him play marse[4] nobody believing he putting up with shut up and go back where you come from in this mine-yuh-own-business catch-arse country where the living hard like rock stone and police shooting you dead dead and leaving you stone-cold in the street like dog. For six cold-no-arse months he up at five cold or no cold, traveling for two hours straight, punching a clock, working like a robot: punch a clock eat, punch a clock pee, punch a clock work, punch a clock leave—clock the punch! Two more hours, underground and over ground is all the same, it dark like hell self, till he back in his basement where the sun on long-leave.[5] But he don't mind, not Totoben, not today—he not giving a blast, damn, or shit if they calling him nigger, for today Emmanuel Sandiford Jacobs dead dead and Totoben in full sway, riding high, riding hard on University Avenue,[6] T-shirt pull up high high over his belly which big round black and shining like it carrying six months of baby in it—a real don't-give-a-damn belly that walking down University Avenue past all them war memorials celebrating empire which is nothing but shooting and loot-ing dress up in fancy costume. Past the Immigration Department where all like Totoben visiting plenty time and coming out feeling like they don't belong in Canada, past all those hospitals like Sick Kids and Mount Sinai and Toronto General where plenty black people like Totoben working and not like doctor or nurse either, past the court houses that Totoben and others like him knowing only too well, and the police station just over there on Dundas Street, and don't forget the American embassy either that marking another empire, except this one living and not dead yet. Totoben walking down University Avenue, drinking some rum with the boys, playing some marse and feeling like he back home.

Look! Is not Boysie that, the little Indian boy from down the lane—look how he get fat—you see how he working himself up on that woman?

Uh uh. I hear he doing well for himself, but Lord help me he should be shame to let anyone see what he doing with that woman, eh eh! you notice she not Indian neither—his poor mother putting she orini[7] over she head and bawling—is a good thing she not alive, god rest her soul, and seeing this shame. He should wear a mask the way he wining and wining on that woman . . . but I never know Indian could wine so—I thought was only black people wining like that, well I think my eyes seeing everything today—wait! is not Bluesman that in the band behind? Lord, he up here too!—I wonder if Immigration knowing that. Is what Canada coming to? Every piece a riff raff up here and look how he cocking a leg over that woman—Lord preserve me! is Gloria that and she coming from a decent home. Her mother dying from shame if she seeing her daughter today— look how he jerking up himself—oh my blessed Savior! You don't see it look like she enjoying sheself—uh uh, her poor mother! I telling you is this kind of behavior that giving black people a bad name. But wait—look, is Maisie that! Is long time since I see her—Lord, but she get even bigger— life up here must be agreeing with her. She still pretty though and it look-ing like she still liking man and man still liking her huh! Now see here! Look at what she doing, wining her all, every and what-you-may-call-it round and round that bottle, and is like she seeing heaven—is like these people losing all shame (if they ever had any) right here on University Avenue. Is like marse gone to their head and is mad they gone mad to marse in your marse and rum sweet woman sweet man sweet and life sweeter still today and is sweat and jostly and push and. . . .

We keeping our eyes on Totoben dancing down University Avenue and Maisie wining and wining her all around that bottle, but we leaving them up in Toronto for a while and looking back, back to where they coming from and how it is they doing what some calling this commonness on University Avenue in the white people country that more than a million black people invading on the first weekend every August.

> On ships the slaves were packed in the hold on galleries one above the other. Each was given only four or five feet in length and two or three feet in height so that they could neither lie at full length nor sit upright. . . . In this position they lived for the voyage, coming up once a day for exercise and to allow the sailors "to clean the pails." But when the cargo was rebellious or the weather bad, then they stayed below for weeks at a time. The close proximity of so many naked human beings, their bruised and festering flesh, the foetid air, the prevailing dysen-

tery, the accumulation of filth, turned these holds into a hell. During the storms the hatches were battened down, and in a close and loathsome darkness they were hurled from one side to another by the heaving vessel, held in position by the chains on their bleeding flesh. No place on earth, observed one writer of the time, concentrated so much misery as the hold of a slave ship. (Lamming 97)

What connecting Maisie and Totoben on the slave ship to Totoben and Maisie on University Avenue up in Canada is moving—the moving of their bodies. And the stopping of that moving. From the very first time when the Europeans putting them in the slave coffle in Africa and forcing Maisie and Totoben onto the slave ship, the owners trying and controlling their moving—where they going, what they eating, who they sleeping with. When Totoben and Maisie entering the slave ship, they having nowhere to move, and once again they moving under heavy manners. Once they landing in the New World—Brazil, Tobago, the United States—anywhere, it don't matter—is the same thing. They living on plantations where massa watching and trying to control all their moving, the moving of their thinking, their speaking and their singing, the moving of their hands on the drum skin giving praise to their gods, even the moving of their feelings, so that mothers finding their loving toward their children coming to nothing when massa taking them away and selling them. Totoben and Maisie seeing the moving of their loving going nowhere when massa selling them one from the other, even their moving toward their gods—their drumming, their dancing, and the movings of their tongue—all these massa trying and controlling. The only moving massa wanting is when Totoben and Maisie working for him in the fields, and when they not moving as he wanting he using the whip.

The crossroads! Where the world of the living bucking up the world of the spirit and filling up with the what could be happening in every meeting. Is early early in the morning—fore day morning at jouvay time[8] and four bands of masqueraders meeting and colliding at the crossroads! their sounds and embracing every living thing in the sea and sound of steel-steel-pans beating their way up and out of the holds of slave ships, beating their way up and out from slaving into the freedom of sound wrested from oil drum and steel pans into the new new of music. At the crossroads! what you hearing is the sound of Africa cutting loose and moving across the Atlantic to surface again and again in the music of the boys from behind the bridge[9] striking fear in the hearts of whites and middle-

class black people, the boys from behind the bridge who hiding their cutlasses inside their steel pans and when the time right is take they taking
them out and chopping their way to supremacy and everybody running,
pants tearing as they climbing walls and fleeing the sound of Africa turning and turning around and across the Atlantic.

The crossroads! Where tongue licking up against tongue and Yoruba
meeting English meeting Ga meeting Twi meeting French meeting Ibo
meeting Spanish. The crossroads! Home of Eshu-Elegbara[10] where all things
happening and the present past and future coming together and out of
them coming what nobody never seeing before, but which plenty more
than the future and what wasn't there before appearing and becoming
more than what was there and the time lasting as long as when you blinking your eye, or as short as the age of the time self.

People carnivalling and playing marse in Brooklyn; they playing marse
in Montreal, in Toronto and Miami, they playing marse in Calgary, and in
Antigua, in St. Lucia, and Jamaica; they playing marse in New York and
Notting Hill, moving and moving and in the moving they throwing out
the seeds that defying the holding in the ships crawling across the Atlantic
with Totoben and Maisie.

Some calling this thing that Totoben and Maisie doing, this playing marse,
European; some saying is Indian, and others saying is a Creole thing—all
mix up mix up. And then again some saying is a African thing. If you
wanting you could be starting with the French who running coming to
Trinidad from Grenada, Guadeloupe, Martinique in 1784. The Spanish
calling it the Cedula of population[11] that saying that as long as you white
and Catholic you can be coming to Trinidad. The Spanish giving away
land they stealing from the native people to French people and they hop-
ing that this stopping the British invading the island. Then again in 1789
more French people fleeing Haiti and the rising up of Africans against Europeans, they fleeing the example Toussaint and Dessalines[12] setting when
they insisting that Africans must be having their freedom to move and
move and move out of the nowhere of slavery into history. Toussaint and
Dessalines playing ol' marse with history and making bassa bassa[13] with
the plans of France; they beating Napoleon at his own game and driving
the French right out of Haiti. Then they putting on the costumes of the
Jacobins and with their Napolen hats and coattails they turning themselves into black Jacobins and parading through history and ending Napoleon and his empire earlier than he expecting.

Although Spain bringing plenty French people to Trinidad with Totoben
and Maisie as their slaves, the British still taking over the island in 1897.

When the French people coming they bringing their Carnival with them and every year around Christmas time the governor declaring martial law and the white French people going from house to house singing Christmas songs; they going into streets and dancing and wearing masks and costumes; and they dancing at parties. Although massa letting Totoben and Maisie have some free time and they dancing in their yard and eating, all at massa expense, is only white people and free colored people who having Carnival. Sometimes free colored people breaking out of their color and dressing up like king and queen and lord and lady. And white men blacking up their faces and playing *negue jadin* which taking the garden Negro in *negre jardin* and turning it into garden nigger, and the white women dressing up like the mulatto and black women their husbands sexing and sleeping with and all the while they dancing to the music that Totoben and Maisie making on their drums because that is the only way they taking any part in the white people Carnival.

Then again maybe we could be starting in Africa with the Yoruba and Ibo of Nigeria, the Ashanti and Fon of Ghana, Dahomey and Guinea and their dances, their masquing, and the rituals they performing and keeping their gods happy. In the New World, Totoben and Maisie, remembering these in the *Bamboula, Ghouba* and the *Kalinda*[14] stick dances, and even if they not dancing in the streets because the French not wanting them nowhere round them, the remembering running deep and strong and they only waiting for the right time.

Sometimes Maisie and Totoben hiding their dreaming for freedom behind Carnival time at Christmas and in 1805 they gathering together in regiments with kings, queens, princes, and princesses and they dressing up in fancy costumes and singing songs rebelling against their not moving and they plotting their overthrowing of massa. And when massa finding out he punishing them bad bad. But in 1838 slavery and its half-sister, apprenticeship,[15] really over and Totoben and Maisie saying: "Ah hah! is free we free now," and all the free-up Africans taking their new new moving onto the streets and celebrating and the white people not liking the bacchanal of Totoben and Maisie and pulling right back.

"Nothing but the vilest of the vile . . . now think of appearing in the streets. Why not forbid it altogether?"[16] Is so one newspaper talking about Carnival in 1856. But Totoben and Maisie celebrating their moving for the first time in the New World, and they unforgetting all that massa thinking they forgetting or not remembering, and Africa sailing right across the middle passage of the Atlantic and coming to land right at the crossroads where the Moko Jumbie[17] tingling your spine as it walking high high above the crowds like the dreams of the Africans who freeing up their moving. Papa Bois and Mama Deleau and Jab Molassi[18]—all of them coming and taking root in Trinidad and driving out the European massa who controlling the moving of Totoben and Maisie for so long. And the French pulling back into their pretty pretty houses, and the colored middle class that wanting to be white but loving black deep inside pulling back and they leaving the street wide wide open and clear for the powerful moving of Totoben and Maisie who catching the African spirit and dancing and fighting and sporting and fighting some more, because is plenty plenty anger they holding down in those four hundred years when they not moving and is so it bursting out and everybody, Indian, Chinese, European, even the black and brown middle classes frighten too bad and pulling back back and Totoben and Maisie moving as they wanting.

Is the moving that changing things that everybody frighten of—the moving of what the whites calling "savage songs" into calypso:

> (The) disgusting and indecent African custom of carrying a stuffed figure of a woman on a pole, which was followed by hundreds of negroes yelling out a savage Guinea song (*Port of Spain Gazette* 22).

The moving of tamboo bamboo bands, pot covers, dustpan covers, and bottle and spoon into steel pan, into pan into orchestra, so that today every music machine program with the sweet-too-bad sound of pan music.

You must be starting in 1838 if you wanting to understand this thing that Totoben and Maisie doing—1838, the year of emancipation for all the Totobens and Maisies in the English colonies; 1838—four years after the apprenticeship period that starting in 1834 when Totoben and Maisie finally free and doing what they wanting, eating what they wanting, drinking what they wanting, working where they wanting, walking where they wanting, and *moving* where they wanting. Or so Maisie and Totoben thinking.

So is true the French "starting" Carnival, but a free French man or woman playing marse in a colony they owning and Totoben and Maisie, who coming over in the hold of a slave ship, playing marse as free man and woman after three or four hundred years of slavery is two different things. And for a while there Totoben and Maisie controlling the streets and pushing everybody back—back back until they controlling what they never controlling before—their own moving, and so they playing marse in the streets, at the crossroads, fore day morning at jouvay time. And is

Totoben and Maisie time now for putting on white masks and playing like white just like their former massa blacking his face and playing *negue jadin:* "Every negro, male and female, wore a white flesh coloured mask, their woolly hair carefully concealed by handkerchiefs. . . . [W]henever a black mask appeared it was sure to be a white man" (*Port of Spain Gazette* 24).

Totoben making fun of massa and missis and suddenly "Canboulay! Canboulay! Canboulay!" running from mouth to mouth and excitement spreading like wildfire during slaving time. "Cannes brules! Cannes brules! The canes burning!" and turning into "Canboulay"—and monsieur, madame, massa and missis getting Totoben and Maisie from all the plantations round about and whipping and beating them to be fighting the fires and reaping the cane before the fire destroying everything. Sometimes Maisie and Totoben working all day and all night and putting out the cane fires.

Now that Totoben and Maisie free up and having their moving, they taking revenge and turning the tables and putting black varnish on their face "they carrying chains and sticks and they yelling and singing and cracking whips" and they carrying on just like massa used to and they making fun of slavery. Massa newspaper saying that Totoben and Maisie making "an unremitting uproar, yelling, drumming and blowing of horns" as they remembering when they fighting the cane fires. Totoben and Maisie carrying their lighted flambeaux and their sticks for their stick fighting through the streets shouting "Canboulay! Canboulay!" and is so through marse they remembering their slaving time especially on August first, the date Massa changing the laws and freeing them.

From the time the English bekas[19] taking over from the Spanish they controlling how Totoben and Maisie playing marse and even trying to stamp it out.

—In 1833 beka saying that Totoben and Maisie not respecting the Sabbath and he arresting two people and holding them in the cage. Then beka saying that nobody must be wearing masks before February eighteenth: "Any person found masked in the streets will be immediately arrested and dealt with according to the law" (*Port of Spain* Gazette 20).

—In 1838 beka not liking what Totoben and Maisie doing any better and he still talking about the

> desecration of the Sabbath. . . . We will not dwell on the disgusting and indecent scenes that were enacted in our streets— we will not say how many we saw in a state so nearly approaching nudity as to outrage decency and shock modesty—we will

not particularly describe the African custom of carrying a stuffed
figure of a woman on a pole, which was followed by hundreds
of negroes yelling out a savage Guinea song (we regret to say
that nine-tenths of these people were Creoles)—we will not
describe the ferocious fight between the "Damas" and the
"Wartloos" which resulted from mummering—but we will say
at once that the custom of keeping Carnival by allowing the
lower order of society to run about the streets in wretched
masquerade belongs to other days, and ought to be abolished
in our own. (*Port of Spain Gazette* 22)

—By 1843 beka telling Totoben and Maisie that they can only be wearing masks for two days and not three and he protecting his Sabbath by
saying that Carnival only beginning on Sunday night.
    —In 1846 beka saying that Totoben and Maisie must not be wearing
masks ever again: "We trust this will prove a final . . . stop to the orgies
which are indulged in by the dissolute of the town at this season of the
year, under pretence of Masking" (*Port of Spain Gazette* 23). But people not
happy and they rumbling and beka pulling back and saying that people
could be going in bands from house to house and putting on masks when
they getting close to the houses.
    Beka ears not liking the drum and trying to ban it although Totoben
and Maisie needing it not only for their Carnival but when they practicing
their religion: "Since midnight on Sunday, this festival has broken the slum-
ber of our peaceable citizens with its usual noisy revelry and uproarious
hilarity" (*Port of Spain Gazette* 22). All the while Totoben and Maisie playing marse on the street, their brothers and sisters who beka calling "colored" not joining them, but they going from house to house playing music
and they not liking the government interfering with Carnival anymore
than Totoben and Maisie.
    —In 1858 beka saying again no more masking and writing about "the
noise, tumult and barbarian mirth" (*Port of Spain Gazette* 28). Then beka
calling on his police who arresting Totoben and Maisie who wearing masks
and even people who not wearing masks. Totoben and Maisie fighting
back: "a band of Negroes 3,000–4,000 strong passing the police station, armed
with hatchets, woodmen's axes, cutlasses, bludgeons and knives . . . had
the bold temerity to give a derisive shout of triumphant defiance to the
police" (*Port of Spain Gazette* 28). Then beka calling out the military to stop
Totoben and Maisie moving and driving them off the street.
    After 1858 Totoben and Maisie, who beka calling "the idle and the va-

grant" and who "taking advantage of the general laxity to outrage public decency" controlling Carnival even more and the middle-class Creoles pulling back inside their houses. They calling Totoben and Maisie bad-johns, dunois, makos, matadors, prostitutes and stickmen and say they belonging to the jamette class (*Port of Spain Gazette* 47) and how they living in barrack yards and having no use for respectable society.

Totoben and Maisie bringing all the anger they feeling to the street and they fighting with whips and sticks, midnight robbers talking pretty and taking your money, and sailors throwing powder over you. Jab Molassi paint up in black and frightening everybody and Maisie and Totoben dressing up like cow with horns, playing fisherman and even pretending to be crazy; some people carrying chains, some carrying snakes, the jab jabs snapping their whips and Totoben dressing like he pregnant.

Maisie, the jamette, opening up her bodice and showing off her breasts and no man telling her what she can be doing and not doing. Totoben dressing up like a woman in a lacy nightgown or sometimes he only wearing a blood cloth like he seeing his monthlies and he playing marse in the "Pissenlit" band and wining and singing songs that beka calling obscene.

—In 1874 beka calling for a Vagrancy Law and a Reformatory School because he not liking Totoben and Maisie going around in bands and behaving like vagabonds: "Herds of disreputable males and females . . . organized into bands and societies for the maintenance of vagrancy, immorality and vice. . . . [T]he name and season (of Carnival) is but a cloak . . . for the shameless celebration of heathenish and vicious rites of some profligate god whose votaries rival in excesses the profligacies and brutalities of Pagan Rome or Heathen India" (*Port of Spain Gazette* 32).

—In 1875 beka saying that he using the Habitual Criminals Act against Totoben and Maisie who forming themselves in bands and fighting each other: "The bands, which under different names infest the colony and are fruitful souces of immorality and crime" (*Port of Spain Gazette* 32).

—In 1876 beka police using their batons without mercy on Totoben and Maisie.

—In 1877, 1878, 1879 a beka captain name Baker controlling Totoben and Maisie during Carnival and in 1880 beka journalists describing them as making a "fearful howling of a parcel of semi-savages emerging God knows where from, exhibiting hellish scenes and the most demoniacal representations of the days of slavery as they were 40 years ago" (*Port of Spain Gazette* 32).

—In l881 the same beka captain name Baker once again trying to get Totoben and Maisie to give up their sticks, their drums and their flambeaux, but they fighting back and dropping plenty blows on. Beka calling out the army to control the moving of Totoben and Maisie, but Totoben and Maisie tasting their moving for the first time in the New World and it sweet sweet and they hitting back because Carnival and marse is their freeing-up time. They fighting back when the army saying that Sunday is a sacred day and trying to ban marse; they fighting back when the Catholics and other Christians saying how Totoben and Maisie and all their African brothers and sisters pagan and how they desecrating a Christian festival. Totoben and Maisie fighting back when the upper classes saying that Africans not belonging in their upper-class celebration and they using their Kalinda sticks: "Canboulay! Canboulay!" Plenty people feeling the hurt—man, woman and child—and everybody calling this the Canboulay riots and although their brothers and sisters getting hurt, Totoben and Maisie injuring thirty-eight police and the beka captain calling out soldiers for them. The beka governor having to go to Totoben and Maisie and telling them that he not wanting to stop their moving but asking them please to keep the peace.

Beka still not giving up and he outlawing the Canboulay procession and banning Totoben and Maisie from carrying sticks, but they still doing it behind beka back.

—In 1883 beka banning the drum!

—In 1884 beka saying no noisy instruments! no lighted torches! and no sticks! and again the police attacking Maisie and Totoben and their bands but they fighting and killing the police officer who in charge.

—In 1917 beka saying no wearing of masks again!

—In 1934 beka saying in the Theatre and Dance Hall Ordinance Act that Totoben and Maisie must not be showing any lewdness and still Totoben and Maisie playing their marse.

And so every year the English bekas controlling Totoben and Maisie a little bit more—no more masquing on Sunday, no more carrying of sticks, Carnival beginning on Monday morning at six in the morning, but still Maisie and Totoben coming strong in Congo band and Shango band, they coming strong in Cattle and Cow band; they playing marse like Dirty Sailor, Sailor Ashore, Fancy Sailor, King Sailor or Stoker; they coming strong like Wild Indian, Red Indian, Blue Indian and Black Indian; they dressing up like Jab Jabs coming from hell and they playing East Indian Burroquite, Spanish Burroquite and Pajaro; they coming strong playing Sebucan and Maypole that coming from Latin America and England, they even playing Yankee Minstrel and blacking up their face that black already and painting on white lips; they playing Tennesse Cowboy, Clown and Bat and they coming strong in bands that telling about history with names like "Quo Vadis" and "Serpent of the Nile" or bands like "A Day at Helsinki," "The People of Iceland" or "Spanish Vagabonds" (*Port of Spain Gazette* 35). Totoben and Maisie coming strong because they knowing that their moving through the streets is a remembering of how their moving always threatening those who wanting and controlling them.

As beka getting more and more control over Carnival Totoben and Maisie "colored" and black brothers and sisters who living in the middle class coming back to the Carnival and the whites joining in and through playing marse it looking like everybody even the Indians[20] moving and creolizing around Carnival.

> During the Carnival season, an entire population is gradually released from moral and civic obligations, and the diverse social, economic, and religious groups become closely united in a single mass activity. Heterogeneous as the wandering Carnival bands are, they intermingle vast numbers of people who, by indulging in similar activities with thousands of other people, become conscious of a unity, a social cohesion, a oneness with the crowd itself. During this time the Haitian peasant experiences the widest range of partial integration that he is likely to realize during the year. (Dunham 42)

But is still Totoben and Maisie who driving it: "In a true sense, Carnival 'belongs' to the black, lower class. It is they who, through most of its history, have been the outstanding participants. But whilst Carnival is a direct expression of the folk, it also acts like a magnet for the coloured population"(*Port of Spain Gazette* 95).

When the English banning the drum, Totoben and Maisie moving around that and using bamboo and making the tamboo bamboo bands[21] and when they banning tamboo bamboo they using pieces of iron, parts of cars, metal boxes, dustbins and even piss pots, all the time they moving towards pan[22] and making their music through their moving.

Totoben and Maisie moving their savage songs into calypso and they singing in French patois, and then in English and they rude rude and mimicking everything and everybody who putting them down *sans humanité*.[23] When the English stopping Totoben and Maisie from singing their calypsos in public because they say they obscene, they moving them into calypso tents.[24]

Totoben and Maisie moving through English and French and singing their songs that full of picong[25] and wit and anger and singing about richman and poorman how richman wearing trousereen and poorman wearing garberdine and how the yankees gone and Sparrow taking over the prostitutes.[26] And is so the moving of Maisie and Totoben words tie up tight tight with their moving on the street. The crossroads! Where the spirit of word meeting the spirit of music and driving each other and Totoben and Maisie who singing calypso marking it with their struggling just Totoben and Maisie beating it out in steel.

When World War II breaking out the beka name English governor telling Totoben and Maisie that they can't be having their Carnival, but when the war over Totoben and Maisie coming back even stronger in 1946. Totoben and his friends like Winston "Spree" Simon[27] using gasoline oil drums and they tuning their pain in steel and turning the pans into instruments—turning the weapons of war—old oil drums that leaving over from the World War II—into music and they making another art form for Carnival: "Steel pan came out of pain. The culture was born in life's shadowed places. It came out of the ghetto areas out of the need to express one's self" (Rudder 31).

Destination Tokyo, Renegades, Invaders, Desperadoes, Casablanca—is names like these that Totoben and his friends from behind the bridge who playing the steel pan giving themselves, and just like the names Totoben and Maisie giving themselves when they singing calypso—Exploiter, Roaring Lion, Tiger, Lord Kitchener, Lord Melody, The Mighty Sparrow, Calypso Rose—the names talking about how Totoben and Maisie moving from slave shack to the street, about how Totoben and Maisie ready to fight for their moving:

> I spend so much a money to buy this costume
> now I ready to jump
> you better give me room
> I make so much a plan just to play this mas
> now is time to play
> give me room to pass
> I want to jam down
> roll down
> shake down
> all around town
> dis mas is for you and you and you and you
> so move, move you blocking up the place
> so move move

> I want to shake my waist
> the people want to jam
> so get out of the band
> I say move
> move—
>   *Black Stalin, "Move" (1991)*

Totoben and Maisie knowing that they needing the music and the drums and the singing to keep moving: "[O]– Carnival Day we roam the street for the two days because the music is carrying you. You have to get a music that can drive people, keep them moving constantly. . . . [W]hen a man goes behind his mas, whatever that mas is, he comes out and says on that particular day, this is how I feel" (Rudder, 16).

For Totoben and Maisie who living in John John and behind the bridge where the downpressed and downtrodden living, playing marse is how they expressing themselves, and is in the music and dance and even the fighting you seeing and feeling the violence they living with all year round.

> But this Carnival, putting on his costume not at dawn, Aldrick had a feeling of being the last one, the last symbol of rebellion and threat to confront Port of Spain. . . . Once upon a time the entire Carnival was expressions of rebellion. Once there were stick fighters who assembled each year to keep alive in battles between themselves the practice of a warriorhood born in them; and there were devils, black men who blackened themselves further with black grease to make of their very blackness a menace, a threat. They moved along the streets with horns on their heads and tridents in hand. They threatened to press their blackened selves against the well-dressed spectators unless they were given money. And there were the jab jabs, men in jester cosutumes, their caps and and shoes filled with tinkling bells, cracking longs whips in the streets, with which they lashed each other with full force. . . . And these little fellars waiting for the band to get underway so they could glide up to the steeldrums and touch one, or wave to a brother or cousin who was playing one of the pans, or help the men push the stands on which the big steeldrums were mounted. . . . This is the guts of the people, their blood; this is the self of the people that they screaming out they possess, that they scrimp and save and whore and work and thief to drag out of the hard rockstone

and dirt to show the world they is people. He felt: "This is people taller than cathedrals; this is people more beautiful than avenues with trees."

. . . For two full days Aldrick was a dragon in Port of Spain moving through the loud, hot streets, dancing the bad-devil dance, dancing the stickman dance, dancing Sylvia and Inez and Basil and his grandfather and the Hill and the fellars by the Corner, leaning against the wall, waiting for the police to raid them. He was Manzanilla, Calvary Hill, Congo, Dahomey, Ghana. He was Africa, the ancestral Masker, affirming the power of the warrior, prancing and bowing, breathing out fire, lunging against his chains, threatening with his claws, saying to the city: I is a dragon. I have fire in my belly and claws on my hands; watch me! Note me well, for I am ready to burn down your city. I am ready to tear you apart, limb by limb. (Lovelace, 123–25)

And the European beka still controlling marse and trying to stop Totoben and Maisie moving, so they passing a regulation that saying Maisie and Totoben must be stopping their marse before 12 midnight on the Tuesday before Ash Wednesday, and the law still on the books to this day. Even when Africans running the country they trying and controlling Totoben and Maisie so in 1956 Dr. Eric Williams who everybody calling De Doc, the first black prime minister of Trinidad and Tobago,[28] sponsoring and supporting Totoben and Maisie as a way of controlling them: "Every government is afraid of a million people on the street. There's no government that's not afraid of a million people in the street" (Rudder, 18).

You better move and move and move. . . . Moving, the metaphor for what the New World promising. Moving towards progress, away from the Old World towards the bettering of life—except for Totoben and Maisie who the European bekas bringing through time and space to the New World and then trying to stop them moving. Everybody but Totoben and Maisie living the promise that is moving in the New World—moving up from low beginnings, moving to a better life or to a new life, but not Totoben and Maisie. Is only Maisie, Totoben and their African brothers and sisters who not moving to the New World for a better life. The bekas who calling themselves Puritans, and those who fleeing the bassa bassa of the Old World, and those who coming after the Africans expecting and bettering their living: the Jews, the Italians, the Greeks, the Poles—the poor that the Statue of Liberty begging the world to be giving to America. All except Totoben and Maisie who not choosing and moving to the New World but who coming in chains. Everybody who moving to the New World either moving to better themselves, or even if they not bettering themselves in money they finding a safe place from those who persecuting them—everybody except Totoben and Maisie. Maisie and Totoben losing everything when the bekas moving them to the New World—they losing their culture, their religion, their language, and their tongue, and all the while beka trying and holding Totoben and Maisie back from the dream that is moving.

For everybody who coming to the New World, the dream that calling is the dream of moving: moving through space to the new land; moving through time to the future; working hard and moving up; moving out to the suburbs from the cramped city always moving. Although Totoben and Maisie moving through space and time, beka cutting them off in time and telling them they having no past and that their past not worth anything. Beka also stopping them from moving forward and making progress like everybody else doing and telling each other to do.[29] The American beka in the United States making up the public and national lie that everybody could be moving up to the sky if they wanting and even becoming president. Everybody that is except Totoben and Maisie. And beka making rules about where Totoben and Maisie living, where they going to school; where they walking, where they working, where they taking their sick bodies, and where they burying them. And although the American bekas taking those rules off the law books and saying everybody free, he still controlling Totoben and Maisie. Today, the beka police still telling young Totoben where he moving and if he not looking sharp he shooting down Totoben stone cold. Totoben and Maisie still living in ghettos and beka even start saying once again that Totoben and Maisie born stupid and bad and that governments throwing good money behind bad if they creating space for Totoben and Maisie to move and move and move and move. . . . So, for one day, two days—Totoben and Maisie taking back the streets, those same streets that the police patrolling every day—to dance down, wine down, parading and presenting their dreadness, making real the unreal:

> An elderly woman shook herself free of her elaborate costume which fell like waxed wings facing the sun. . . . [S]he had woken up with forty different dreams when she thought about making a costume for Carnival. She could only use four of them. She made a sea dragon costume for her little grandson, two turtles for her granddaughters and a sea queen for herself. She had thirty-six more dreams left for next year's. But "listen young

man," she said, "I is someone who bound to dream again before then" (Owusu 30).

For one—two days—the doors to the prison that the black skin making
for Totoben and Maisie opening up and they escaping into promise of
moving. And so Totoben and Maisie jamming and jocking[30] their waist all
the way down University Avenue in Toronto, in Notting Hill, in Port of
Spain, in Miami and wherever they making marse they creating something new with the language of their moving.

For a long time is Totoben as man, as stickfighter, fighter, warrior who
controlling marse: "I Lawa (le Roi) with stick, with fight, with woman,
with dance, with song, with drum, with everything" (*Port of Spain Gazette*
xvi). And when Totoben disappearing as stickfighter and chantwell[31] he
living on in the calypsonian and the steelbandsman. In Totoben black nationalism and manness coming together and fighting the racism American
service men bringing to Trinidad along with their yankee dollars when
they coming to the American base at Chaguaramus racism during World
War II. And Sparrow the calypsonian singing about how he taking over
the prostitutes which he getting cheap cheap since the "Yankees gone and
Sparrow take over now."[32]

Is only Maisie who living in the barrack yards and who belonging to
the jamette class who playing marse with Totoben when it first starting.
And Maisie the jamette is sister to other jamettes like Sara Jamaica, Long
Body Ada and Techselia and Boadicea fighting with stick man and woman
alike. As the years going by Maisie from the middle class joining Maisie
from the streets and remembering how to wine and together they taking
their wining into the public spaces. Maisie taking over the street and strut-
ting her sexiness up and down Port of Spain, Toronto, Notting Hill, New
York, Miami and she not frighten because today is her day and she wining
and wining:

> Shake up de bam bam,
> roll up de bum bum
> wine wine wine Virginia wine Virginia. . . .
> Virginia say give me room
> I want to wine
> Virginia say I don't care
> Is my time
> women will slander
> men will admire

. . . .
she wine on de pan man
she wine on de pan stan
woi woi woi
shake up de bam bam
roll up de bum bum

Blue Boy, "Virginia" (1992)

Maisie brown, Maisie black, Maisie white, Maisie African, Maisie Indian and Maisie Chinese and Maisie wining—round her staff, round her
bottle, round anything sometimes but a man. Women wining round their
space—their inside space, the space of their becoming, where anything
happening—the crossroads that is their space—their inner space where
woman meeting woman meeting man as Blue Boy singing:

> Virginia dey shame about de native dance
> Virginia is culture we inheriting
> Is part of our history
> A gift to the body
> So how come we discussing immorality
> You like playing sailor
> So wine for your lover
> Wine wine wine
> Shake up your bum bum
> Roll up your bam bam

And is like Maisie taking over Carnival—taking over the streets with
her rampant, raucous, strident and her sweet-too-bad sexuality, wining
and wining around and around on something, anything—but a man. Is
the one time Maisie showing her sexuality open open and not feeling
threatened, is the one time Maisie freeing up and not dealing with men if
she not wanting to and she wining and wining on anything.

> Externalization, catharsis, sexual stimulus, and sexual release
> seem to be the fundamental psychological functions of the sea-
> sonal crowd dance. There is every indication that at one time
> the seasonal dances were associated conceptually with some
> fertility cult (the planting season and emphasis on the sexual
> form of the dances) but this significance has been submerged
> in the function of sexual catharsis. The emphasis on the sexual

function is confirmed by the increased birth rates at a reasonable time after Mardi Gras. . . . To release or to externalize energy is the psychological function of practically every dance
which is not purely formal. . . . Closely bound up with
externalization of energy is the function of escape from emotional conflict through the dance, an escape that is a form of
externalization, usually voluntary. In the seasonal dance, primary gratification is derived from the complete externalization
of inhibition . . . an escape sanctioned by country wide license.
. . . [T]he Mardi Gras acts as both a stimulus and release of
energy, chiefly sexual. This release process might be called sexual catharsis. (Dunham 42)

And so long time after leaving Africa, Maisie and Totoben still having
"the instinct to dance the ritual dance of procreation" (Rohlehr, 1) although
they unremembering the meaning. Totoben and Maisie knowing that these
dances not having to do with having babies, but their bodies remembering
the instinct and that it not easy or safe to get rid of it.

The crossroads! That is Trinidad is where Carib, Arawak and Taino meeting European and dying; where African meeting European and dying and
living, where Asian meeting European and African and living and dying;
the crossroads! Where anything can be happening, where Eshu-Elegbara
ruling. Totoben and Maisie wining around the space of the crossroads and
creating the callaloo[33] that is Carnival and creating the moving out of
Trinidad to away and big country and foreign. Totoben and Maisie moving
from the islands, by boat and by plane they moving overseas to foreign,
they moving in time and space once again, to be bettering themselves,
following their money and their raw material that the banks and compa-
nies taking overseas and abroad. They following Barclays Bank, Shell, Le-
ver Brothers and Frys Cocoa to England; they following Texaco and Amoco
to the United States, and they following the Bank of Nova Scotia, the Royal
Bank of Canada, and Alcan to Canada. And in England Carnival turning
to ole marse[34] when the natives confronting Totoben and Maisie in Notting
Hill in 1976:

Then the police Mas arrived, more than 300 men in blue costumes and helmets. They carried no instruments except one
percussive item, a baton concealed in their costumes. They
started their ritual dance in silence, except for the radios and
sirens. The revellers moved back into a tight space in front of

Acklam Hall as the blue Mas formed a loop around them. All
possible exits were blocked, tension mounted and loud pleas
rose above the cacophony of voices. The police charged into
the besieged crowd "to arrest pickpockets." It was frightening.
Half of the people who initally tried to run fell over, children
trampled underfoot, bleeding and crying. Those who tried to
help also went down in the stampede. . . . The inevitable response came. Some of the cornered youth broke through the
rain of batons and broke the siege. As soon as they regrouped
they launched an offensive which surprised the police by its
effectiveness. They knew the terrain intimately. Their only
weapons: bricks from nearby building cites, cans and bottles.
For four hours these untrained youths waged a guerilla battle
with the police on the streets of Notting Hill, and won. When
the police retreated only the sirens of ambulances stirred the
still of the night. The streets were empty; the red, gold and
green still flapped in the wind from the third floor window.

In the morning all the newspapers were simply and literally
fuming with rage. . . . The initial baton charge (by the police)
which provoked the reaction was ignored by almost all the
newspapers. Black casualties were ignored in favour of photo-
graphs of bleeding policemen being rushed to hospital. . . .

The young warriors of Notting Hill have a noble history. They
were the descendants of the stickmen of the famous Arouca
riots of l891 who beat off police constables sent to break up the
drum dance. (Owusu 3)

Totoben and Maisie in 1976 keeping faith with Totoben and Maisie in
1858, 1881, and 1884 and resisting beka controlling them. In London the
English bekas wanting to move Totoben and Maisie from Notting Hill and
putting them in Hyde Park, and in Toronto they moving Toronto Totoben
and Maisie first one way then another because "The police have never
liked Caribana—if it were not for Caribana's economic infusion, the police
would have stopped it. It would make a lot of people happy if it was
moved."[35] And finally in 1991 the Canadian bekas getting their way and
moving it from University Avenue which having so much meaning for
Totoben and Maisie who living up there in the cold and they putting it
down on the Lakeshore where is only into Lake Ontario the people can be
running if any ruckshun breaking out. The people who running it saying
they making more money from it by moving it, but it giving beka another
way to control Totoben and Maisie even more.

Move and move and move—Totoben and Maisie moving to the promising and promises of the mother country, big country and away and when
England not wanting them anymore they moving to Canada and America
and they seeding and sporing these countries with their desiring and doing better, only they finding that while no plantations waiting for them,
beka still not wanting Totoben and Maisie moving and they streaming them
into low-level jobs. And when Totoben and Maisie hearing a beka name
Botha from South Africa saying that they must be learning that there are
certain greener pastures that they never owning, they knowing that the
other bekas who running England and Canada and the United States thinking the same thing. Totoben thinking of the jobs he not getting and Maisie
about the money she not earning; Totoben and Maisie thinking of the
moving they not doing, and so they taking their bodies to the streets, to
the crossroads of their minds, and they moving, bearing the sounds of
their ancestors on University Avenue past the United States embassy, past
the police station, past the courts, past the hospitals where Totoben and
Maisie working in the kitchens, and cleaning the floors, past statues glori-
fying wars between one beka country and another to the Lakeshore[36] where
the only place they having to move to if ruckus breaking out is the lake.

In Canada Totoben and Maisie turning Carnival into Caribana in 1967
for Canada's Centennial celebrations and everybody liking it so much, they
doing it every year and bringing plenty money into Toronto. And brip
brap just so what Totoben and Maisie doing no longer African or black and
Sam Lewis, a black beka, and chairman of the Caribana Committee saying
on the radio, the Canadian Broadcasting Corporation: "I can't repeat this
enough. Caribana is *not* a black festival necessarily. It is a *Canadian* festival
that reflects black and Caribbean culture."[37] Is where Totoben and Maisie?
Still there on University Avenue wining in the *Canadian* festival of Caribana.
Totoben and Maisie laughing and laughing and knowing that is not just so
Caribana turning Canadian and they wondering how the black beka, Lewis,
turning Caribana into "not a black festival." Totoben and Maisie knowing
that if Canadian elastic enough and including them who black and Caribbean in their wining and their playing marse and their struggling for respect then and only then Caribana becoming Canadian.

Totoben and Maisie knowing that every year their wining and dancing
making millions for businesses in Toronto,[38] yet they still not getting the
support they needing from the government or from businesses and every
year they running a debt. People who running Caribana looking at Caribana
as a "marketing tool" and Totoben and Maisie laughing fit to kill because
they knowing what the doing in Trinidad and in Toronto and Notting Hill
and New York is not no marketing tool. Totoben and Maisie who organiz-

ing Caribana trying and trying and looking for ways and making money from Caribana, and is like they trying and putting reins on a hurricane, because playing marse not working in the way white bekas making things work.

Totoben and Maisie facing the same problem in Toronto as they facing in Notting Hill: "It is Europe's largest street festival and clearly has the potential to be self-funding if the money generated by Carnival goes back into the Carnival and the Black community. However contracts are given to Cockspur Rum and Kiss FM" ("Carnival under Siege" 37). Caribana is the biggest festival in Canada, and yet Totoben and Maisie still scrunting.[39]

The police still seeing Totoben and Maisie moving as a catastrophe waiting to happen and they putting them behind barricades on the Lakeshore so that if you watching Totoben and Maisie playing marse, you mustn't be jumping up in the bands. And they bringing out the troops because they not understanding that what Totoben and Maisie doing is freeing up and they not looking for trouble unless trouble troubling them. So they watching Totoben and Maisie close close:

> What creates the tension is the understandable angry reaction
> to the fact that it is so heavily policed and shackled into a small
> area. The Carnival was literally surrounded by coach loads of
> police on standby, with as many roadblocks as would be em-
> ployed in a war or state of emergency. To African Caribbean
> people, Carnival is much more than a dance in the street; it
> represents our sense of collective freedom and right to be free.
> Imagine the humiliation and anger of our community when
> we are herded around a few square miles, then told to get out
> of the area by dusk. There were 36 crimes, 46 arrests and 1
> fatal stabbing and there were one million people. ("A Carnival
> under Siege" 37)

The police not understanding that Totoben and Maisie who standing and watching and Maisie and Totoben who dancing in the band is one and the same; they not understanding that Carnival and marse meaning that you crossing from looking to dancing and back again to looking, from not moving to moving and back again to not moving. For Totoben and Maisie marse is moving and not moving; is man dressing up as woman and woman dressing up as dirty sailor and playing man; is woman loving man yet wining on anything—but a man; is Crazy the calypsonian singing "if you can't get a woman, take a man!" And marse is living and dying. And then living again.

When the Canadian bekas putting Totoben and Maisie behind the barricades and telling them they must only be watching, they controlling Totoben and Maisie moving again. When the beka police in Toronto even putting up a sign at the end of the route that saying "STOP MUSIC" at the end of the parade route, Totoben and Maisie recognizing it from way way back in Trinidad where beka trying for over a hundred years and controlling their moving and their playing marse. The beka police in Canada even sending helicopters overhead and watching Totoben and Maisie because with one million Totobens and Maisies anything is possible.

Totoben and Maisie understanding and tasting the power of the crossroads of Eshu-Elegbara and the power of anything happening; they breaking up space into rhythm which is time and time and space making one; they knowing when they reaching the crossroads where living and dying meeting, they forgetting the jobs they not getting, the money they not making and so they taking to the streets and to the crossroads of their minds bearing the sounds of their ancestors on University, on the Lakeshore where if they running the only place they running is into the lake, but they urging and freeing up, they keeping moving as they wining and dancing their history and is sweat and jostle and push and shove and sway hip wine hip up down and around down University Avenue as the last band coming, only is not a band but a whole set of white men dress up in dirty white overalls with broom and dust pan and they cleaning up and reconquering University Avenue for one more year, doing work that black men and women like Totoben and Maisie doing, sweeping and washing the street clean clean of the stain of sweatandjostleandpushandpulseandbeatand the nightmare of Maisie, Bluesman, Boysie, and Totoben and his belly who conquering their own universe on University Avenue with their moving for the blinking of an eye. In time. And space. And just so the war over for one more year—is sweatandbeatand jostleandpulseand. . . .

Afterword

Yanick Lahens

Translated by Marie-Agnès Sourieau

Reading these essays about Caribbean creolization—that is, the forms resulting from the encounter and the blending of different cultures in the
Caribbean—leads me to ask myself where my own discourse should stand.

On the one hand, I find that my thinking here cannot be independent
from my lived experience. I have approached these texts as one does a
native land, with a double sense of recognition and discovery: recognition
of comforting familiarities and discovery of surprises produced by distance.
Above all, I have encountered the essentially manifold reality of the Caribbean—which must be transcended through reflection and creation—with
the scattering, doubling, and dissemination of—and the tensions between—
what is comprehensible and what is not. For "Nowhere has geography
been in better harmony with history. The tragically scattered land expresses
the dramatic dispersal of the people. Coming from where? Shipwrecked!
Native people? Rather, a circular current whose origins and whereabouts
are unknown. Except for a few stops, here and there, which even when
extended, do not presume the end of the voyage" (Fignolé 21).

On the other hand, under the cover of creoleness we are talking about
human beings whose "memory as far back as it can be remembered would
be painfully wounded" (Lahens 16). But this painful, multiple, irremedi-
able encounter from which we were born was nevertheless rich in promises at the very same time that it branded our flesh and our memory. Since
then, our self-awareness has oscillated endlessly between a difficult en-
trenchment here and a call for elsewhere that remains unfulfilled. Because we cannot grasp this awareness, we have often borrowed others:
Indian, African, European, Asian, as if in this multiplicity of our origin we
refused to take sides: "in search as we were of a fixed, stable, forever elusive identity" (Lahens 14). And today, as the same questions return under

different guises, I ask at the outset: How can we become, in a way that is ours, masters of our own space?

Without trying to get rid of our history—because it is not enough to want to be rid of one's history, one has to be able to—and instead of tirelessly seeking to stick back together the broken pieces of our identity, why not use this multiplicity precisely to invent the future that, more than does any other region, we represent?

Indeed, if we accept the paradox according to which humanity is one and diversity is infinite, then the Caribbean is its most perfect metaphoric expression. As a collection, these texts illustrate this paradox in the very impulse that drives them to relate their Creole convergence—that is, the foundation of the colonial monogenesis. In the diversity of their expression, processes, echoes, and through the problematics that they raise, these texts evoke the existence of a hispanophone, francophone, anglophone, and Dutch Créolité, though none—not even Jean Métellus—addresses the atypical Haitian case. Therefore, it is easy to observe with Maryse Condé that though they may be "historically conspicuous, the conditions of Créolité do not intersect." I might be tempted to add: "and that's just fine!"

The familiar elements of Caribbean unity can be assessed through reading and analyzing the diverse cultural facts compiled by the authors of this anthology—facts which, at a given time in this American and Caribbean context, led to the slow process of creolization. It is this unity that I would like to address first, examining the issues at the heart of these texts, then offering my own observations to illuminate the Haitian situation—since I know it best.

Unity

All the authors of the anthology agree that the term Creole, créole, referred first to a biological reality: a European, and especially a Spaniard, born in the Caribbean islands or in America. Frank Martinus Arion suggests that the concept derives from an Afro-Portuguese Creole spoken on the West Coast of Africa from the fifteenth century. The verb criar from which it stems means to be born locally. We then come to the broader meaning: that of the native being not necessarily a European. Condé quotes Loreto Todd who, in *Pidgins and Creoles,* also defines the Spanish word criollo as native of the locality, the country. This word would be a colonial corruption of criadillo, itself a diminutive of criado, which means educated, domesticated in contrast to savage, left wild. These meanings—born locally and domesticated—do not necessarily include the racial mixture, but they are going to prevail in the Caribbean as well as in Latin America. Carlos Guillermo Wilson and Antonio Benítez-Rojo stress that Creole cultures first began to appear between the late sixteenth and early seventeenth centuries in the different towns and villages of Spanish America; the principal agents of propagation of this culture were the Creoles (whites, Mulattoes, and Blacks born in the New World), particularly those from the second and third generation. Different economic, ethnologic, social, and political factors seemed to have played a role in the formation of this Creole culture.

In Suriname, Astrid Roemer tells us, the freshly liberated Afro-Surinamese called themselves Creoles as the most appropriate name after the abolition of slavery in the Americas in 1863 and at the end of the system of control by the state in 1873. In Haiti, the term Creole first referred— without any distinction—to the black and mulatto freed slaves, as well as the black slaves born in slavery, in order to distinguish them from the Bossales born in Africa, freshly arrived in Santo-Domingo and who, because of the intensification of the slave trade, represented more than half of the population of the island in 1770 (Barthélémy 1989, 13). It is only later, through a shift in meaning, that the term was used to define the elements and the process that engendered both Creole culture and Creole languages—generated from the contacts between autochthonous French or English and languages from Africa. On the other hand, the interaction among the African, European, and Amerindian cultures expressed itself in all spheres of life, and it is important to consider several factors of differentiation that result from the colonial universe, such as ethnicity, class, gender, age, place of residence, education, and occupation.

For instance, just as Benítez-Rojo stresses the role of the plantation, Martinus Arion rightly points out that the power of the big house on the plantation was in reality only apparent, since it was totally dependent upon the cabins that surrounded it for its wealth, as well as for the care of the children. It is indeed by means of the black women who took care of the white children that the cultural influence of the cabins were felt in the big houses. Songs, proverbs, folk tales, food, and language have invested this space to create the culture of Créolité.

Turning now to the language issue, we can also detect elements of unity. Two distinct tendencies exist today regarding the search for the genesis of the Creole language: some locate its origin in the African languages, others in the European. These assertions often conceal a hidden determination either to minimize the relation of Créole to French or, alternatively, to make it a debased by-product of French. However, most of the authors of this anthology who deal with this question see in Creole languages an original linguistic creation of the Caribbean world, even when the awareness of this originality is a recent phenomenon, as is the case in of St. Lucia. Merle Collins points out that very early on she noted the difference of status between Creole and English but that the term Creole only recently has been accepted; until then Creole was referred to by the expression "our way of speaking."

Quoting authors such as Edouard Glissant, Simone Schwarz-Bart, Earl Lovelace, and Wilson Harris, Condé presents Créole as a process of self-assertion. In Haiti, such authors as Félix Morisseau-Leroy, Frank Etienne, Georges Castera, Lionel Trouillot, and Pierre Richard Narcisse have claimed Créole as either political or personal identity. So the Creole language has always been at stake in the Caribbean, especially since colonial or local powers have attempted to restrict or suppress it. However, a survey of the last fifty years of Haiti's political history reveals that the political issues surrounding Haitian Créole are far more complex than is generally believed. Indeed, Créole has served as a demagogic screen to hide the incompetence—a total inability to solve real problems—of the government of the last thirty years; and it is still used today as a populist screen.

In his study of the origins of Haitian Créole, Jean Métellus considers that Caribbean people, Haitians in particular, have taken up the wrong fight in making Creole a hobbyhorse. And this for two reasons: first, Creole derives from a French language that was not yet homogenized at the time of colonization; second, Creole is not the only factor of national unity. As he concludes his essay on the linguistic problems specific to Haiti, Métellus considers as a mistake the extreme emphasis that intellectuals and politicians have placed on language as the most important element of cultural cohesion. He believes religion to be a stronger factor. Is the weakness of Créole that Métellus describes an essential weakness? Is it possible for Creole to develop, and should it do so? What means should then be implemented for this evolution? In this case, does religion have more structuring elements than language? These questions should remain open for discussion among Haitian anthropologists, philosophers, and linguists.

What, precisely, is the nature of the religious problem in the Caribbean? Here is the definition that Lahenec Hurbon, the Haitian specialist of religion in the Caribbean offers: "[T]he deportation to the New World of millions of Black slaves has led to the reconstitution in the Americas of African beliefs and practices under various forms and names: Candomble in Brazil, Santeria in Cuba, Obea in Jamaica, Shango in Tinidad, Vaudou in Haiti" (1979, 35). Roemer's essay has allowed us to discover the Winti

religion of Suriname, with a genesis similar to that of Vaudou. The practices of both religions evolved from the same historical events:

> Upon their arrival, the slaves are divided up on the planta-
> tions. In workshops and cabins, a systematic mixing of ethnic
> groups is carried out: slaves must lose the memory of their fam-
> ily, lineage and origins. Deprived of their humanity, they are
> then able to become totally submissive. Meetings and gather-
> ings are forbidden except when they are held under the master's
> vigilant watch.
>
> At work as well as during religious ceremonies, slaves are
> constantly threatened by the whip of the commander, watched
> by the manager and the steward, and the prosecutor—always
> White. It is in such a context of violent uprooting, absolute
> control of their slightest movements, and imposition of Chris-
> tianity, that the slaves try to revive their cultural and religious
> traditions, which represent great powers of survival, both indi-
> vidual and collective. The ancestral spirits, these so-called su-
> pernatural forces, are regularly called upon and celebrated in
> secrecy, away from the masters; the sacraments of the Catholic
> Church would serve as a hiding screen and support to the Afri-
> can beliefs. (Hurbon 1993, 28)

This genesis brings out, then, the strong syncretic character of Vaudou
and other Caribbean religions. Furthermore, Gérard Barthélémy shows
how these rhythmic and danced religions would nurture the formation of
groups because, though slaves were forbidden to form groups and to organize themselves socially, "music through dancing and especially rhythmic
motions were to constitute . . . the only means of socialization since rhythm
allows the emergence of collective expression while foregoing any pre-
established social structure" (Barthélémy, n.d.). To this day, this characteristic marks the entire evolution of Vaudou: it has no centralized or single
hierarchy, which enables everybody to mingle occasionally with others
while allowing the free development of individual and family practices.

This mingling also occurs during Carnival through dancing and rhythm.
Philip and Benítez-Rojo show its importance in the Creole culture of the
Caribbean. Yet, while Benítez-Rojo tangentially refers to Carnival as a
manifestation of rhythm and performance, Philip makes it the principal
object of her essay, showing how this cultural element has imposed itself
despite governmental bans and restrictions from the eighteenth century

until today. In Haiti, Carnival has the same origin and, over the years, has become an urban event, whereas the Rara, which begins on Ash Wednesday and ends on Easter Sunday or Monday, is more rural and more clearly linked to Vaudou. In the past few years, however, this tendency has changed because of the increasing migration of the rural population to our cities, transforming Rara into a more urban phenomenon. Significantly, Carnival is now—as it was in the past—an important political issue in Haiti: any government must ensure the success of Carnival or at least provide the best conditions for its course. I would like to go even further than Philip, and point out that what happens during Carnival, at least in Haiti, is a remarkable capacity for autoregulation by thousands of men and women gathered in one place. However, this autoregulation has been less successful in the framework of the growing urban population: Haiti's recent political turmoil resulted in a lesser police presence and led to growing acts of violence during recent pre-Carnival exercises and the 1995 Carnival itself, leaving many dead and injured.

Diversity

Curiously, only two or three of the essays deal with marooning along with the process of creolization that has shaped the character of our region. In my view, however, these two processes are inseparable. If, as the essays show, creolization consisted of the gathering of scattered elements and the creation of a new coherence in accordance with history (as in the relationships among people within the space of the plantation or its surroundings), marooning, on the other hand, was an attempt—common to all lands of slavery—to create in an out-of-reach, wild space, a counterculture opposed to that of the plantation. The effect of marooning was to impose, in a more radical way, another form of cultural coherence. Although both creolization and marooning involved struggle, they involved different strategies: the first involved an indirect, insidious confrontation and a search for integration; the second a more direct, violent, and definite opposition fueled by a distinct refusal to integrate.

The weight of these elements becomes significant in the nature of the creolization of a place. For instance, while marooning had great importance in the size of the contributions of African cultures to the Cuban, Garifuna, and Haitian cultures, it was nearly absent in Barbados. In the same way, the length of the colonial presence also shapes these spaces and marks cultural differences. These differences have taken multiple forms that could be classified according to: (a) the degree of marooning, (b) differences within the same island, (c) regional characteristics, and (d) the colonizing countries.

Marooning alone represents an undeniable politicocultural catalyst. What did marooning consist of? It was the act of leaving the space of the plantation to take refuge in the mountains and create a clandestine space. It is possible to classify differences among Caribbean nations by this criterion. Some countries, such as Haiti, were strongly influenced by marooning, while others, such as Barbados, were not. Between these two extremes, we find some countries that experienced marooning to a lesser degree than Haiti—the French Antilles, for instance—as well as countries where marooning had a lesser impact because of the nature of their population and of the different origins of the less Africanized population. But we find everywhere—in the United States, in Brazil and in the other islands of the Caribbean—the same ability to organize marooning with defensive strategies (collective gardens, ambushes, surveillance of the geographic zone of retreat) as well as offensive ones (plundering of the plantations, fires, poisoning of the masters). Therefore another culture developed, a counter-plantation culture that systematically opposed plantation culture.

According to Hurbon, "What will happen in Saint Domingue from 1791 and 1793, namely the beginning of a long war for the total independence of the country that would last twelve years, was due to the singular evolution of the contradictions of slavery in this area, and not to the existence of some Black heroes or Black messiahs" (1979, 35). Indeed, it is important to remember that because of the intensification of the slave trade, the newly arrived slaves from Africa in 1770 represented more than half of the population of Saint Domingue. We find in these communities the figure of the maroon as founding base, whereas in other islands, such as Trinidad, Suriname, Barbados, or the Dominican Republic, we do not.

If in Cuba the differences between the east and west of the island created specific regional and cultural characters, in Haiti it is the difference between Creole culture and Bossale culture that takes on an obvious social relevance. Very early on, three types of Blacks could be distinguished: the freed black slaves, distinct from the Mulattoes; the Creole black slaves; and finally, the Bossale slaves. In Haiti, marooning simply curbed the process of creolization from developing to the degrees to which it developed in the countries of Latin America and elsewhere in the Caribbean. Gérard Barthélémy, in *Le pays en dehors,* has judiciously pointed out that 1804 obstructed the classic process of creolization. It is not surprising that this "creolization" from a new kind of Bossale was carried out in a completely different way than what the Creoles had known at the time of slavery. From then on, these two cultures were doomed to live alongside each other, each defining itself in relation to and against the other. This process has continued through the twentieth century and has created what Barthélémy calls an "interior colonization." Indeed, the impression is that within the same space, two great forces are mixing and clashing with each other: the Creole force will attempt to absorb most elements of Western culture to which it is closest due to its economic power, education, and phenotype, while the Bossale force will attempt to maintain its coherence—thus its strength—beyond structures of state control or any form of modern organization. Barthélémy writes:

> The Bossales, excluded from the sharing of plunder after independence, and wishing to remain that way, occupied part of the space let free by the Creoles' social advancement, therefore reinforcing the establishment of marooning. In addition to the plantations that the Creoles took over from the Whites, the Creoles inherited their language, culture, religion and state organization, while the Bossales built on this abandoned terrain a milieu (a peasantry and gardens), a religion (Vaudou), a language (Creole), and a family structure (1989, 24).

Erna Brodber brings out the existence of another regional culture, the one that links Barbados to some American colonies that were established at the same time, by the same populations, and which had never changed hands. Unlike Jamaica or Trinidad, these regions were never subjected to French, Dutch, or Spanish influences, and they never experienced marooning.

The impact of the colonizing countries upon the regions that they have dominated, and still do, is quite obvious. So obvious in fact, that even as we read the essays in this anthology—their very forms and their tensions on some specific problems—we could easily speak of anglophone, francophone, hispanophone, and Dutch Caribbean subcultures. Moreover, as we consider the process of creolization, we should ask if the *créolité* of the francophone Caribbean exactly matches the "creoleness" of the anglophone or the *creolidad* of the hispanophone islands. Indeed, tensions regarding the question of language are stronger in the francophone Caribbean, which again indicates the influence of France, so normative in this respect. As for the "creoleness" of the anglophone Caribbean, it refers more to cultural and behavioral practices than to a question of language. In the hispanophone space, as Chiqui Vicioso and Carlos Guillermo Wilson show well, the question of color seems to be a most sensitive factor, since creolization has always, more or less, officially meant the occultation of the black contribution.

Finally, I am not sure that Haiti has ever defined itself as being inherently Creole in spite of some attempts in the nineteenth century and early twentieth century to make it an illegitimate daughter of France. From the end of the nineteenth century to this day, indigenisme—whose validity under its various names (noirisme, négritude, roots), I have no intention of examining here—has always wanted to bear witness, on the political, discursive and artistic levels, to the existence of this Bossale culture.

Some Concluding Thoughts

Maximin, Roemer, Condé, Harris, and Philip bear witness to the possibility of being creative in total freedom within the Creole space. Haitian writers seem to have settled their linguistic struggles and write today in one or the other language without guilt. And the new Haitian literature emerging in English might soon succeed in sweeping away any remaining inhibitions. In this respect, the problematic raised by Pépin and Confiant does not apply to literary creation in Haiti.

To inhabit créolité is not to systematically and unconditionally praise the country, but it is "to consent to be confronted by the Universal" (Dahomey 132), since identity is acquired through the other. We can, therefore, suggest that the transformations of the past twenty years in Haiti are due to an opening of the Bossale country (by means of migration, by means of information) onto the world outside Haitian Creole and onto the world at large. A new process is here under way that deserves to be watched—the end of inner colonization, contact between the cultures of modernity and the Bossale culture. Maybe we will witness a new process of creolization, new artistic expressions, and a different dynamic in the quest of identity, since until now the question of identity has always been problematic of the island's intellectual *petit bourgeois*. The common people simply assert themselves.

Further, it is imperative that Caribbean nations avoid reducing the universal to their old colonizing country by overlooking the fact that today it is the particular story that becomes universal. But universalization must not, in any way, mean standardization, because universalization within the new world order could also signify the Americanization of the world, regardless of cultural differences. It is a matter of balancing simultaneously what is happening in Rwanda, in the former Yugoslavia, in Tchetchenia, in the Middle East, and at home. Indeed, a failure to establish a minimum of common principles regarding these events runs the risk of rendering the planet uninhabitable. These principles imply a questioning of one's own traditions as well as those of others.

Moreover, we must be wary of accepting modernity as a whole at a time when in modern societies some people are challenging (and rightly so) the very foundations of this modernity. Modernity has allowed the individual to stand out in all the magnificence of his/her freedom—and this has been exceptionally valuable at the philosophical and political levels as well as at the level of artistic creation. But individuals have forgotten, indeed rejected, other values of group solidarity and the spontaneous humanism of traditional societies. Rather than focusing on an unceasing and exclusive search for an everlasting identity, it seems to me that we should seek to create with others—all the others—a world where individualism and humanism do not exclude each other.

In this respect, Harris's analysis seems to me absolutely relevant. How, through the most deeply buried imaginary and the most archaic representations, can we recover another vision of the world that makes us aware of the unity beyond the artificial borders and the easy analogies of our mass-media culture?

Notes

Introduction

1. Translation by Balutansky and Sourieau.
2. The text of Walcott's Nobel Lecture (1993) is not paginated. In our second reference to this text, we have provided our own pagination of the published version.
3. Gilroy attributes the metaphor of the rhizome to Gilles Deleuze and Félix Guattari, who use it to express the multiramified syncretic interdependency of the cultural and ethnic dynamics in the Caribbean (see Deleuze and Guattari 1980a and 1980b).
4. With minor alterations, our translation is based on Mohamed Taleb-Khyar's translation, published as "In Praise of Creoleness" in *Callaloo* 13/4 (903).
5. We are indebted to the participants at the April 1995 conference on Creole Cultures in Latin America and the Caribbean, held at the University of Delaware, whose discussions of the terms *Creole* and *creolization* clearly pointed to the ongoing questions and disparities regarding these terms in historical, cultural, and linguistic studies. We are particularly grateful to Franklin W. Knight, who generously shared with us a manuscript version of his chapter "Pluralism, Creolization, and Culture," in which he outlines the historical and cultural development of these terms. This chapter has been published in the *UNESCO General History of the Caribbean*, vol. 3 (1997).
6. We could also mention writers like Earl Lovelace, Erna Brodber, Jamaica Kincaid, Michelle Cliff, and many others from the anglophone islands; or novelists Maryse Condé, Simone Schwarz-Bart, Marie Chauvet, Edouard Glissant, Patrick Chamoiseau, among other francophone writers; or Alejo Carpentier, Carlos Guillermo Wilson, Rosario Ferré, Ana Lydia Vega, Julia Alvarez, among other hispanophone writers.
7. As cited in Staples (1).
8. Naipaul's various positions on what he considers to be the tragic history of the Caribbean are well documented in his own novels and essays, and most Caribbeanists have argued that Naipaul sees the Caribbean from the outside—that he evaluates its history and cultural manifestations from a Eurocentric position. Though Naipaul's perspective has changed over the years, a recent

articulation of his position vis-à-vis the multiplicity of the Caribbean is quite revealing of his skepticism regarding the search for identity (see Cessole 5).

9. We place the term *post-colonial* in quotation marks because the validity of these concepts in relation to the Caribbean has already been challenged, both in their theoretical use and as descriptions of reality. See, for instance, the essays in the special issue of *Callaloo* (16/4) on "Post-Colonial Discourse."

10. For an example (among many) of the exploration of the phenomenon of cultural syncretism, see Clifford (1988).

Antillean Journey

1. Translation by Eshleman and Smith.
2. In Damas (1972, 43), translation by Balutansky and Sourieau.
3. In Damas (1972, 74), translation by Balutansky and Sourieau.
4. *Lucioles* was a short-lived literary journal published in Fort-de-France, Martinique, in 1927.
5. From Leiner's interview in *Tropiques* 14. This is a reprint of the literary journal published in Fort-de-France between 1939 and 1944.
6. Translation by Eshleman and Smith (38–40).
7. In Damas (1972, 119), translation by Balutansky and Sourieau.
8. Translation by Balutansky and Sourieau.

Chapter 2: The Caribbean: Marvelous Cradle-Hammock and Painful Cornucopia

1. This information is gleaned from the following works of scholars of Garifuna culture: Lopez Garcia, Suazo, Savaranga, Avila; I also refer to the papers of Melecio R. Gonzales and Jorge Bernardez in the Primero and Segundo Encuentro Cumbre Garifuna, held in New York in 1991 and Los Angeles in 1992, respectively.
2. As a Sevillian soldier, Las Casas had participated in the killings and conquests of the Indians in Quisqueya and Cuba; he later became the first ordained Dominican Catholic priest in the New World, the Apostle of the Indians, and later the Bishop of Chiapas (see Sauer).
3. For more details of this practice, see Jackson (1988) and Birmingham-Pokorny (1993).
4. The works I refer to here are my novels *Chombo* (1981) and *Los nietos de Felicidad Dolores* (1991) and my poems "In Exilium," and "Desarraigado" (*Pensamientos* 1977).

Chapter 3: Who's Afraid of the Winti Spirit?

1. It appears that Winti is a very old form of religious experience. For instance, in the Old Testament, it is introduced for the first time in the mention of ecstatic groups of people who, through the rhythm of music, brought themselves into

a trance during which individuals spoke in another voice; no doubt, people originally thought that it was the voice of the local god (1 Samuel 10:5–6). Winti is experienced and interpreted in exactly the same way.

2. In a search for notions of humanity all over the world, Fons Elders, a Dutch professor, wrote an interesting article about the Dogon people of Mali, "The Hidden Qualities of an African World View," which offers remarkable similarities with the Winti philosophy that bear quoting at length. I cite from the unpublished manuscript:

> The first striking feature is a profound spirituality, a characteristic which is difficult to grasp by our secularist profane outlook on reality, and by our individualistic life experience. . . . A central notion in the world view of the Dogon is AMMA. AMMA, a sound and a word that show a perfect symmetry from right to left and from left to right, is usually translated with God, and subsequently interpreted as the closest analogy of the Dogon religion with the Christian or Moslim notion of God. The question remains whether this notion can be interpreted as an analogon to the notion of a transcendent god or principle, or whether it has to be understood as a unifying, more immanent idea. . . . During a dialogue with our guide Amadinge who cooperated with Griaule for his Dictionaire de Dogon, we asked him about Amma. Referring to Amma as God, as Marcel Griaule happens to do, Amadinge answered my question positively about Amma as God. However, when I quoted the same Griaule, who writes that Amma is also referred to as air, water, fire and earth, he answered that this is right. When I then asked him if we humans are also air, water, fire and earth, he confirmed this statement. On the question if we are also Amma, if both can be described as air, water, fire and earth, he said, literally: "We are also Amma." From this explanation I am inclined to deduce that the hypothesis of a unifying concept such as Amma has to be understood as an immanent reality, perhaps not so different from Spinoza's Natura naturans, natara naturata—nature being its own subject and object. This interpretation fits into the description of the African spirituality where the polarity of give and take is so strikingly present.

Chapter 4: Three Words toward Creolization

1. The word *criollo* (antecedent to *Créole* and *Creole* appears for the first time in Mexico in *Geografia y descripción general de las Indias* (1571–74) by Juan López de Velasco (see Arrom). In Cuba it appears in a document of March 1607, upon

the confiscation of the departing governor Pedro de Valdés' ship *La Criolla*, built in Havana around 1605.

Chapter 5: Dominicanyorkness: A Metropolitan Discovery of the Triangle

1. A plant with big, white, bell-shaped flowers.
2. Italics indicate that the passage is in English in the original.
3. Caribbean food.
4. Caribbean food.
5. Religious ceremony of the Taino people, which tells their oral history, accompanied by drums and maracas.
6. Deities in the Afro-Caribbean religion of Santería.
7. Patriots from the Dominican Republic.
8. Julia de Burgos, a poet from Puerto Rico.

Chapter 7: A Brief History of My Country

1. A song and dance ritual of the Tainos.

Chapter 8: Writing and Creole Language Politics: Voice and Story

1. In this essay, *Kriol*, the Folk Research Centre spelling, refers to the languages influenced by French and Creole to those influenced by English.
2. See, for example, Allsopp, Dalphinis, and Devonish.
3. News item, Grenada Broadcasting Corporation, June 10–17, 1994.
4. In Grenada, the late C. A. Francis has left a considerable amount of unedited, unpublished research on Grenadian Creole.
5. For discussion of the concept "nation language," see Brathwaite (1993).
6. A reference to efforts made by the Alliance Française to organize gathering of Kriol speakers.

Chapter 9: The Stakes of Créolité

1. In *Éloge*, the authors created a stir by declaring themselves Creoles and claiming as the foundation of their Caribbeanness the *interactional* or *transactional aggregate* of Caribbean, European, African, Asian, and Levantine cultural elements united on the same soil by the yoke of history. Though they acknowledged their debt to Edouard Glissant and other predecessors, they affirmed that their definition of Caribbeanness went beyond that defined by Glissant in *Le discours antillais*.

Chapter 10: Créolité without the Creole Language?

1. See Césaire (1978, 1988, 1989).
2. See Harris (1960 and 1990); see also Drake (1986).

Chapter 11: The Victory of the Concubines and the Nannies

1. Cola Debrot's novel, *Mijn zuster de Negerin* (1935), was translated into English by Estelle Reed as *My Sister the Negro* (*Antillianese Cahiers* 3 [2 June 1958]).

2. Francesco Carletti's travelogue was first published in Italian in 1958 as *Ragionamenti del mio viaggioo intorno al mondo* and translated into Dutch by J. A. Verhaart-Bodderij (The Hague: Kruseman's Uitgeversmastschappij N., 1965). The English translations from Dutch are by Frank Martinus Arion.

3. See for instance, Beryl Gilroy's historical novel, *Stedman and Joanna: A Love in Bondage* (New York: Vantage Press, 1991).

4. Gilberto Freyre's study *Casa grande e Senzala* (1933) was translated into English as *Masters and Slaves: A Study in the Development of Brazilian Civilization* (New York: A. Knopf, 1946).

5. I discuss many such rhymes in *Krioolse Kinderrijmen in het Nederlands en de oorsprong van de Limerick* (*Creole Nursery Rhymes in Dutch and the Origin of the Limerick*). In *Homenahe na Raul Romer.* (Instituto Lingwistio Antiano [I.L.A.], 1989).

Chapter 13: Race, Space, and the Poetics of Moving

1. The Trinidad Carnival is referred to as Carnival in all subsequent references.

2. Ezra Pound, in his work *The ABC of Writing*, defined languages according to their most distinctive features: phanopoesis, beautiful to look at (Chinese); melopoesis, beautiful sounding (Greek); and logopoesis, logical (English). I have added the quality of kinopoesis, dynamic and quick moving (African).

3. A circular movement made with the hips during dancing that is integral to African-Canadian dance.

4. To play marse is to take part in the Carnival parade, usually wearing a costume.

5. Under colonial regimes civil servants from England were granted extended holidays to return home. The practice was known as "home leave" and was continued after independence when the civil servants were no longer English but from the former colony itself. "Long leave" was used synonymously for "home leave."

6. This avenue is situated within the business area of the City of Toronto; down its center are to be found several statues commemorating Canadian participation in World War I and World War II.

7. Head covering worn by South Asian women in Trinidad.

8. Carnival festivities begin at 6:00 A.M. on the Monday before Ash Wednesday. This is referred to as jourvert or jouvay, from the French *jour ouvert:* open day.

9. "Behind the bridge" is a colloquial expression for the socially and economically depressed area in Port of Spain also known as Laventille.

10. Eshu-Elegbara is regarded by the Yoruba of Nigeria as the god of the crossroads as well as a messenger of the gods.

11. Instituted by Spain in 1783, the Cedula of population stipulated that only Catholic immigrants could enter Trinidad.

12. Toussaint l'Ouverture and Jean Jacques Dessalines were liberators of Saint Domingue from French rule, making the Haitian revolution the only successful slave revolt in history. Haiti was the second country, after the United States, to achieve independence in the New World.

13. Yoruba words meaning destruction.

14. The cultures of Guinea, Dahomey, the Yoruba, and Ibo of Nigeria as well as the Ashanti of Ghana were the sources of these dances and rituals.

15. For the five years prior to 1838—the year slavery was finally abolished—slaves were supposed to serve an apprenticeship period in preparation for freedom. During apprenticeship their lives were little different from when they were slaves.

16. As quoted in the Pearse, "Carnival in Nineteenth-Century Trinidad," *Caribbean Quarterly* 4, nos. 3 and 4 (1956): 22.

17. Moko Jumbies in colorful costumes played (and still play) marse on stilts.

18. Familiar and traditional folk figures derived from the African pantheon of gods who were an integral part of Carnival. Papa Bois's home was the woods, and he was considered the protector of animals; Mama Deleau was literally mother of the waters. The Jab Molassi, meaning "molasses devil," roamed the streets demanding money and frightening spectators.

19. Caribbean demotic word for a white person.

20. After the abolition of slavery, the colonial governments brought in indentured workers from India to work on the sugar plantations.

21. Musical bands in which the instruments are pieces of bamboo, cut at different lengths, which the players strike against the ground. The sound varies depending on the length of the bamboo.

22. Pan was formerly known as "steel pan," because steel drums (used to ship oil) were initially tuned and used as musical instruments.

23. The *sans humanité* (without humanity) tradition is one in which calypsonians sang in a fearless manner about any subject.

24. Initially, tents (usually bamboo and coconut) were erected during Carnival season so that calypsonians could perform. Even though calypsonians no longer now perform in tents, their performance venues are still called tents.

25. Sharp, satirical wit.

26. In the calypso "Jean and Dinah," the calypsonian The Mighty Sparrow sang of American sailors and soldiers leaving Trinidad, where the United States held a military base, which resulted in the lowering of rates from prostitutes.

27. Winston "Spree" Simon is credited for the creation of pan.

28. On August 31, 1962, Dr. Eric Williams led the nation of Trinidad and Tobago to independence.

29. Bonnie Barthold makes this argument in *Black Time: Fiction of Africa, the U.S. and the Caribbean* (New Haven: Yale University Press, 1991).

30. The movement of the hips backward and forward during dancing, simulating the sexual act.

31. Chantwells, or singers, eventually developed into calypsonians.

32. The Mighty Sparrow, in "Jean and Dinah."

33. A gumbo-type dish.

34. At jourvert celebrations masqueraders are said to be playing "ole marse," arising out of the tradition of wearing old clothes. This is in contrast to "fancy marse," or "pretty marse," which happens later in the day on Monday and on Tuesday, when masqueraders wear costumes that are usually highly decorated.
35. Romaine Pitt, in an interview with the writer in Toronto in 1991.
36. An expressway named after the fact that it runs along the shoreline of Lake Ontario in the city of Toronto.
37. Sam Lewis, in an interview with the Canadian Broadcasting Corporation (CBC) on 2 August 1991 in Toronto.
38. According to research carried out in 1990 by Decima Research, Caribana generated $187 million in that year. As of 1994, the figure has exceeded $200 million.
39. Caribbean demotic word meaning economic hardship.

Works Cited

Allsopp, Richard. 1972. *Why a Dictionary of Caribbean English Usage?* Cave Hill: University of the West Indies, Caribbean Lexicography Project.

Alonso, Manuel. [1849] 1967. *El Gibaro: Cuadro costumbres de la isla de Puerto Rico.* Facsimile. San Juan: Institute of Puerto Rican Culture.

Antoni, Robert. 1992. *Divina Trace.* Woodstock, N.Y.: Overlook Press.

Archer, Marie-Thérèse. 1986. *La créologie haïtienne.* Port-au-Prince: Le Natal.

Arrom, José Juan. 1971. "Criollo: Definición y matices de un concepto." In *Certidumbre de América.* Madrid: Gredos.

Ashcroft, Bill, Gareth Griffiths, and Helen Tiffin. 1989. *The Empire Writes Back.* London and New York: Routledge.

Avila, José Francisco, ed. 1991. *U.S.A. Garifuna.* Allen, Tex.: Avila.

Barros, J. 1987. *Haïti de 1804 à nos jours.* Paris: L'Harmattan.

Barthélémy, Gérard. N.d. "L'esclave debout." Unpublished manuscript.

———. 1989. *Le pays en dehors.* Port-au-Prince: Editions Deschamp.

Barthold, Bonnie. 1991. *Black Time: Fiction of Africa, the U.S., and the Caribbean.* New Haven: Yale University Press.

Bazin, Jean, and Alba Benza. 1976. Preface to *La Raison graphique* by Jack Goody. Paris: Minuit.

Benítez-Rojo, Antonio. 1992. *The Repeating Island.* Translated by James Maraniss. Durham and London: Duke University Press.

Bentolila, Alain. 1976. *Petit dictionnaire Créole-Francais.* Paris: Hatier/Caraïbes.

Bernabé, Jean, Patrick Chamoiseau, and Raphaël Confiant. 1989. *Éloge de la créolité.* Paris: Gallimard.

Birmingham-Pokorny, Elba, ed. 1993. *Denouncement and Reaffirmation of Afro-Hispanic Identity in Carlos Guillermo Wilson's Works.* Miami: Ediciones Universal.

Bolivar, Simon. 1951. "Message to the Congress of Angostura." In *Selected Writings of Bolivar,* vol. 1: *1810–1822,* edited by Vicente Lecuna and Harold A. Bierck Jr. New York: Colonial Press.

Boxer, Charles Ralph. 1963. *Race Relations in the Portuguese Colonial Empire, 1415–1825.* Oxford: Clarendon.

Brathwaite, Edward Kamau. 1971. *The Development of Creole Society in Jamaica, 1770–1820.* Oxford: Clarendon.

————. 1993. *History of the Voice: The Development of Nation Language in Anglophone Caribbean Poetry.* London: New Beacon.

Breton, Marcela, ed. 1995. *Rhythm and Revolt: Tales of the Antilles.* New York: Plume.

Cabrera, Lydia. 1970. *La sociedad secreta abakua narrada por viejos adeptos.* Miami: Chichereku.

————. 1980. *Yemaya y Ochun.* Miami: Chichereku.

Carletti, Francesco. 1965. *Ragionamenti del mio viaggioo intorno al mondo.* Translated into Dutch by J. A. Verhaart-Bodderij. The Hague: Kruseman's Uitgeversmast-schappij N.

"A Carnival under Siege." 1991. *Spare Rib* (September).

Castellanos, Jorge. 1984. *Placido.* Miami: Ediciones Universal.

Cérol, Marie-Josée [Ama Mazama]. 1992. "Introduction au Créole Guadeloupéen." In *L'Héritage de Caliban.* Pointe-à-Pitre: Editions Jasor.

Césaire, Aimé. 1983. *Aimé Césaire: The Collected Poetry.* Edited by Clayton Eshleman and Annette Smith. Berkeley: University of California Press.

————. 1988. *Cahier d'un retour au pays natal.* Paris: Présence Africaine.

————. 1978. "Entretien avec Aimé Césaire par Jacqueline Leiner." *Tropiques.* Paris: Réedition Jean-Michel Place.

————. 1989. *Et les chiens se taisaint.* Paris: Présence Africaine.

Cessole, Bruno, de. 1995. Interview avec V. S. Naipaul. *Le Figaro Littéraire* 20 (April).

Chamoiseau, Patrick. 1992. *Texaco.* Paris: Gallimard.

Chaudenson, Robert. 1978. "Créole et langage enfantin: Phylogenèse et ontogenèse." *Langue française* 37.

————. "Les langues Créoles." 1992. *La Recherche* 248, vol. 23 (November).

Clifford, James. 1988. *The Predicament of Culture: Twentieth-Century Ethnography, Literature, and Art.* Cambridge, Mass.: Harvard University Press.

Confiant, Raphaël. 1988. *Le nègre et l'amiral.* Paris: Grasset.

Cozigon, Paul. 1993. *La République Haïtienne.* Paris: Karthala.

Cruz, Isabelo Zenon. 1974–75. *Narciso descubre su trasero.* Humacaco, P.R.: Editorial Furidi.

Cubena [Carlos Guillermo Wilson]. 1981. *Chombo.* Miami: Ediciones Universal.

————. 1991. *Los nietos de Felicidad Dolores.* Miami: Ediciones Universal.

————. 1977. *Pensamientos del Negro Cubena.* Los Angeles.

Cudjoe, Selwyn R., ed. 1990. *Caribbean Women Writers: Essays from the First International Conference.* Wellsley, Mass.: Calaloux.

D'Aguiar, Fred. 1994. *The Longest Memory.* New York: Pantheon.

D'Ans, André Marcel. 1968. *Le Créole français d'Haiti.* Paris: Mouton.

Dahomey, Jacky. "Habiter la créolité ou le heurt de l'universel." *Chemins critiques: Revue Haitiano-Caribéenne* 1/3 (December 1989): 109–34.

Dalphinis, Morgan. 1981. "African Language Influences in Creoles Lexically Based on Portuguese, English, and French, with Special Reference to Casamance Kriol, Gambia Krio, and St. Lucia Patwa." Ph.D. diss., University of London.

Damas, Léon-Gontran. 1972. *Pigments/Névralgies.* Paris: Présence Africaine.

———. 1947. *Poètes d'expression Française 1900–1945.* Paris: Editions du Seuil.

Dance, Daryl. 1992. *New World Adams: Conversations with Contemporary West Indian Writers.* Leeds: Peepal Tree.

d'Ans, André-Marcel. 1987. *Haïti, Paysage et société.* Paris: Karthala.

Danticat, Edwige. 1994. *Breath, Eyes, Memory.* New York: SOHO.

———. 1995. *Krik? Krak!* New York: SOHO.

Davies, Carol Boyce, and Elaine Savory Fido, eds. 1990. *Out of the Kumbla: Caribbean Women and Literature.* Trenton: Africa World Press.

Debrot, Cola. [1935]. *Mijn zuster de Negerin.* Amsterdam. Translated by Estelle Reed as *My Sister the Negress. Antilliaanse Cahiers* 3/2 (June 1958).

Deleuze, Gilles, and Félix Guattari. 1980a. *Mille Plateaux.* Paris: Minuit.

———. 1980b. "Rhizome." *Ideology and Consciousness* 8.

Depestre, René. 1994. "Les Aventures de la créolité." In *Ecrire la parole de la nuit: La nouvelle littérature antillaise,* edited by Ralph Ludwig. Paris: Gallimard.

Devonish, Hubert. 1986. *Language and Liberation: Creole Language Politics in the Caribbean.* London: Karia.

Dieudonné, Jean. 1987. *Pour l'honneur de l'esprit humain.* Paris: Hachette.

Drake, Sandra. 1986. *Wilson Harris and the Modern Tradition.* New York: Greenwood.

Drewal, Margaret. 1989. "Dancing for Ogun in Yorubaland and in Brazil." In *Africa's Ogun,* edited by Sandra T. Barnes. Bloomington: Indiana University Press.

Dunham, Catherine. 1983. *Dances of Haiti.* Los Angeles: Unversity of California Center for Afro-American Studies.

Eshleman, Clayton, and Annette Smith. 1992. *Lyric and Dramatic Poetry, 1946–1982.* Charlottesville: University Press of Virginia.

Espinet, Ramabai, ed. 1990. *Creation Fire: A CAFRA Anthology of Caribbean Women's Poetry.* Toronto: Sister Vision.

Esteves, Carmen C., and Lizabeth Paravisini-Gebert, eds. 1991. *Green Cane and Juicy Flotsam: Short Stories by Caribbean Women.* New Brunswick: Rutgers University Press.

Ferguson, Moira. 1992. *Subject to Others: British Women Writers and Colonial Slavery, 1670–1834.* New York and London: Routledge.

Fignolé, Jean-Claude. 1991. "Une poétique de la schizophrénie." *Revista Cultural del IFAL* 10 (Winter).

Firmin, Anténor. 1910. *Lettres de Saint-Thomas.* Paris.

Freyre, Gilberto. [1933]. *Casa grande e Senzala.* Translated as *Masters and Slaves: A Study in the Development of Brazilian Civilization.* New York: Knopf, 1946.

Galan, Natalio. 1993. *Cuba y sus sones.* Valencia: Soler.

Garcia, Cristina. 1992. *Dreaming in Cuban.* New York: Ballantine.

Gilroy, Beryl. 1991. *Stedman and Joanna—A Love in Bondage: Dedicated Love in the Eighteenth Century.* New York: Vantage Press.

Gilroy, Paul. 1993. *The Black Atlantic: Modernity and Double Consciousness.* Cambridge, Mass.: Harvard University Press.

Glissant, Edouard. 1964. *Le quatrième siècle.* Paris: Editions du Seuil.

———. 1975. *Malemort.* Paris: Editions du Seuil.

———. 1981. *Le discours antillais*. Paris: Editions du Seuil.

———. 1990. *Poétique de la relation*. Paris: Gallimard.

González, José Luis. 1989. *El pais de cuatro pisos y otros ensayos*. Rio Piedras, P.R.: Ediciones Huracan.

Gratiant, Gilbert. 1927. *Lucioles*.

Harris, Wilson. 1990. *The Four Banks of the River Space*. London: Faber and Faber.

———. 1960. *The Palace of the Peacock*. London: Faber and Faber.

———. 1983. *The Womb of Space: The Cross-Cultural Imagination*. Westport: Greenwood.

Hurbon, Lahenec. 1979. *Culture et dictature en Haiti*. Port-au-Prince: Editions Deschamp.

———. 1993. *Les mystères du vaudou*. Paris: Editions Gallimard.

Jackson, Richard L. 1988. *Black Literature and Humanism in Latin America*. Athens: University of Georgia Press.

Jourdain, Elodie. 1946. "Le Créole de la Martinique." Ph.D. diss., Université de la Sorbonne.

Kent, George E. 1973. "A Conversation with George Lamming." *Black World* 22/5 (March).

Khyar, Mohamed B. Taleb. 1990. "In Praise of Creoleness." Translation of Bernabé, Chamoiseau, and Confiant's *Eloge de la créolité*. *Callaloo* 13/4 (Fall).

Kortenaar, Neil Ten. 1995. "Beyond Authenticity and Creolization: Reading Achebe Writing Culture." *PMLA* 110/1 (January): 30–42.

Kristeva, Julia. 1986. *The Julia Kristeva Reader*. Edited by Toril Moi. London: Blackwell.

Kundera, Milan. 1991. "Beau comme une rencontre multiple." *L'Infini* 34: 50–62.

———. 1993. *Les testaments trahis*. Paris: Gallimard.

Lahens, Yanick. 1990. *Entre l'ancrage et la fuite: l'écrivain haitien*. Port-au-Prince: Editions Deschamp.

Lamming, George. 1984. *The Pleasures of Exile*. London and New York: Allison and Busby.

La Rose, John. 1990. *Kaiso Calypso Music: David Rudder in Conversation with John La Rose*. London: New Beacon.

Las Casas, Bartolomé, de. 1965. *Historia de las Indias*. Mexico City: Fondo de Cultura Economica.

Leiner, Jacqueline. 1978. "Entretien avec Aimé Césaire par Jacqueline Leiner." *Tropiques*. Paris: Jean-Michel Place.

Lionnet, Françoise. 1989. *Autobiographical Voices*. Ithaca: Cornell University Press.

Lopez Garcia, Victor Virgilio. 1991. *Lamumehan Garifuna: Clamoo Garifuaa*. Tela, Honduras: Tornabé.

Lovelace, Earl. 1981. *The Dragon Can't Dance*. Essex: Longman.

Marrero, Levi. 1974. *Cuba: Economia y sociedad II*. Madrid: Playor.

———. 1976. *Cuba: Economia y sociedad V*. Madrid: Playor.

Martinus, Frank [Arion]. 1989. *Krioolse Kinderrijmen in het Nederlands en de oorsprong van de Limerick* [Creole Nursery Rhymes in Dutch and the Origin of the Limerick]. In *Homenahe na Raul Romer*. Amsterdam: Instituto Lingwistio Antiano.

Megenny, William W. 1993. "Common Words of African Origin Used in Latin America." *Hispania* 66 (March): 1–10.

Mordecai, Pamela, and Betty Wilson, eds. 1989. *Her True True Name: An Anthology of Women's Writing from the Caribbean*. Oxford: Heinemann International.

Morejon, Nancy. 1982. *Nacion y Mestizaje en Nicolas Guillén*. Havana: Union.

Morris, Merwyn, ed. 1990. *Contemporary Caribbean Short Stories*. London: Faber and Faber.

Mosonyi, Esteban Emilio. 1993. "Nuestro Legado Linguistico Africano." *Africamérica* 1/1 (January): 22–26.

Naipaul, V. S. 1959. *The Mystic Masseur*. New York: Vanguard.

Nichols, Grace. 1983. *I Is a Long Memoried Woman*. London: Karnac House.

Nugent, Lady Maria. 1966. *Journal of a Voyage to and Residence in the Islands of Jamaica*. Edited by Philip Wright. Kingston.

Opie, Iona, and Peter Opie. 1980. *The Oxford Dictionary of Nursery Rhymes*. Oxford: Oxford University Press.

Ortiz, Fernando. 1960. *La antiqua fiesta afrocubana del Dia de Reyes*. Havana: Ministerio de Relaciones Exteriores.

———. 1981. *Los bailes y el teatro de los negros en el folklore de Cuba*. Havana: Letras Cubanas.

Orville, Xavier. 1977. *Délices et le fromager*. Paris: Bernard Grasset.

———. 1989. *Laissez brûler Laventurcia*. Paris: Bernard Grasset.

———. 1979. *La tapisserie du temps présent*. Paris: Bernard Grasset.

Owusu, Kwesi. 1986. *The Struggle for Black Arts in Britain*. London: Comedia.

Pépin, Ernest. 1992. *L'homme au bâton*. Paris: Gallimard.

———. 1995. *Coulée d'or*. Paris: Gallimard.

———. 1996. *Tambour-Babel*. Paris: Gallimard.

Perse, Saint-John. 1960. *Eloge*. Paris: Gallimard.

Phillips, Caryl. 1994. *Crossing the River*. London: Picador.

Pividal, Raphaël. 1976. *La Maison de l'écriture*. Paris: Editions du Seuil.

Placoly, Vincent. 1983. *Frères Volcans*. Paris: Editions la Brèche.

Porras, Jorge E. "The Spanish Language in the Americas 500 Years After: Unity Within Diversity." 1993. *Diaspora: Journal of the Annual Afro-Hispanic Literature and Culture Conference* 2/2 (Spring): 181.

"Port of Spain Gazette of 1858." 1956. *Caribbean Quarterly* 4.

"Post-Colonial Discourse." 1993. *Callaloo* 16/4 (Fall). Special issue.

Ramchand, Kenneth. 1983. *The West Indian Novel and Its Background*. London: Heinemann.

Rhys, Jean. 1966. *Wide Sargasso Sea*. London: Deutsch/New York: Norton.

Robbe-Grillet, Alain. 1961. *Pour un Nouveau Roman*. Paris: Editions de Minuit.

Rohlehr, Gordon. 1992. "Pelvis Festival." *Sunday Express* (March 1).

Rout, Leslie B., Jr. 1976. *The African Experience in Spanish America*. Cambridge: Cambridge University Press.

Rowell, Charles, ed. 1995. *The Ancestral House: The Black Short Story in the Americas and Europe*. Boulder: Westview.

Rudder, David, with John La Rose. 1990. *Kaiso Calypso Music: David Rudder in Conversation with John La Rose*. London: New Beacon.

Sauer, Carl Ortwin. 1984. *Descubrimiento y dominacion Espanola del Caribe*. Translated by S. Mastrangelo. Mexico: Fondo de Cultura Economica.

Savaranga, Crisanto Uayujuru. 1992. "Conferencia de la cosmovision historica, cultural del pueblo kaliponan (garifuna) kalinagus (garinagus) de Honduras," Tegucigalpa, Honduras, June 17.

Schwarz-Bart, Simone. 1972. *Pluie et vent sur Télumée Miracle*. Paris: Editions du Seuil.

Selvon, Samuel. 1956. *The Lonely Londoners*. London: Heinemann.

Smorkaloff, Pamela Maria, ed. 1994. *If I Could Write This in Fire: An Anthology of Literature from the Caribbean*. New York: New Press.

Staples, Brent. "Con Men and Conquerors." 1994. *New York Times Book Review* (May 22), 1.

Suazo, Salvador. 1991. *Conversemos en garifuna*. Tegucigalpa, Honduras: Editorial Guaymuras.

Todd, Loreto. 1974. *Pidgins and Creoles*. London and Boston: Routledge and Kegan Paul.

Vaval, Duraciné. [1933] 1971. *Histoire de la littérature haïtienne ou "l'âme noire."* Nendeln: Kraus Reprint.

Wa Thiong'o, Ngugi. 1986. *Decolonizing the Mind: The Politics of Language in African Literature*. London: Currey.

Walcott, Derek. 1993. *The Antilles: Fragments of Epic Memory*. New York: Farrar, Strauss and Giroux.

———. 1975. "On Choosing Port of Spain." In *David Frost Introduces Trinidad and Tobago*, edited by Michael Anthony and Andrew Carr. London: Deutsch.

Contributors

Frank Martinus Arion is the pen name of Frank Martinus, who was born and raised in Curaçao (Netherlands Antilles). From 1971 to 1981 he was Professor of Linguistics and Creole Studies at the University of Amsterdam and subsequently in Suriname. Currently Director of the Institute of Ancient Languages at the University of Curaçao, he lectures extensively in the Caribbean. Martinus Arion has published several studies on Creole linguistics. His major work, *Bibliography of Papiamento* (1972), has been reprinted as *Bibliography of Creole Languages* (1975). Excerpts of his novel *Double Play* appeared in *Callaloo* 11/3 (Spring 1988). His novels in Dutch, *Goodbye to the Queen* (1975) and *Noble Savages* (1979), have not yet been translated into English.

Kathleen M. Balutansky is Associate Professor of English at Saint Michael's College, where she teaches twentieth-century and Caribbean literature. She is the author of *The Novels of Alex La Guma: The Representation of a Political Conflict* (1990) and of several articles on anglophone and francophone Caribbean women writers.

Antonio Benítez-Rojo is a Cuban writer of fiction and an authority in the field of Caribbean studies. Until 1980 he lived in Havana, where he was Director of the Editorial Department of Casa de las Americas and later of the Centro de Estudios del Caribe. In 1980 he moved to the United States, where he teaches Hispano-American literature at Amherst College. He is the author of *La isla que se repite: El Caribe y la perspectiva postmoderna* (1989), the introduction of which was listed among the most notable essays in *Best American Essay* 1986 and *Pushcart Prize* 11. This book was translated by James Maraniss as *The Repeating Island: The Caribbean and the Postmodern Perspective* (1992). Benítez-Rojo's collections of short stories include *Tute de* *reyes* (1967), *El Escudo de hojas secas* (1968), *Heroica* (1977), *Fruta verde* (1980) and *The Magic Dog and Other Stories* (1990). A novel, *Sea of Lentils*, originally published in Spanish in 1985, was translated into English in 1990.

Elba D. Birmingham-Pokorny is Professor of Spanish in the Department of English and Foreign Languages at Southern Arkansas University. She is the founder and editor of the journal *Diaspora*, and she has translated Carlos Guillermo Wilson's *Pensamientos del negro Cubena* (1990) and edited two collections of essays, *Denouncement and Reaffirmation of the Afro-Hispanic Identity in Carlos Guillermo Wilson's Works* (1993) and *An English Anthology of Afro-Hispanic Writers of the Twentieth Century.*

Wanda Boeke received her degree from the Translation Program at the University of Iowa and has produced literary translations in the Netherlands, France, and Spain. Her translations of poetry, short stories, and articles have also appeared in Great Britain and the United States in such publications as *Greenfield Review, Poetry International,* and *Dutch Crossing.* Boeke has provided first-time translations of the works of Dutch poet Elly de Waard and novelist Renate Dorrestein.

Erna Brodber was born in Jamaica. She studied history and sociology at the University of the West Indies and social psychology at McGill University and at the University of Washington. Brodber is now a member of the Department of Sociology at the University of the West Indies in Mona. She has published two novels, *Jane and Louisa Will Soon Come Home* (1980) and *Myal* (1988). Her scholarly publications include *Perceptions of Caribbean Women: Towards a Documentation of Stereotypes* (1982).

Maria Cristina Canales is Chair of the Department of Foreign Languages and International Studies at Elms College. A specialist of francophone and hispanophone Caribbean literature, she is a cowriter of a book on oral tradition from Guatemala entitled *Gracias, Matiox, Thanks, Hermano Pedro: A Trilingual Anthology of Guatemalan Oral Tradition* (1996).

Merle Collins was born, raised, and educated in Grenada. She now lives in England. Her collection of poetry, *Because Dawn Breaks* (1985), was followed by the novel *Angel* (1987). She also coedited the anthology *Watchers and Seekers: Creative Writing by Black Women in Britain* (1987).

Maryse Condé was born in Guadeloupe. She studied in France, lived many years in Ghana and Senegal, where she taught French literature, and returned to France in 1972 to study for her doctorate in comparative litera-ture. She taught Afro-Caribbean literature at the Sorbonne in Paris and later at the University of California at Berkeley, the University of Mary-land, the University of Virginia, and Harvard University. Currently she is Professor of Comparative Literature at Columbia. Maryse Condé is known as a literary critic (especially of Caribbean poetry, fiction, and women's writing), novelist, and playwright. Her novels include *Une saison à Rihata* (1981); *Ségou* (2 vols., 1984–85), translated into English as *Segu* by Bar-bara Bray (1987); *Moi, Tituba sorcière* (1986), translated as *I, Tituba Witch of Salem* (1992); *La vie scélérate* (1987), translated as *The Tree of Life* (1992); *En attendant le bonheur* (Heremakhonon) (1988); *Traversée de la mangrove* (1989), translated as *The Crossing of the Mangrove* (1994); *Les derniers rois mages* (1992); *La colonie du Nouveau Monde* (1993); and *La migration des coeurs* (1995).

Raphaël Confiant is from Martinique. He is an essayist and novelist whose work has recently focused on the problematics of "creoleness" in the francophone Caribbean. With Jean Bernabé and Patrick Chamoiseau, Confiant coauthored an essay entitled "Eloge de la créolité" (1989), which was translated into English as "In Praise of Creoleness" (*Callaloo* 13/4). Recently Confiant and Chamoiseau collaborated on a long essay entitled "Lettres créoles" (1991), on creolization in its historical context. Confiant wrote five works of fiction in Creole before publishing three novels in French: *Le Nègre et l'amiral* (1988), *Eau de café* (1991), and *L'Allée des soupirs* (1994).

Robert M. Fedorchek is Professor of Spanish in the Department of Modern Languages and Literatures at Fairfield University. He is the translator of several books of nineteenth-century Spanish short stories, and of a Portu-guese text, *Alves & Co.*, by Jose Maria Eca de Queiros. He has also pub-lished translations and articles in such journals as *Archivum, Hispania, Luso-Brazilian Review, Revista de estudios hispanicos, Romance Notes,* and *Romance Quarterly.*

Wilson Harris was born in Guyana. After attending King's College in Guyana, he practiced land surveying for the Guyanese government until 1958. That year he migrated to England, where he started his fiction-writing career with *The Palace of the Peacock* (1960). This novel was followed by many others, including *The Waiting Room* (1967), *The Age of the Rainmakers* (1971), *The Angels at the Gate* (1982), *Carnival* (1985), *The Four Banks of the River of Space* (1990), to name but a few. Harris's scholarly publications include *Traditions, the Writer, and Society: Critical Essays* (1967), *Explorations* (1981),

The Womb of Space: The Cross-Cultural Imagination (1983), and *The Radical Imagination* (1992). His most recent novel, *Resurrection at Sorrow Hill*, was published in 1993.

Luis A. Jiménez is Chair of Spanish in the Department of Modern Languages at Florida Southern College. He has edited, translated, and written several books and articles, including *Julian del Casal: Estudios criticos sobre su obra, Cinco aproximaciones a la narrativa hispanoamericana*.

Yanick Lahens was born in Haiti, where she returned after studies in France. She teaches Haitian and Comparative Literature at the Ecole Normale Supérieure of Port-Au-Prince. Her scholarly essays and articles have appeared in the Haitian literary journal *Chemin Critiques* and in non-Haitain journals such as *Callaloo*. A collection of short stories, *Tante Résia et les dieux*, was published in 1995.

James Maraniss is Professor of Spanish at Amherst College. He is the author of *On Calderon* and the translator of several books by Antonio Benítez Rojo, including *The Repeating Island* (1992) and *A View from the Mangrove* (1995).

Daniel Maximin is a poet, essayist, and novelist from Guadeloupe. He is currently the Director of Cultural Affairs for Guadeloupe. His three novels are *L'Isolé soleil* (1981), translated by Clarisse Zimra as *Lone Sun* (1990); *Soufrières* (1987); and *L'île et une nuit* (1995).

Jean Métellus was born in Haiti. Although he holds a Ph.D. in linguistics and practices neurology in Paris, where he has lived since 1959, Métellus is best known for his poetry, fiction, and drama. A prolific writer, Métellus has published four collections of poems, *Au pipirite chantant* (1978), *Hommes de plein vent* (1981), *Voyances* (1984), and *Voix nègres* (1992); two plays, *Anacaona* (1986) and *Colomb* (1992); seven novels, *Jacmel au crépuscule* (1981), *La Famille Vortex* (1982), *Une Eau-forte* (1983), *La parole prisonière* (1986), *L'Année dessalines* (1986), *Les cacos* (1989), and *Charles Honoré Bonnefoy* (1990).

Ernest Pépin was born in Guadeloupe, where he is presently Regional Representative of the French Government for Cultural Affairs. He has published three volumes of poetry, *Au verso du silence* (1986), *Salve et salive* (1988), and *Boucan de mots livres* (1990). His first novel, *L'Homme au bâton*, was published in 1992. His most recent novels are *Coulée d'or* (1995) and *Tambour-Babel* (1996). Pépin is also known as a literary critic and essayist on Antillean literature and culture.

M. Nourbese Philip was born in Tobago. After studying economics at the University of the West Indies, she migrated to Toronto, Canada, and studied law. She has published three volumes of poetry, *Thorns* (1968), *Salmon's Courage* (1983), and *She Tries Her Tongue* (1989), for which she received the Casa de las Americas Prize in 1988. Her fiction includes short stories and a novel, *Harriet's Daughter* (1988).

Astrid H. Roemer was born in Suriname. She has published a collection of poetry, *Sasa*, and four novels, including *Neem mijn, terug Suriname* (1974), *Nergens, ergens* (1983), translated as *Somewhere, Nowhere, Schoon en schofterig* (1985); and *Levenslang gedicht* (1987). English translations of some of her short stories have appeared in recent anthologies. Roemer lives in The Hague, where she writes and practices family psychology.

Marie-Agnès Sourieau is Assistant Professor of French at Fairfield University. Her articles on francophone Caribbean literature have been published in *Callaloo*, *French Review*, and *Francophonia* as well as in collective works published in France and Canada.

Lourdes Vázquez is a poet and essayist from Puerto Rico. Her poetry, short stories, and essays have been published in journals from the Caribbean, Latin America, and the United States. Her books of poetry include *Las hembras* (1987), *La rosa mecanica* (1992), *El amor urgente* (1995), and *The Broken Heart* (1996). In 1988 the museum Omar Rayo in Bogota, Colombia, published part of *La rosa mecanica* in its series on Latin American women poets. Vázquez now lives in New York, where she is coeditor of the poetry series La Candelaria.

Sherezada (Chiqui) Vicioso is a poet and essayist from Santo Domingo, in the Dominican Republic. In 1980 she returned to her homeland after having lived in New York City for eighteen years. Her first collection of poetry, *Viaje desde el agua* (1981) was followed by *Internamiento* (1992). Over the years she has published many articles on the sociological problems facing her country and on the life of minorities in the Western world. She is presently working for UNICEF in Santo Domingo.

Carlos Guillermo Wilson was born in Panama. Two of his great-grandparents were francophone immigrants to Panama from St. Lucia, and three of his grandparents were anglophone immigrants to Panama from Barbados, Grenada, and Jamaica. In 1959 he left Panama to study at the Divine Word Seminary in Mississippi and then in Massachusetts. Wilson has taught at Loyola Marymount University, El Camino College, and the University of California at San Diego. Currently he chairs the Department of Spanish and Portuguese at San Diego State University. Under the pen name "Cubena," Wilson has published *Cuentos del negro Cubena* (1977), *Pensamientos del negro Cubena* (1977), *Chombo* (1981), and *Los nietos de Felicidad Dolores* (1991).

Index

Achilles, armor of, 33, 35
aesthetics, decolonized, 96–100. *See also* poetics
African American dialect, linked with Barbados, 73–74
African culture: appropriation of, 28–29, 33–34; influence by, 131, 169n.10; mythology from, 45–46; rejection of, 38–43; stereotypes of, 39–41; uses of, 55–56, 58. *See also* African languages
African diaspora: cultural movement in, 2–3; mythology from, 45–46. *See also* creolization; slavery
African languages: as basis of Creole, 90–91, 113–14, 131, 157; erasure of, 119; as resistance, 102–3; status of, 94–95. *See also* African culture
agelessness, gift of, 29–30
Alhambra, Catholic victory at, 36–37
Alliance Française, 168n.6
Alonso, Manuel, 78
anthologies, list of, 8
Antigua, Carnival in, 129
antillanité (Caribbeanness), 4, 96
Antillean experience: basis of, 7; and language, 77; writing of, 13–19. *See also* Caribbean archipelago; creolization; literature (Caribbean)
Antilles islands: cultural development in, 113–14; language in, 37, 120, 123; and marooning, 161; and transracial attraction, 111

Antoni, Robert, 60–61
Arawak people: language of, 37–39; marriages of, 27
Archer, Marie-Thérèse, 125, 127
arts: and extrahuman faculties, 34–35; science's connections with, 25, 31. *See also* aesthetics; poetics
Arzola, Marina, 85
Ashcroft, Bill, 104–5
authenticity, exclusion engendered by, 106–7
Aztecs, Spanish interest in, 36

Baldwin, James, 73–74
bamboo bands, 142
Barbados: Carnival in, 129; language in, 73–74; marooning in, 160, 162
Barthélémy, Gérard, 157, 159, 161–62
Bazin, Jean, 124
Bean, Manda, 68–69
Beauharnais, Joséphine de, 96
Belize, Garifunas in, 39
Benin, language in, 120
Benítez-Rojo, Antonio, 4–5, 7–8
Bentolila, Alain, 124, 128
Benza, Alban, 124
Bernabé, Jean, 4, 96–97, 105
bilingualism: balance in, 128; implications of, 14, 79–80; reclaiming, 97; shaping of, 89–95; support for, 123
biography, based on testimonials, 85
black, meanings of, 26

Henri Christophe (king of Haiti), 126–27
Hephaestus (Greek god), Legba's link to, 29, 31–35
Hill, Errol, 6
Hispanic writers, and bilingualism, 80
Holland. See Dutch language; Netherlands; Netherlands Antilles
Honduras, Garifunas in, 38–39
House of Spirits (Puerto Rico), 81
humanity: Caribbean as metaphor for, 156; changes in, 27; chasm in, 28–29, 33; choices of, 27–28; extrahuman faculties of, 34–35; gods' gifts for, 31–32; notions of, 167n.2; relationship to languages, 98. See also Creoles
Hurbon, Lahenec, 158–59, 161

I, versus me, 104–5
identity: approach to, 97–98; and authenticity, 106–7; bases for, 110; construction of, 163–64; and decolonized aesthetics, 96–97; definition of, 2–4; elusiveness of, 155–56; as individual, 105; and names, 58; plantation as signifier in, 5–6; of reader, 93–94; and skin color, 64. See also creoleness
illiteracy, causes of, 125–28
imagination: and language choice, 93–94; quantum, 34–35; role of, 27. See also originality
immortality, consolidation of, 32–33
immunity, distinctions of, 32
Incas, Spanish interest in, 36
Indian, as label, 24
Indian (spirit), 81–82
individualism: and identity, 105; and writing, 107
involuntary association: context of, 28–29; explanation of, 34–35; and transfigurative bridges, 25–27
Ireland, language links with, 74–75

Jab Molassi (folk figure), 137, 140
Jamaica: everyday life in, 68–71; Garifunas deported to, 38; Rastafarians in, 104–5
James, C. L. R., 65
Joe Chiss, 69–71
Jourdain, Elodie, 102
Júsuf (general), 36

Kardec, Allan, 81–82
Kinopoesis, of Creole languages, 130–31
kinship ties, and slavery, 46–48
Kipling, Rudyard, 117
Knight, Franklin W., 165n.5
Kriol language: definition of, 168n.1; teaching of, 91–92; understanding of, 89. See also Creole languages
Kristeva, Julia, 131
Kundera, Milan, 2–3, 6

Lam, Wilfredo, 55–56
Lamming, George, 5–6
languages: connections among, 29, 76–77; control of, 102–3, 130; deconstruction of, 103–5; features of, 169n.2; humanity's relationship to, 98; imposition of, 79, 87, 120–21; juxtaposition of, 103–4; naming of, 101; politics of, 71–75, 89–90; reclaiming of, 99–100; reverence for, 18; simplification of, 121–22; status of, 90–95, 121, 123, 130, 158; as subversive, 103–9; syncretism/mixing in, 37–39; written versus spoken, 92–93, 124. See also bilingualism; Creole languages; Dutch language; English language; French language; Spanish language
Las Casas, Bartolomé de, 40, 53–54
Latin America, identity in, 105
Laubach, Charles, 124–25, 128
Lefebvre, C., 120
legal system: and Carnival, 140–41, 145; and Creole immigrants, 146; revolt against, 14
Legba (Haitian loa): Hephaestus's link to, 29, 31–35; implications of, 31; role of, 29–30; roots of, 30–31
Lescot, Elie, 125
Lévi-Strauss, Claude, 45, 125
Lewis, Sam, 151
Lewis-Warner, Maureen, 75
Lionnet, Françoise, 106
literature (Caribbean): anthologies of, 8; approach to, 8, 98–100; becoming native versus racial mixing in, 110–11; characteristics of, 29–30, 59, 84–85, 98–99; control of, 107–9; creoleness applied to, 23; focus of, 7; goals of, 11, 14–15, 84–85, 108, 125; identity in, 6; influences on, 9–10, 78; orality in, 85, 98; and quantum imagination, 34–35;

women: in Barbados, 74; in Carnival, 147–48; role of, 157; and transracial attraction, 112–13; as writers, 8, 85–86. *See also* gender; sex
Wooding, Charles, 48
writers: categorization of, 80; and individualism, 107; irreverence of, 84–85; limitations on, 108; women as, 8, 85–86. *See also* literature (Caribbean)

Yoruba, influence of, 131, 169n.10
Yurumei. *See* Garifuna people